Cooking Healthy
with a Man in Mind

COOKING
HEALTHY

with a

MAN IN
MIND

A Healthy Exchanges® Cookbook

JoAnna M. Lund

with Barbara Alpert

G. P. Putnam's Sons / New York

G. P. Putnam's Sons
Publishers Since 1838
200 Madison Avenue
New York, NY 10016

Diabetic Exchanges Calculated by Rose Hoenig, RD, LD

Before using the recipes and advice in this book, consult your physician or health provider to be sure they are appropriate for you. The information in this book is not intended to take the place of any medical advice. It reflects the author's experiences, studies, research, and opinions regarding a healthy lifestyle. All material included in this publication is believed to be accurate. The publisher assumes no responsibility for any health, welfare, or subsequent damage that might be incurred from use of these materials.

For more information about Healthy Exchanges products, contact:
Healthy Exchanges, Inc.
P.O. Box 124
DeWitt, Iowa 52742-0124
(319) 659-8234

Library of Congress Cataloging-in-Publication Data

Lund, JoAnna M.
Cooking healthy with a man in mind / JoAnna M. Lund with Barbara Alpert.
p.   cm.
"A Healthy exchanges cookbook."
Includes index.
ISBN 0-399-14265-7
1. Cookery   2. Low-calorie diet   Recipes.   3. Low-fat diet—Recipes.   4. Low-cholesterol diet—Recipes.   5. Diabetes—Diet therapy—Recipes.   6. Reducing diets—Recipes.   7. Men—Nutrition.   I. Alpert, Barbara.   II. Title.
TX714.L85   1997   96-35509 CIP
641.5'63—dc20

Printed in the United States of America

3   5   7   9   1 0   8   6   4   2

This book is printed on acid-free paper. ♾

Book design by Richard Oriolo

This cookbook is dedicated in loving memory to my parents, Jerome and Agnes McAndrews. My father delighted in praising my mother's creative talent in the kitchen. He was especially proud of her ability to stir up fantastic meals almost like magic from even the barest cupboard. We came from hardworking "working-class" stock and money was often scarce, but love was abundant! Mom demonstrated her love for us by preparing mouthwatering foods lovingly made "from scratch." My fondest childhood memories are of family meals shared around our modest kitchen table.

In this collection of "man-pleasing" recipes, I've chosen the types of foods my mother cooked that my father so enjoyed. I've simply taken my "magic whisk" and stirred out the excess fats, sugars, calories, and sodium, while stirring in health and ease of preparation. Daddy would approve because my meals are still economical in cost and extravagant in taste just like Mom's. I like to think I left the loving in the ingredients just the way she did.

In recognition of the "tummy-filling" recipes in this collection, I'm sharing a poem my mother wrote many years ago about food and thanks. While she composed these words in celebration of Thanksgiving Day, I believe we should be thankful for the bounties most of us enjoy every day in our great nation. No wonder we are the envy of the rest of the world!

Our Bountiful Table

We thank You, Lord, for our bountiful table laden with
    food You have blest.
We invite You to stay in our hearts and homes and
    always be our guest.
May the happiness we enjoy on this
    and every day
Spread throughout the world, granting peace and
    love along the way.

—*Agnes Carrington McAndrews*

Acknowledgments

---■---

Without some very special men in my life, this book would not have been possible. I am so thankful that my "common folk" healthy recipes have pleased my guys, from my two-year-old grandson to my seventy-something father-in-law. Every time I serve "my men" a dish prepared in *The Healthy Exchanges Way*, they smack their lips in satisfaction. No other compliment will ever mean as much. For both tasting and encouraging, I want to publicly express my thanks:

To Cliff Lund, my "truck-drivin' man." It takes a really special husband to leave his long-haul trucking profession of more than twenty years to work full-time with his wife in her business, whatever it is. But then, to have that business be healthy recipes? Cliff has lost more than thirty pounds just coming along for the ride as the "official taste tester" of Healthy Exchanges.

To James Dierickx and Thomas Dierickx, my two "guinea pig" sons. Many a recipe has been created with their taste buds in mind. James is fond of spicy Mexican food, and Tommy loves anything with "hamburger milk gravy" as the starting point.

To John Taylor, my son-in-law. He had the good taste to marry my daughter and has gladly shared in tasting duties—especially desserts—whenever back in Iowa visiting.

To Zachary James Dierickx and Joshua Michael Dierickx, my precious grandsons. Their squeals of delight over Grandma's healthy food, especially for "pie, Grandma, pie," is music to my ears.

To Cleland Lund, my father-in law. He's a willing taster whenever I ask for his opinion, especially if the recipe includes macaroni and tomatoes.

To Charlie Tonn, my business guardian angel from the Iowa Small Business Development Center (SBDC). He never makes decisions for me, but he surely taught me how to think things through. The fact that he loves my desserts doesn't hurt anything.

To John Volkman, my friendly hometown lender. When I visited with him back in 1991 about borrowing money to finance the printing of a self-published cookbook, he immediately saw my vision with me. And after I served him a piece of cheesecake, the loan was a sure thing.

To John McEwen, my visionary dream facilitator. After just one visit to "The House That Recipes Built" (my nickname for our Healthy Exchanges office in DeWitt, Iowa) and one "man-pleasing" meal, he chose to help me share my recipes with the rest of the world.

To John Duff, my editor. From that first tasting of Triple Layer Party Pie in 1994, he continues to encourage me to create my "common folk" healthy recipes and write in my "Grandma Moses"–style of writing.

I also must give praise to God for giving me the talent to create recipes. I gladly take credit for the chopping of the onions and even for the washing of the dishes, but not for the recipes that flow like water from my mind. Creating recipes is every bit as much fun today as it was back in 1991 when I began my personal quest for "man-pleasing" recipes. With God's blessings, I'll still be stirring up new ones for "my men" and everyone else for many years to come.

The "Truck-Drivin' Man" Gets His Say at Last . . .

------------■------------

When it comes to this particular book, I like to say that *I'm* the man JoAnna Lund had "in mind" when she started out cooking healthy more than six years ago. At that time, I had no idea how our lives would be changed by her decision to find a new road for herself, one that would lead to a healthy lifestyle and a weight loss of 130 pounds.

I'm proud of her accomplishment, and I'm happy to have been part of her inspiration to pull it off. But there's more to it. I'm like most men: if food doesn't look, taste, and smell good, I just won't eat it. After all, I know the way to the nearest fast-food place or truck stop.

What made Healthy Exchanges work for both of us was that JoAnna's recipes took into consideration the kind of foods both she *and* her family liked. She stirred up spicy Mexican and hearty Italian dishes because she knew they were my favorites. She invented more than a few ways for Tommy to enjoy his best-loved food, cheeseburgers. She won James over by figuring out how to make kolaches almost as good as his grandma's. And she treated Becky to healthy pies brimming with her preferred flavors like bananas and butterscotch.

In my opinion, *Cooking Healthy with a Man in Mind* is JoAnna's best collection of recipes yet. Every page promises something so good to eat, the men in your family will ask for seconds with a smile. I've tasted every single dish in here, and if you leave out the ones with broccoli in 'em (there aren't too many, I'm happy to report . . .), I liked them all!

Eat hearty!

Clifford Lund

Contents

----------■----------

THE RECIPES

Introduction

----------------■----------------

I magine driving down the Interstate, alone or with your family in tow. Suddenly you see a sign: **Wanted: Hungry Men with Healthy Appetites!**

You'd be inclined to head for the nearest exit . . . and you'd be heading right for my little restaurant, JO's Kitchen Cafe—the home of filling, satisfying, man-pleasing food that's already received the seal of approval from truckers, factory workers, traveling salesmen, and growing teenage boys.

But if DeWitt, Iowa, isn't on your itinerary anytime soon, don't despair. For *Cooking Healthy with a Man in Mind,* I've collected more than two hundred of my best-loved Healthy Exchanges recipes, dishes I've served to men of all ages and backgrounds and even had tested by hundreds of visitors at a taste-testing buffet a few months ago. In addition, every one of them has received my husband, Cliff's, unqualified approval, and if my "truck-drivin' man" (who now trucks me around instead) agrees that these common-folk healthy recipes are not only tummy filling but deliver real taste satisfaction, you can be sure they'll appeal to men everywhere!

He Needs to Eat Healthy—But Believes No "Good-for-You" Recipe Tastes Good

If, as the proverb says, the way to a man's heart is through his stomach, I think the best way to get a man to eat healthy is to serve him food that looks and tastes like the dishes he loves. If you set a good-sized slab of a delicious-looking, spicy, meaty casserole or a dish of great coleslaw in front of him, and he smacks his lips after every bite, he's going to pay attention when you tell him, afterward, that he's just devoured something that's not only good, but good for him.

When I started creating Healthy Exchanges recipes six years ago, I began with the idea that the dishes I prepared had to appeal to my "truck-drivin' man," Cliff. But unlike all those times I tried to serve the family traditional "low-cal" dishes my husband considered "diet slop" and rejected, I invented healthy versions of recipes we all loved—Mexican and Italian specialties, biscuits and gravy, luscious pies—and won over their hearts and tummies.

My very first dish is still one of Cliff's favorites, and one that men often mention when they tell me which of my recipes they like best. Mexicalli Pie is made with ground beef (the leanest you can buy), chunky salsa, reduced-fat cheese, and even topped with a few ounces of Fritos, but it looks and tastes like the real thing while delivering much less fat than a traditional Mexican dish. It's impossible to eat a big slice of this tangy, satisfying entree and not feel like you've eaten real food. In fact, those crunchy bits on top make it taste like a real splurge.

I remember Cliff's reaction when I served it to him for the first time. He finished his serving and told me, "Boy, this is good." I told him then that it was healthy, and he said, "I don't care. It tastes great. Can I have some more, please?" So I went to the kitchen and got him another piece. I realized then that as long as I fixed that kind of food, I'd have his cooperation—and the help I needed to succeed.

Just last week a woman (who had no idea it was my first recipe) told me that Mexicalli Pie is her husband's favorite. And mothers have told me that it took only one serving for their teenage sons to become converts to *The Healthy Exchanges Way*. I feel blessed that the very first recipe I created was such a man-pleasing one because it gave me the courage and the inspiration to go forward with more.

Most men tell me that "diet" is the four-letter word they fear the most. Sometimes, they complain, just because *she's* trying to diet, he's stuck with tasteless casseroles, meatless mystery meals, midget-sized portions, and frustrated taste buds! Or maybe she's doing it for *his own good*—he's just had a mild heart attack, or his cholesterol level is too high, or he's been diagnosed with diabetes. "We're going to eat healthy from now on," she announces. "We could both lose a few pounds."

I always say that it's not enough for a recipe to be healthy. It also has to taste and look good. Otherwise, men won't eat it. Your kids won't eat it. And eventually even the most dedicated dieter will feel so deprived she'll give up.

When I finally made the connection between food and feelings, I used what I learned to make over family favorites so they were delicious as well as nutritious. Because the meals I served were tasty and satisfying enough for my entire family to enjoy, all of us benefited from the change to healthy eating. I lost 130 pounds (and have kept it off for over six years), Cliff has lost about 30 pounds just coming along for the ride, and my kids and grandsons have developed an appetite for healthy cooking—as long as the dishes are prepared *The Healthy Exchanges Way.*

What Makes Healthy Food Appeal to Men?

Any woman who's ever cooked for a man knows the kinds of things men like: potatoes and gravy, big pieces of meat (not just fish or chicken), and dessert at every meal. But getting a man to eat healthy isn't about **getting a man to change**—we all know how difficult it can be to change anything about a man!—but instead **changing the way you prepare the foods he likes to eat.**

I've had some people tell me, "Oh, he never notices what he's eating, as long as he's filled up when he leaves the table." If you've ever wondered about that, let me share some of my own unscientific research into whether men care whether what they're eating is good for them, or not.

If there ever was a manly profession, it'd have to be long-haul trucking. Well, one afternoon not long after I began creating healthy recipes, I was giving Cliff, my own long-haul trucker, his Sunday lunch. I'd made a Banana Split Pie and gave him a piece to try for the first time. He took one bite, then put his fork down and said, "Wow! You'd better get up to the store quick before they close and buy what you need so you can make me one of these to take to my dispatcher. She'll never believe that it's healthy!" He licked his plate clean, then added, "You know, if you ever open a restaurant, people are going to come for your desserts alone!" (And he was right!)

After that, I used to send all kinds of leftovers with him in the refrigerator he carried in his truck. Once the word got out that he was taking my desserts and salads along, other truckers would call him on his CB and want to know where the nearest mile marker was, so they could meet up with him and share some of that precious cargo!

Okay, you may say, but Cliff doesn't really count, because he already knew he was getting a healthy dessert. Well, here's another:

A few months later, I was talking on the radio in Des Moines, Iowa, telling my story and describing how to make that same Banana Split Pie. I also told how to order my cookbook and newsletter. Well, listening to the interview that day was a man driving his tractor doing spring field work. He had nothing to write with, so he stopped the tractor and scribbled the address in the dust on the fender. When he went in for lunch, he asked his wife to send for my book and newsletter.

She wrote to me that afternoon to order them, saying, "I didn't hear the program, but you must have been one heck of a talker to get my husband interested in healthy recipes in the middle of the cornfield." I met her at a cooking demo recently, and she told me that her husband loves my recipes as much today as he did when he first heard about Banana Split Pie.

Why is Banana Split Pie so irresistible to men? Maybe it's the combination of flavors that triggers the taste buds of the typical male. Just hearing me talk about the pie's ingredients—the coolness of the pineapple, the "filling-ness" of the banana and strawberries, plus a tiny bit of chocolate, and a couple of maraschino cherries chopped up on top—seems to get their attention.

A salesman who heard me talking about that pie actually pulled over to the side of the road and *wrote the recipe down*. He was one of those guys who eats in every greasy spoon along the interstate. When he got home that night, he gave the recipe to his wife and asked her to fix the pie. (How often do you hear of men stopping their cars to write down a healthy recipe? There must be something *magical* about that pie!)

His wife wasn't used to hearing a request like this from her husband, but she mixed up the pie and served it that night. He must have thought it was a winner, because two days later, when he was in eastern Iowa, he drove thirty miles out of his way to meet me and get a copy of my cookbook. He couldn't say enough about how much he enjoyed that pie!

If a Man Eats Healthy, the Kids Will Follow

If you can please the man of the house with a healthy recipe, more often than not it will please the rest of the family, too. I believe that kids typically get their eating habits from their fathers. Because Dad is a bit of a mystery figure, often sharing a family meal only at night, the children pay attention to what he does, what he says—*and* what he eats. If you can win his approval for a healthy recipe, the kids will share his enthusiasm!

What does it take to satisfy a man at the table? Often, it's the taste of dishes his mother used to make, or the kind of substantial family favorites that both look hearty and please the taste buds. When I create recipes with a man in mind, I know I've got a winner when I serve potatoes and gravy (not the old-fashioned kind, of course, but my healthy version is so delicious, men can't tell the difference!), or when I plunk a slab of a meaty casserole onto the plate. It doesn't look like diet food, it doesn't taste like diet food, and as the factory workers who've been eating lunch from my Health Wagon Catering Bus have told me, they don't care if it's healthy as long as it tastes *good*.

What's Different about Cooking Healthy with a Man in Mind?

As usual, let me begin my "research" with Cliff. Back in 1991, he led a pretty normal lifestyle for a long-haul trucker—home about one day a week and on the road the other six. He thought French fries were the only potatoes worth ordering, and that all food should be served in huge quantities and really fast, just the way the truck stops did.

In fact, here's the way he puts it: Cliff wants **Real Food served Real Fast in Real Quantities with a Real Smile—the way he got it from Truck Stop Waitresses!**

When I started serving him my Healthy Exchanges recipes, his life changed forever. He liked them so much, he told his friends he'd never eaten so well in all the years we'd been married. When he asked if he could take healthy leftovers along in his portable fridge, I felt as if I'd won a kind of victory—and when he began to lose weight without trying, he became my greatest supporter.

(He's also always welcome in my test kitchen—but I wish I could persuade him to help with the dishes!)

Now that I've talked to and received letters from men from all over the country, I know that Cliff is pretty typical. With the exception of the few foods he really doesn't like (and that other men may like), he's a reliable median of what it takes to please a man when it comes to cooking.

These days, when men meet me, they usually say, "Boy, if I've got to eat healthy, I'm so glad that my wife found your recipes. And your pies are out of this world!" In fact, men seem to really relate to me. This is exceedingly unusual in the diet/healthy food business. Maybe it's because I tend to remind them of their wives, mothers, daughters, or sisters that they're immediately drawn to me.

Most of all, they see me as a friend who wants them to eat well, instead of a threatening diet cop who does plate patrol or a seductive female who's all false promises about what eating healthy really means.

When Cliff and I were traveling through Texas recently, we met a couple who summed it up perfectly. The woman, who'd been trying to cook for her diabetic husband, told me that, once she found Healthy Exchanges, her kitchen "was no longer a disaster area." The man said simply, "Your food looks and tastes like you put the lovin' back in."

What Will the Food Be Like?

I'm sure you remember reading about the government's suggestions for a Food Pyramid, with certain recommended numbers of servings of fruits, vegetables, breads, proteins, and fats to be consumed each day. Well, I like to say that a man's "Food Pyramid" just isn't the same as the government's. Men need meat. They need chocolate. They need bananas. They need corn. Most of all, they need dessert. (If you're looking for the quickest superhighway to get what you want from a man, make sure you serve him from the dessert fast lane!)

Men will get what they need *and* what they want from Healthy Exchanges. My Men's Healthy Food Pyramid may win more votes than anything cooked up in Washington! But they'll get it in a healthy, enjoyable way. Don't expect to find in this book the dozens of grilled and broiled fish and chicken recipes that are at the heart of almost every healthy cookbook. That kind of food might have been all right when you were looking for a quick fix or a crash diet, but it's just not a way to eat and live well for a lifetime.

Why "Cooking Healthy
with a Man in Mind"?

When I was trying to decide what to call this cookbook, I did some grassroots research, talking to all the men I met at bookstores and cooking demos, media appearances and transplant support groups. I told them I was thinking of calling it **Cooking Healthy with a Man in Mind.** Well, to a man their eyes lit up, they smiled, and they said, "It's about time." Then they added, "I can't wait to get my hands on the book—and on the food!"

I sure do like knowing that my recipes make their mouths water.

Is Cooking Healthy with a Man
in Mind *for You?*

Because of Healthy Exchanges, the old days of preparing a separate meal for the family dieter are over for good. The cardiac patient and diabetic don't have to be outcasts from the family dinner table any longer. Healthy Exchanges recipes provide what every table needs—a way for everyone to eat healthy without sacrificing flavor. The portions are realistic, not diet sized, the dishes resemble family favorites in appearance and taste, and they're prepared quickly from easy-to-find ingredients.

I wrote *Cooking Healthy with a Man in Mind* for three distinct audiences.

- It's a welcome bible for the man who now must eat healthy for medical reasons but needs friendly advice about what foods to eat and how to prepare them so they'll taste like the food he's always loved. Maybe he's developed heart or cholesterol problems, or been diagnosed as diabetic. Many wives don't know where to begin, particularly if they don't share their husband's medical problem, but this book can help them learn a new way of cooking.

- It's the *ideal* cookbook for any man who does his own cooking, whether he's a bachelor, divorced, a widower, or a husband who cooks for his family. The recipes are simple, made of commonly available ingredients, and easy to fix.

- It's the best gift a man married to a "professional dieter" could give his wife, so she can stop preparing a diet meal for herself and a separate meal for her husband and children. He's more than willing to eat what she does, and enjoy the health benefits too, but the food has to be as delicious and soul-satisfying as what he's enjoyed in the past.

And, of course, it's the perfect book for every woman who wants to cook healthy for herself *and* for the man in her life.

Every **Healthy Exchanges** recipe provides:

Weight Loss Choices™/Exchanges that can be used with many national weight-loss programs

Calories, Fat and Fiber Grams, Proteins, Carbohydrates, and Sodium

Diabetic Exchanges

This book is also jam-packed with dozens of healthy cooking and easy food preparation tips as well as secrets I've discovered during my years of recipe creating and testing. You'll hear in their own words from men who've already tried Healthy Exchanges cooking and have become enthusiastic fans.

Because I want you to feel confident about eating well in a healthy way, I'll also provide inside information on:

- what brands cook up best

- why ingredients you believe are diet no-nos are fine when used in moderation and measured amounts

- how to "beef up" servings while holding the line with fats and sugars

- how to streamline your preparations so you can prepare foods faster than you can get a pizza delivered

In addition, I'll tell you just what you need to know to:

- furnish your own Healthy Exchanges kitchen
- shop for the best low-fat and low-sugar healthy brand-name products

If your goal is better health, if your appetite demands substantial and good-tasting foods served up quickly, and if you're ready to make a few easy changes in what you eat—let's start cooking healthy together!

JoAnna M. Lund and the Creation of Healthy Exchanges

-------■-------

For twenty-eight years I was the diet queen of DeWitt, Iowa. I tried every diet I ever heard of, every one I could afford, and every one that found its way to my small town in eastern Iowa. I was willing to try anything that promised to "melt off the pounds," determined to deprive my body in every possible way in order to become thin at last.

I sent away for expensive "miracle" diet pills. I starved myself on the Cambridge Diet and the Bahama Diet. I gobbled Ayds diet candies, took thyroid pills, fiber pills, prescription and over-the-counter diet pills. I went to endless weight-loss support group meetings—but I managed to turn healthy programs such as Overeaters Anonymous, Weight Watchers, and TOPS into unhealthy diets . . . diets I could never follow for more than a few months.

I was determined to discover something that worked long-term, but each new failure increased my desperation that I'd never find it.

I ate strange concoctions and rubbed on even stranger potions. I tried liquid diets like Slimfast and Metrecal. I agreed to be hypnotized. I tried reflexology and even had an acupuncture device stuck in my ear!

Does my story sound a lot like yours? I'm not surprised. No wonder the weight-loss business is a billion-dollar industry!

Every new thing I tried seemed to work—at least at first. And losing that first five or ten pounds would get me so excited, I'd believe that this new miracle diet would, finally, get my weight off for keeps.

Inevitably, though, the initial excitement wore off. The diet's routine and boredom set in, and I quit. I shoved the pills to the back of the medicine chest; pushed the cans of powdered shake mix to the rear of the kitchen cabinets; slid all the program materials out of sight under my bed; and once more I felt like a failure.

Like most dieters, I quickly gained back the weight I'd lost each time, along with a few extra "souvenir" pounds that seemed always to settle around my hips. I'd done the diet-lose-weight-gain-it-all-back "yo-yo" on the average of once a year. It's no exaggeration to say that over the years I've lost 1,000 pounds—and gained back 1,150 pounds.

Finally, at the age of forty-six I weighed more than I'd ever imagined possible. I'd stopped believing that any diet could work for me. I drowned my sorrows in sacks of cake donuts, and wondered if I'd live long enough to watch my grandchildren grow up.

Something had to change.

I had to change.

Finally, I did.

I'm just over fifty now—and I'm 130 pounds less than my all-time high of close to 300 pounds. I've kept the weight off for more than six years. I'd like to lose another ten pounds, but I'm not obsessed about it. If it takes me the rest of my life to accomplish it, that's okay.

What I *do* care about is never saying hello again to any of those unwanted pounds I said good-bye to!

How did I jump off the roller coaster I was on? For one thing, I finally stopped looking to food to solve my emotional problems. But what really shook me up—and got me started on the path that changed my life—was Operation Desert Storm in early 1991. I sent three children off to the Persian Gulf War—my son-in-law, Matt, a medic in Special Forces; my daughter, Becky, a full-time college student and member of a medical unit in the Army Reserve; and my son James, a member of the Inactive Army Reserve reactivated as a chemicals expert.

Somehow, knowing that my children were putting their lives on the line got me thinking about my own mortality—and I knew in my heart the last thing they needed while they were overseas was to get a letter from home saying that their mother was ill because of a food-related problem.

The day I drove the third child to the airport to leave for Saudi Arabia, something happened to me that would change my life for the better—and forever. I stopped praying my constant prayer as a professional dieter, which was simply "Please, God, let me lose ten pounds by Friday." Instead, I began praying, "God, please help me not to be a burden to my kids and my family."

I quit praying for what I wanted, and started praying for what I needed—and in the process my prayers were answered. I couldn't keep the kids safe—that was out of my hands—but I could try to get healthier to better handle the stress of it. It was the least I could do on the homefront.

That quiet prayer was the beginning of the new JoAnna Lund. My initial goal was not to lose weight or create healthy recipes. I only wanted to become healthier for my kids, my husband, and myself.

Each of my children returned safely from the Persian Gulf War. But something didn't come back—the 130 extra pounds I'd been lugging around for far too long. I'd finally accepted the truth after all those agonizing years of suffering through on-again, off-again dieting.

There are no "magic" cures in life.

No "magic" potion, pill, or diet will make unwanted pounds disappear.

I found something better than magic, if you can believe it. When I turned my weight and health dilemma over to God for guidance, a new JoAnna Lund and Healthy Exchanges were born.

I discovered a new way to live my life—and uncovered an unexpected talent for creating easy "common folk" healthy recipes, and sharing my commonsense approach to healthy living. I learned that I could motivate others to change their lives and adopt a positive outlook. I began publishing cookbooks and a monthly food newsletter, and speaking to groups all over the country.

I like to say, *"When life handed me a lemon, not only did I make healthy, tasty lemonade, I wrote the recipe down!"*

What I finally found was not a quick fix or a short-term diet, but a great way to live well for a lifetime.

I want to share it with you.

Food Exchanges
and Weight-Loss
Choices

--------■--------

Healthy Exchanges® Weight Loss
Choices™/Exchanges

If you've ever been on one of the national weight-loss programs like Weight Watchers or Diet Center, you've already been introduced to the concept of measured portions of different food groups that make up your daily food plan. If you are not familiar with such a system of weight-loss choices or exchanges, here's a brief explanation. (If you want or need more detailed information, you can write to the American Dietetic Association or the American Diabetes Association for comprehensive explanations.)

The idea of food exchanges is to divide foods into basic food groups. The foods in each group are measured in servings that have comparable values. These groups include Proteins/Meats,

Breads/Starches, Vegetables, Fats, Fruits, Skim Milk, Free Foods, and Optional Calories.

Each choice or exchange included in a particular group has about the same number of calories and a similar carbohydrate, protein, and fat content as the other foods in that group. Because any food on a particular list can be "exchanged" for any other food in that group, it makes sense to call the food groups *exchanges* or *choices*.

I like to think we are also "exchanging" bad habits and food choices for good ones!

By using Weight Loss Choices™ or exchanges you can choose from a variety of foods without having to calculate the nutrient value of each one. This makes it easier to include a wide variety of foods in your daily menus and gives you the opportunity to tailor your choices to your unique appetite.

If you want to lose weight, you should consult your physician or other weight-control expert regarding the number of servings that would be best for you from each food group. Since men generally require more calories than women, and since the requirements for growing children and teenagers differ from those of adults, the right number of exchanges for any one person is a personal decision.

I have included a suggested plan of weight-loss choices in the pages following the exchange lists. It's a program I used to lose 130 pounds, and it's the one I still follow today.

(If you are a diabetic or have been diagnosed with heart problems, it is best to meet with your physician before using this or any other food program or recipe collection.)

Food Group Weight Loss
Choices™ Exchanges

Not all food group exchanges are alike. The ones that follow are for anyone who's interested in weight loss or maintenance. If you are a diabetic, you should check with your health-care provider or dietitian to get the information you need to help you plan your diet. Diabetic exchanges are calculated by the American Diabetic Association, and information about them is provided in *The Diabetic's Healthy Exchanges Cookbook* (Putnam).

Every Healthy Exchanges recipe provides calculations in three ways:

- Weight Loss Choices/Exchanges
- Calories, Fat, Protein, Carbohydrates, and Fiber Grams, and Sodium in milligrams
- Diabetic Exchanges calculated for me by a Registered Dietitian

Healthy Exchanges recipes can help you eat well and recover your health, whatever your health concerns may be. Please take a few minutes to review the exchange lists and the suggestions that follow on how to count them. You have lots of great eating in store for you!

Proteins

Meat, poultry, seafood, eggs, cheese, and legumes.
One exchange of Protein is approximately 60 calories. Examples of one Protein choice or exchange:

1 ounce cooked weight of lean meat, poultry, or seafood

2 ounces white fish

1½ ounces 97% fat-free ham

1 egg (limit to no more than 4 per week)

¼ cup egg substitute

3 egg whites

¾ ounce reduced-fat cheese

½ cup fat-free cottage cheese

2 ounces cooked or ¾ ounces uncooked dry beans

1 tablespoon peanut butter (also count 1 fat exchange)

Breads

Breads, crackers, cereals, grains, and starchy vegetables. One exchange of Bread is approximately 80 calories. Examples of one Bread Choice/exchange:

1 slice bread or 2 slices reduced-calorie bread (40 calories or less)

1 roll, any type (1 ounce)

½ cup cooked pasta or ¾ ounce uncooked (scant ½ cup)

½ cup cooked rice or 1 ounce uncooked (⅓ cup)

3 tablespoons flour

¾ ounce cold cereal

½ cup cooked hot cereal or ¾ ounce uncooked (2 tablespoons)

½ cup corn (kernels or cream style) or peas

4 ounces white potato, cooked, or 5 ounces uncooked

3 ounces sweet potato, cooked, or 4 ounces uncooked

3 cups air-popped popcorn

7 fat-free crackers (¾ ounce)

3 (2½-inch squares) graham crackers

2 (¾ ounce) rice cakes or 6 mini

1 tortilla, any type (6-inch diameter)

Fruits

All fruits and fruit juices. One exchange of Fruit is approximately 60 calories. Examples of one Fruit choice or exchange:

1 small apple or ½ cup slices

1 small orange

½ medium banana

¾ cup berries (except strawberries and cranberries)

1 cup strawberries or cranberries

½ cup canned fruit, packed in fruit juice or rinsed well

2 tablespoons raisins

1 tablespoon spreadable fruit spread

½ cup apple juice (4 fluid ounces)

½ cup orange juice (4 fluid ounces)

½ cup applesauce

Skim Milk

Milk, buttermilk, and yogurt. One exchange of Skim Milk is approximately 90 calories. Examples of one Skim Milk choice or exchange:

1 cup skim milk

½ cup evaporated skim milk

1 cup low-fat buttermilk

¾ cup plain fat-free yogurt

⅓ cup nonfat dry milk powder

Vegetables

All fresh, canned, or frozen vegetables other than the starchy vegetables. One exchange of Vegetable is approximately 30 calories. Examples of one Vegetable choice or exchange:

½ cup vegetable

¼ cup tomato sauce

1 medium fresh tomato

½ cup vegetable juice

Fats

Margarine, mayonnaise, vegetable oils, salad dressings, olives, and nuts. One exchange of fat is approximately 40 calories. Examples of one Fat choice or exchange:

1 teaspoon margarine or 2 teaspoons reduced-calorie margarine

1 teaspoon butter

1 teaspoon vegetable oil

1 teaspoon mayonnaise or 2 teaspoons reduced-calorie
*   mayonnaise*

1 teaspoon peanut butter

1 ounce olives

¼ ounce pecans or walnuts

Free Foods

Foods that do not provide nutritional value but are used to enhance the taste of foods are included in the Free Foods group. Examples of these are spices, herbs, extracts, vinegar, lemon juice, mustard, Worcestershire sauce, and soy sauce. Cooking sprays and artificial sweeteners used in moderation are also included in this group. However, you'll see that I include the caloric value of artificial sweeteners in the Optional Calories of the recipes.

You may occasionally see a recipe that lists "free food" as part of the portion. According to the published exchange lists, a free food contains fewer than 20 calories per serving. Two or three servings per day of free foods/drinks are usually allowed in a meal plan.

Optional Calories

Foods that do not fit into any other group but are used in moderation in recipes are included in Optional Calories. Foods that are counted in this way include sugar-free gelatin and puddings, fat-free mayonnaise and dressings, reduced-calorie whipped toppings, reduced-calorie syrups and jams, chocolate chips, coconut, and canned broth.

Sliders™

These are 80 Optional Calorie increments that do not fit into any particular category. You can choose which food groups to *slide* them into. It is wise to limit this selection to approximately three per day to ensure the best possible nutrition for your body while still enjoying an occasional treat.

Sliders™ may be used in either of the following ways:

1. If you have consumed all your Protein, Bread, Fruit, or Skim Milk Weight Loss Choices for the day, and you want to eat additional foods from those food groups, you simply use a Slider. It's what I call "healthy horse trading." Remember that Sliders may not be traded for choices in the Vegetables or Fats food groups.

2. Sliders may also be deducted from your Optional Calories (OC) for the day or week. ¼ Sl equals 20 OC; ½ Sl equals 40 OC; ¾ Sl equals 60 OC; and one Sl equals 80 OC. This way, you can choose the food groups to *slide* into.

Healthy Exchanges® Weight Loss Choices™

My original Healthy Exchanges program of Weight Loss Choices™ was based on an average daily total of 1,400–1,600 calories per day. That was what I determined was right for my needs, and for those of most women. Because men require additional calories (about 1,600–1,900), here are my suggested plans for women and men. (*If you require more or fewer calories, please revise this plan to your individual needs.*)

Each day, women should plan to eat:

2 Skim Milk servings, 90 calories each
2 Fat servings, 40 calories each
3 Fruit servings, 60 calories each
4 Vegetable servings or more, 30 calories each
5 Protein servings, 60 calories each
5 Bread servings, 80 calories each

Each day, men should plan to eat:

2 Skim Milk servings, 90 calories each
4 Fat servings, 40 calories each

3 Fruit servings, 60 calories each
4 Vegetable servings or more, 30 calories each
6 Protein servings, 60 calories each
7 Bread servings, 80 calories each

Young people should follow the program for Men but add 1 Skim Milk serving for a total of 3 servings.

You may also choose to add up to 100 Optional Calories per day, and among 28 Sliders per week at 80 calories each. If you choose to include more sliders in your daily or weekly totals, deduct those 80 calories from your Optional Calorie "bank."

A word about **Sliders**™: These are to be counted toward your totals after you have used your allotment of choices of Skim Milk, Protein, Bread, and Fruit for the day. By "sliding" an additional choice into one of these groups, you can meet your individual needs for that day. Sliders are especially helpful when traveling, stressed-out, eating out, or for special events. I often use mine so I can enjoy my favorite Healthy Exchanges desserts. Vegetables are not to be counted as Sliders. Enjoy as many Vegetable Choices as you need to feel satisfied. Because we want to limit our fat intake to moderate amounts, additional Fat Choices should not be counted as Sliders. If you choose to include more fat on an *occasional* basis, count the extra choices as Optional Calories.

Keep a daily food diary of your Weight Loss Choices, checking off what you eat as you go. If, at the end of the day, your required selections are not 100 percent accounted for, but you have done the best you can, go to bed with a clear conscience. There will be days when you have ¼ Fruit or ½ Bread left over. What are you going to do—eat two slices of an orange or half a slice of bread and throw the rest out? I always say that "Nothing in life comes out exact." Just do the best you can . . . *the best you can.*

Try to drink at least eight 8-ounce glasses of water a day. Water truly is the "nectar" of good health.

As a little added insurance, I take a multi-vitamin each day. It's not essential, but if my day's worth of well-planned meals "bites the dust" when unexpected events intrude on my regular routine, my body still gets its vital nutrients.

The calories listed in each group of Choices are averages. Some choices within each group may be higher or lower, so it's important to select a variety of different foods instead of eating the same three or four all the time.

Use your Optional Calories! They are what I call "life's little extras." They make all the difference in how you enjoy your food and appreciate the variety available to you. Yes, we can get by without them, but do you really want to? Keep in mind that you should be using all your daily Weight Loss Choices first to ensure you are getting the basics of good nutrition. But I guarantee that Optional Calories will keep you from feeling deprived—and help you reach your weight-loss goals.

Sodium, Fat, Cholesterol, and Processed Foods

---■---

re Healthy Exchanges Ingredients Really Healthy?
When I first created Healthy Exchanges, many people asked about sodium, about whether it was necessary to calculate the percentage of fat, saturated fat, and cholesterol in a healthy diet, and about my use of processed foods in many recipes. I researched these questions as I was developing my program, so you can feel confident about using the recipes and food plan.

Sodium

Most people consume more sodium than their bodies need. The American Heart Association and the American Diabetes Association recommend limiting daily sodium intake to no more than 3,000 mg. per day. If your doctor suggests you limit your sodium even more, then *you really must read labels.*

Sodium is an essential nutrient and should not be completely eliminated. It helps to regulate blood volume and is needed for normal daily muscle and nerve functions. Most of us, however, have no trouble getting "all we need" and then some.

As with everything else, moderation is my approach. I rarely ever have salt on my list as an added ingredient. But if you're especially sodium sensitive, make the right choices for you—and save high-sodium foods such as sauerkraut for an occasional treat.

I use lots of spices to enhance flavors, so you won't notice the absence of salt. In the few cases where it is used, it's vital for the success of the recipe, so please don't omit it.

When I do use an ingredient high in sodium, I try to compensate by using low-sodium products in the remainder of the recipe. Many fat-free products are a little higher in sodium to make up for any flavor that disappeared along with the fat. But when I take advantage of these fat-free, higher-sodium products, I stretch that ingredient within the recipe, lowering the amount of sodium per serving. A good example is my use of fat-free canned soups. While the suggested number of servings per can is two, I make sure my final creation serves at least four and sometimes six. So the soup's sodium has been "watered down" from one-third to one-half of the original amount.

Even if you don't have to watch your sodium intake for medical reasons, using moderation is another "healthy exchange" to make on your own journey to good health.

Fat Percentages

We've been told that 30 percent is the magic number—that we should limit fat intake to 30 percent or less of our total calories. It's good advice, and I try to have a weekly average of 15 to 25 percent myself. I believe any less than 15 percent is really just another restrictive diet that won't last. And more than 25 percent on a regular basis is too much of a good thing.

When I started listing fat grams along with calories in my recipes, I was tempted to include the percentage of calories from fat. After all, in the vast majority of my recipes, that percentage is well below 30 percent This even includes my pie recipes that allow you a realistic serving instead of many "diet" recipes that tell you a serving is ½₂ of a pie.

Figuring fat grams is easy enough. Each gram of fat equals nine calories. Multiply fat grams by nine, then divide that number by the total calories to get the percentage of calories from fat.

So why don't I do it? After consulting four registered dietitians for advice, I decided to omit this information. They felt that it's too easy for people to become obsessed by that 30 percent figure, which is after all supposed to be a percentage of total calories over the course of a day or a week. We mustn't feel we can't include a healthy ingredient such as pecans or olives in one recipe just because, on its own, it has more than 30 percent of its calories from fat.

An example of this would be a casserole made with 90 percent lean red meat. Most of us benefit from eating red meat in moderation, as it provides iron and niacin in our diets, and it also makes life more enjoyable for us and those who eat with us. If we *only* look at the percentage of calories from fat in a serving of this one dish, which might be as high as 40 to 45 percent, we might choose not to include this recipe in our weekly food plan.

The dietitians suggested that it's important to consider the total picture when making such decisions. As long as your overall food plan keeps fat calories to 30 percent, it's all right to enjoy an occasional dish that is somewhat higher in fat content. Healthy foods I include in **MODERATION** include 90 percent lean red meat, olives, and nuts. I don't eat these foods every day, and you may not either. But occasionally, in a good recipe, they make all the difference in the world between just getting by (deprivation) and truly enjoying your food.

Remember, the goal is eating in a healthy way so you can enjoy and live well the rest of your life.

Saturated Fats and Cholesterol

You'll see that I don't provide calculations for saturated fats or cholesterol amounts in my recipes. It's for the simple and yet not so simple reason that accurate, up-to-date, brand-specific information can be difficult to obtain from food manufacturers, especially since the way in which they produce food keeps changing rapidly. But once more I've consulted with registered dietitians and other professionals and found that because I use only a few products that are high in saturated fat, and use them in such limited quantities, my recipes are suitable for patients concerned about controlling or lowering cholesterol. You'll also find that whenever I do use one of these ingredients *in moderation,* everything else in the recipe, and in the meals my family and I enjoy, is low in fat.

Processed Foods

Some people have asked how "healthy" recipes can so often use "processed foods"—ready-made products like canned soups, prepared pie crusts, frozen potatoes, and frozen whipped topping? Well, I believe that such foods, used properly (that word **moderation** again) as part of a healthy lifestyle, have a place as ingredients in healthy recipes.

I'm not in favor of spraying everything we eat with chemicals, and I don't mean that all our foods should come out of packages. But I do think we should use the best available products to make cooking easier and foods taste better. I take advantage of good low-fat and low-sugar products, and my recipes are created for busy people like me who want to eat well and eat healthy. I don't expect people to visit out-of-the-way health food stores or find time to cook beans from scratch—*because I don't.* There are lots of very good processed foods available in your local grocery store, and they can make it so much easier to enjoy the benefits of healthy eating.

I certainly don't recommend that everything you eat come from a can, box, or jar. I think the best of all possible worlds is to start with the basics: rice, poultry, fish, or beef, and raw vegetables—then throw in a can of reduced-sodium/97 percent fat-free soup (a processed food) and end up with an appetizing, easy-to-prepare, healthy meal.

Most of us can't grow fresh food in the backyard, and many

people don't even have a nearby farmer's market. But instead of saying "Well, I can't get to the health food store so why not eat that hot fudge sundae?" you gotta play ball in your private ball field, not in someone else's. I want to help you figure out ways to make living healthy **doable** and **livable** *wherever you live,* or you're not going to stick with it.

I've checked with the American Dietetic Association, the American Diabetes Association, and with many registered dietitians, and I've been assured that sugar-free and fat-free processed products that use substitutes for sugar and fat are safe when used in the intended way. This means a realistic serving, not one hundred cans of diet soda every day of the year! Even carrots can turn your skin orange if you eat far too many, but does anyone suggest we avoid eating carrots?

Of course, it is your privilege to disagree with me and to use whatever you choose when you prepare your food. I never want to be one of those "opinionated" people who think it's their God-given right to make personal decisions for others and insist that their way is the *only* way.

Besides, new research comes out every day that declares one food bad and another food good. Then a few days later, some new information emerges, saying that the opposite is true. When the facts are sifted from the fiction, the truth is probably somewhere in between. I know I feel confused when what was bad for you last year is good for you now, and vice versa.

Instead of listening to unreasonable sermons by naysayers who are nowhere around when it comes to make a quick and healthy meal for your family, I've tried to incorporate the best processed foods I can find into my Healthy Exchanges recipes. I get stacks of mail from people who are thrilled to discover they can eat good-tasting food and who proudly use processed foods in the intended way. I think you will agree that my commonsense approach to healthy cooking is the right choice for many. Because these foods are convenient, tasty, and good substitutes for less healthy products, people are willing to use them long-term.

So don't let anyone make you feel ashamed for including these products in your healthy lifestyle. Only you can decide what's best for you and your family's needs. Part of living a healthy lifestyle is making those decisions and *getting on with life.*

JoAnna's Ten Commandments of Successful Cooking

------■-------

A few minutes spent before you start cooking will save you hours in the kitchen. The best use of your time, energy, and money is not only reading these suggestions for conquering the kitchen but also applying them to your daily cooking.

1. **Read the entire recipe from start to finish** and be sure you understand the process involved. Check that you have all the equipment you will need *before* you begin.

2. **Check the ingredient list** and be sure you have *everything* and in the amounts required. Keep cooking sprays handy—while they're not listed as ingredients, I use them all the time (just a quick squirt!).

3. **Set out *all* the ingredients and equipment needed** to prepare the recipe on the counter near you *before* you start. Remem-

ber that old saying, *A stitch in time saves nine*. It applies in the kitchen, too.

4. **Do as much advance preparation as possible** before actually cooking. Chop, cut, grate, or do whatever is needed to prepare the ingredients and have them ready before you start to mix. Turn the oven on at least 10 minutes before putting food in to bake, to allow the oven to preheat to the proper temperature.

5. **Use a kitchen timer** to tell you when the cooking or baking time is up. Because stove temperatures vary slightly by manufacturer, you may want to set your timer for 5 minutes less than the suggested time just to prevent overcooking. Check the progress of your dish at that time, then decide if you need the additional minutes or not.

6. **Measure carefully.** Use glass measures for liquids and metal or plastic cups for dry ingredients. My recipes are based on standard measurements. Unless I tell you it's a scant or full cup, measure the cup level.

7. **For best results, follow the recipe instructions exactly.** Feel free to substitute ingredients that *don't tamper* with the basic chemistry of the recipe, but be sure to leave key ingredients alone. For example, you could substitute sugar-free instant chocolate pudding for sugar-free instant butterscotch pudding, but if you used a 6-serving package when a 4-serving package was listed in the ingredients, or you used instant when cook-and-serve is required, you won't get the right result.

8. **Clean up as you go.** It is much easier to wash a few items at a time than to face a whole counter of dirty dishes later. The same is true for spills on the counter or floor.

9. **Be careful about doubling or halving a recipe.** Though many recipes can be altered successfully to serve more or fewer people, *many cannot*. This is especially true when it comes to spices and liquids. If you try to double a recipe that calls for one teaspoon pumpkin-pie spice, for example, and you double the spice, you may end up with a too-spicy taste. I

usually suggest increasing spices or liquid by 1½ times when doubling a recipe. If it tastes a little bland to you, you can increase the spice to 1¾ times the original amount the next time you prepare the dish. Remember: you can always add more, but you can't take it out after it's been stirred in.

The same is true with liquid ingredients. If you wanted to **triple** a recipe like my Macho Burritos because you were planning to serve a crowd, you might think you should use three times as much of every ingredient. Don't, or you could end up with Burrito Soup! The original recipe calls for 1¾ cup of chunky tomato sauce, so I'd suggest using 3½ cups of sauce when you **triple** the recipe (or 2¾ cups if you **double** it). You'll still have a good-tasting dish that won't run all over the plate.

10. **Write your reactions next to each recipe once you've served it.**

Yes, that's right, I'm giving you permission to write in this book. It's yours, after all. Ask yourself: Did everyone like it? Did I have to add another half teaspoon of chili seasoning to please my family, who like to live on the spicier side of the street? You may even want to rate the recipe on a scale of 1☆ to 4☆, depending on what you thought of it. (Four stars would be the top rating—and I hope you'll feel that way about many of my recipes.) Jotting down your comments while they are fresh in your mind will help you personalize the recipe to your own taste the next time you prepare it.

This is such a simple way to keep track of everything that goes into my mouth as well as my husband's. I made the Taco Casserole the other night and did my husband ever flip over it! He wanted seconds and thirds!

—K.S., IA

My Best Healthy Exchanges Tips and Tidbits

-------■--------

Measurements, General Cooking Tips, and Basic Ingredients

The word **moderation** best describes **my use of fats, sugar substitutes,** and **sodium** in these recipes. Wherever possible, I've used cooking spray for sautéing and for browning meats and vegetables. I also use reduced-calorie margarine and no-fat mayonnaise and salad dressings. Lean ground turkey *or* ground beef can be used in the recipes. Just be sure whatever you choose is at least *90 percent lean.*

I've also included **small amounts of sugar and brown sugar substitutes as the sweetening agent** in many of the recipes. I don't drink a hundred cans of soda a day or eat enough artificially sweetened foods in a 24-hour time period to be troubled by sugar substitutes. But if this is a concern of yours and you *do not* need to watch your sugar intake, you can always replace the sugar substitutes with processed sugar and the sugar-free products with regular ones.

I created my recipes knowing they would also be used by hypoglycemics, diabetics, and those concerned about triglycerides. If you choose to use sugar instead, be sure to count the additional calories.

A word of caution when cooking with **sugar substitutes:** Use **saccharin**-based sweeteners when **heating or baking.** In recipes that **don't require heat, Aspartame** (known as NutraSweet) works well in uncooked dishes but leaves an aftertaste in baked products.

I'm often asked why I use an **8-by-8-inch baking dish** in my recipes. It's for portion control. If the recipe says it serves four, just cut down the center, turn the dish, and cut again. Like magic, there's your serving. Also, if this is the only recipe you are preparing requiring an oven, the square dish fits into a tabletop toaster oven easily and energy can be conserved.

To make life even easier, **whenever a recipe calls for ounce measurements** (other than raw meats) I've included the closest cup equivalent. I need to use my scale daily when creating recipes, so I've measured for you at the same time.

Most of the recipes are for **4 to 6 servings.** If you don't have that many to feed, do what I do: freeze individual portions. Then all you have to do is choose something from the freezer and take it to work for lunch or have your evening meals prepared in advance for the week. In this way, I always have something on hand that is both good to eat and good for me.

Unless a recipe includes hard-boiled eggs, cream cheese, mayonnaise, or a raw vegetable or fruit, **the leftovers should freeze well.** (I've marked recipes that freeze well with the symbol of a **snowflake.**❄) This includes most of the cream pies. Divide any recipe up into individual servings and freeze for your own "TV" dinners.

Another good idea is **cutting leftover pie into individual pieces and freezing each one separately** in a small Ziploc freezer bag. Then the next time you want to thaw a piece of pie for yourself, you don't have to thaw the whole pie. It's great this way for brown-bag lunches, too. Just pull a piece out of the freezer on your way to work and by lunchtime you will have a wonderful dessert waiting for you.

Unless I specify **"covered" for simmering or baking,** prepare my recipes **uncovered.** Occasionally you will read a recipe that asks you to cover a dish for a time, then to uncover, so read the directions carefully to avoid confusion—and to get the best results.

Low-fat cooking spray is another blessing in a Healthy Exchanges kitchen. It's currently available in three flavors . . .

- **Olive-oil flavored** when cooking Mexican, Italian, or Greek dishes

- **Butter flavored** when the hint of butter is desired

- **Regular** for everything else

A quick spray of the butter-flavored kind makes air-popped popcorn a low-fat taste treat, or try it as a butter substitute on steaming hot corn on the cob. One light spray of the skillet when browning meat will convince you that you're using "old fashioned fat," and a quick coating of the casserole dish before you add the ingredients will make serving easier and cleanup quicker.

I use reduced-sodium **canned chicken broth** in place of dry bouillon to lower the sodium content. The intended flavor is still present in the prepared dish. As a reduced-sodium beef broth is not currently available (at least not in DeWitt, Iowa), I use the canned regular beef broth. The sodium content is still lower than regular dry bouillon.

Whenever **cooked rice or pasta** is an ingredient, follow the package directions, but eliminate the salt and/or margarine called for. This helps lower the sodium and fat content. It tastes just fine; trust me on this.

Here's another tip: When **cooking rice or noodles,** why not cook extra "for the pot"? After you use what you need, store leftover rice in a covered container (where it will keep for a couple of days). With noodles like spaghetti or macaroni, first rinse and drain as usual, then measure out what you need. Put the leftovers, covered with water, in a bowl, then store in the refrigerator, covered, until they're needed. Then, measure out what you need, rinse and drain them, and they're ready to go.

Does your **pita bread** often tear before you can make a sandwich? Here's my tip to make it open easily: cut the bread in half, put the halves in the microwave for about 15 seconds, and they will open up by themselves. *Voilà!*

When **chunky salsa** is listed as an ingredient, I leave the degree of "heat" up to your personal taste. In our house, I'm considered a wimp. I go for the "mild" while Cliff prefers "extra-hot." How do we compromise? I prepare the recipe with mild salsa because he can always add a spoonful or two of the hotter version to his serving, but I can't enjoy the dish if it's too spicy for me.

Proteins

I use eggs in moderation. I enjoy the real thing on an average of three to four times a week. So, my recipes are calculated on using whole eggs. However, if you choose to use egg substitute in place of the egg, the finished product will turn out just fine and the fat grams per serving will be even lower than those listed.

If you like the look, taste, and feel of **hard-boiled eggs** in salads but haven't been using them because of the cholesterol in the yolks, I have a couple of alternatives for you. (1) Pour an 8-ounce carton of egg substitute into a medium skillet sprayed with cooking spray. Cover skillet tightly and cook over low heat until substitute is just set, about 10 minutes. Remove from heat and let set, still covered, for 10 minutes more. Uncover and cool completely. Chop set mixture. This will make about 1 cup of chopped egg. (2) Even easier is to hard-boil "real eggs," toss the yolk away, and chop the white. Either way, you don't deprive yourself of the pleasure of egg in your salad.

In most recipes calling for **egg substitutes,** you can use 2 egg whites in place of the equivalent of 1 egg substitute. Just break the eggs open and toss the yolks away. I can hear some of you already saying, "But that's wasteful!" Well, take a look at the price on the egg substitute package (which usually has the equivalent of 4 eggs in it), then look at the price of a dozen eggs, from which you'd get the equivalent of 6 egg substitutes. Now, what's wasteful about that?

Whenever I include **cooked chicken** in a recipe, I use roasted white meat without skin. Whenever I include **roast beef or pork** in a recipe, I use the loin cuts because they are much leaner. However, most of the time, I do my roasting of all these meats at the local deli. I just ask for a chunk of their lean roasted meat, 6 or 8 ounces, and ask them not to slice it. When I get home, I cube or dice the meat and am ready to use it in my recipe. The reason I do this is threefold. (1) I'm getting just the amount I need without leftovers. (2) I don't have the expense of heating the oven. (3) I'm not throwing away the bone, gristle, and fat I'd be cutting away from the meat. Overall, it is probably cheaper to "roast" it the way I do.

Did you know that you can make an acceptable meat loaf without using egg for the binding? Just replace every egg with ¼ cup of liquid. You could use beef broth, tomato sauce, even applesauce, to name just a few alternatives. For a meat loaf to serve 6, I always use 1 pound of extra-lean ground beef or turkey, 6 tablespoons of dried fine bread crumbs, and ¼ cup of the liquid, plus anything else healthy that strikes my fancy at the time. I mix well and place the mixture in an 8-by-8-inch baking dish or 9-by-5-inch loaf pan sprayed with cooking spray. Bake uncovered at 350 degrees for 35 to 50 minutes (depending on the added ingredients). You will never miss the egg.

Anytime you are **browning ground meat** for a casserole and want to get rid of almost all of the excess fat, just place the uncooked meat loosely in a plastic colander. Set the colander in a glass pie plate. Place in microwave and cook on HIGH for 3 to 6 minutes (depending on the amount being browned), stirring often. Use as you would for any casserole. You can also chop up onions and brown them with the meat if you want to.

Milk and Yogurt

Take it from me—nonfat dry milk powder is great! I *do not* use it for drinking, but I *do* use it for cooking. Three good reasons why:

1. It is very **inexpensive.**

2. It does not **sour** because you use it only as needed. Store the box in your refrigerator or freezer and it will keep almost forever.

3. You can easily **add extra calcium** to just about any recipe without added liquid.

I consider nonfat dry milk powder one of Mother Nature's modern-day miracles of convenience. But do purchase a good national name brand (I like Carnation), and keep it fresh by proper storage.

In many of my pies and puddings, I use nonfat dry milk powder and water instead of skim milk. Usually I call for ⅔ cup nonfat dry milk powder and 1¼ to 1½ cups water or liquid. This way I can get the nutrients of two cups of milk, but much less liquid, and the end result is much creamier. Also, the recipe sets up more quickly, usually in 5 minutes or less. So if someone knocks at your door unexpectedly at mealtime, you can quickly throw a pie together and enjoy it minutes later.

You can make your own **"sour cream"** by combining ¾ cup plain fat-free yogurt with ⅓ cup nonfat dry milk powder. What occurs by doing this is fourfold: (1) The dry milk stabilizes the yogurt and keeps the whey from separating. (2) The dry milk slightly helps to cut the tartness of the yogurt. (3) It's still virtually fat free. (4) The calcium has been increased by 100 percent. Isn't it great how we can make that distant relative of sour cream a first kissin' cousin by adding the nonfat dry milk powder? Or, if you place 1 cup of plain fat-free yogurt in a sieve lined with a coffee filter, and place the sieve over a small bowl and refrigerate for about 6 hours, you will end up with a very good alternative for sour cream. To **stabilize yogurt** when cooking or baking with it, just add 1 teaspoon cornstarch to every ¾ cup yogurt.

If a recipe calls for **evaporated skim milk** and you don't have any in the cupboard, make your own. For every ½ cup evaporated skim milk needed, combine ⅓ cup nonfat dry milk powder and ½ cup water. Use as you would evaporated skim milk.

You can also make your own **sugar-free and fat-free sweetened condensed milk** at home. Combine 1⅓ cups nonfat dry milk powder and ½ cup cold water in a 2-cup glass measure. Cover and microwave on HIGH until mixture is hot but *not* boiling. Stir in ½ cup Sprinkle Sweet or Sugar Twin. Cover and refrigerate at least 4 hours. This mixture will keep for up to two weeks in the refrigerator. Use in just about any recipe that calls for sweetened condensed milk.

For any recipe that calls for **buttermilk,** you might want to try Jo's Buttermilk: Blend one cup of water and ⅔ cup dry milk powder (the nutrients of two cups of skim milk). It'll be thicker than this mixed-up milk usually is, because it's doubled. Add 1 teaspoon white vinegar and stir, then let it sit for at least 10 minutes.

One of my subscribers was looking for a way to further restrict salt intake and needed a substitute for **cream of mushroom soup.** For many of my recipes, I use Healthy Request Cream of Mushroom soup, as it is a reduced-sodium product. The label suggests two servings per can, but I usually incorporate the soup into a recipe serving at least four. By doing this, I've reduced the sodium in the soup by half again.

But if you must restrict your sodium even more, try making my Healthy Exchanges **Creamy Mushroom Sauce.** Place 1½ cups evaporated skim milk and 3 tablespoons flour in a covered jar. Shake well and pour mixture into a medium saucepan sprayed with butter-flavored cooking spray. Add ½ cup canned sliced mushrooms, rinsed and drained. Cook over medium heat, stirring often, until mixture thickens. Add any seasonings of your choice. You can use this sauce in any recipe that calls for one 10¾-ounce can of cream of mushroom soup.

Why did I choose these proportions and ingredients?

- 1½ cups evaporated skim milk is the amount in one can.

- It's equal to three milk choices or exchanges.

- It's the perfect amount of liquid and flour for a medium cream sauce.

- 3 tablespoons flour is equal to one Bread/Starch choice or exchange.

- Any leftovers will reheat beautifully with a flour-based sauce, but not with a cornstarch base.

- The mushrooms are one vegetable choice or exchange.

- This sauce is virtually fat free, sugar free, and sodium free.

Fruits and Vegetables

If you want to enjoy a **"fruit shake"** with some pizazz, just combine soda water and unsweetened fruit juice in a blender. Add crushed ice. Blend on High until thick. Refreshment without guilt.

You'll see that many recipes use ordinary **canned vegetables.** They're much cheaper than reduced-sodium versions, and once you rinse and drain them, the sodium is reduced anyway. I believe in saving money wherever possible so we can afford the best fat-free and sugar-free products as they come onto the market.

All three kinds of **vegetables—fresh, frozen, and canned—** have their place in a healthy diet. My husband, Cliff, hates the taste of frozen or fresh green beans, thinks the texture is all wrong, so I use canned green beans instead. In this case, canned vegetables have their proper place when I'm feeding my husband. If someone in your family has a similar concern, it's important to respond to it so everyone can be happy and enjoy the meal.

When I use **fruits or vegetables** like apples, cucumbers, and zucchini, I wash them really well and **leave the skin on.** It provides added color, fiber, and attractiveness to any dish. And, because I use processed flour in my cooking, I like to increase the fiber in my diet by eating my fruits and vegetables in their closest-to-natural state.

To help keep **fresh fruits and veggies fresh,** just give them a quick "shower" with lemon juice. The easiest way to do this is to pour purchased lemon juice into a kitchen spray bottle and store in the refrigerator. Then, everytime you use fresh fruits or vegetables in a salad or dessert, simply give them a quick spray with your "lemon spritzer." You just might be amazed by how well this little trick keeps your produce from turning brown so fast. You may also want to purchase Fruit Fresh, which helps keep bananas and apples from turning brown.

The next time you warm canned vegetables such as carrots or green beans, drain and heat the vegetables in ¼ cup beef or chicken broth. It gives a nice variation to an old standby. Here's how a simple **white sauce** for vegetables and casseroles can be made without using added fat: Spray a medium saucepan with butter-flavored cooking spray. Place 1½ cups evaporated skim milk and 3 tablespoons flour in a covered jar. Shake well. Pour into sprayed saucepan and cook over medium heat until thick, stirring constantly. Add salt and pepper to taste. You can also add ½ cup canned drained mushrooms and/or 3 ounces (¾ cup) shredded reduced-fat cheese. Continue cooking until cheese melts.

Zip up canned or frozen green beans with **chunky salsa:** ½ cup to 2 cups beans. Heat thoroughly. Chunky salsa also makes a wonderful dressing on lettuce salads. It only counts as a vegetable, so enjoy.

Another wonderful **South of the Border** dressing can be stirred up by using ½ cup chunky salsa and ¼ cup fat-free Ranch dressing. Cover and store in your refrigerator. Use as a dressing for salads or as a topping for baked potatoes.

For **gravy** with all the "old time" flavor but without the extra fat, try this almost effortless way to prepare it. (It's almost as easy as opening up a store-bought jar.) Pour the juice off your roasted meat, then set the roast aside to "rest" for about 20 minutes. Place the juice in an uncovered cake pan or other large flat pan (we want the large air surface to speed up the cooling process) and put it in the freezer until the fat congeals on top and you can skim it off. Or, if you prefer, use a skimming pitcher purchased at your kitchen gadget store. Either way, measure about 1½ cups skimmed broth and pour into a medium saucepan. Cook over medium heat until heated through, about 5 minutes. In a covered jar, combine ½ cup water or cooled potato broth with 3 tablespoons flour. Shake well. Pour flour mixture into warmed juice. Combine well using a wire whisk. Continue cooking until gravy thickens, about 5 minutes. Season with salt and pepper to taste.

Why did I use flour instead of cornstarch? Because any left-overs will reheat nicely with the flour base and would not with a cornstarch base. Also, 3 tablespoons of flour works out to 1 Bread/Starch exchange. This virtually fat-free gravy makes about 2 cups, so you could spoon about ½ cup gravy on your low-fat mashed potatoes and only have to count your gravy as ¼ Bread/Starch exchange.

Desserts

Thaw **lite whipped topping** in the refrigerator overnight. Never try to force the thawing by stirring or using a microwave to soften. Stirring it will remove the air from the topping that gives it the lightness and texture we want, and there's not enough fat in it to survive being heated.

How can I **frost an entire pie with just ½ cup of whipped topping?** First, don't use an inexpensive brand. I use Cool Whip Lite or La Creme Lite. Make sure the topping is fully thawed. Always spread from the center to the sides using a rubber spatula. This way, ½ cup topping will literally cover an entire pie. Remember, the operative word is *frost;* don't pile the entire container on top of the pie!

Here's a way to **extend the flavor (and oils) of purchased whipped topping:** Blend together ¾ cup plain nonfat yogurt and ⅓ cup nonfat dry milk powder. Add sugar substitute to equal 2 tablespoons sugar, 1 cup Cool Whip Lite and 1 teaspoon of the flavoring of your choice (vanilla, coconut, or almond are all good choices). Gently mix and use as you would whipped topping. The texture is almost a cross between marshmallow cream and whipped cream. This is enough to mound high on a pie.

For a different taste when preparing sugar-free instant pudding mixes, use ¾ cup plain fat-free yogurt for one of the required cups of milk. Blend as usual. It will be *thicker and creamier.* And, no it doesn't taste like yogurt. Another variation for the sugar-free instant vanilla pudding is to use 1 cup skim milk and 1 cup crushed pineapple juice. Mix as usual.

For a special treat that tastes anything but "diet," try placing **spreadable fruit** in a container and microwave for about 15 seconds. Then pour the melted fruit spread over a serving of nonfat ice cream or frozen yogurt. One tablespoon of spreadable fruit is equal to 1 fruit serving. Some combinations to get you started are apricot over chocolate ice cream, strawberry over strawberry ice cream, or any flavor over vanilla. Another way I use spreadable fruit is to make a delicious **topping for a cheesecake or angel food cake.** I take ½ cup of fruit and ½ cup Cool Whip Lite and blend the two together with a teaspoon of coconut extract.

Here's a really **good topping** for the fall of the year. Place 1½ cups unsweetened applesauce in a medium saucepan or 4-cup glass measure. Stir in two tablespoons raisins, 1 teaspoon apple pie spice, and two tablespoons Cary's sugar-free maple syrup. Cook over medium heat on the stove or process on HIGH in microwave until warm. Then spoon about ½ cup warm mixture over pancakes, French toast, or fat-free and sugar-free vanilla ice cream. It's as close you will get to guilt-free apple pie!

A quick yet tasty way to prepare **strawberries for shortcake** is to place about ¾ cup of sliced strawberries, 2 tablespoons Diet Mountain Dew, and sugar substitute to equal ¼ cup sugar in a blender container. Process on Blend until mixture is smooth. Pour mixture into bowl. Add 1¼ cups sliced strawberries and mix well. Cover and refrigerate until ready to serve with shortcakes.

The next time you are making treats for the family, try using **unsweetened applesauce** for some or all of the required oil in the recipe. For instance, if the recipe calls for ½ cup cooking oil, use ½ cup applesauce. It works and most people will not even notice the difference. It's great in purchased cake mixes, but so far I haven't been able to figure out a way to deep-fat fry with it!

Another trick I often use is to include tiny amounts of "real people" food, such as coconut, but extend the flavor by using extracts. Try it—you will be surprised by how little of the real thing you can use and still feel you are not being deprived.

If you are preparing a pie filling that has ample moisture, just line **graham crackers** in the bottom of a 9-by-9-inch cake pan.

Pour the filling over the top of the crackers. Cover and refrigerate until the moisture has had enough time to soften the crackers. Overnight is best. This eliminates the added **fats and sugars of a piecrust.**

When **stirring fat-free cream cheese to soften it,** use only a sturdy spoon, never an electric mixer. The speed of a mixer can cause the cream cheese to lose its texture and become watery.

Did you know you can make your own **fruit-flavored yogurt?** Mix 1 tablespoon of any flavor of spreadable fruit spread with ¾ cup plain yogurt. It's every bit as tasty and much cheaper. You can also make your own **lemon yogurt** by combining 3 cups plain fat-free yogurt with 1 tub Crystal Light lemonade powder. Mix well, cover, and store in refrigerator. I think you will be pleasantly surprised by the ease, cost, and flavor of this "made from scratch" calcium-rich treat. P.S.: You can make any flavor you like by using any of the Crystal Light mixes—Cranberry? Iced tea? You decide.

Sugar-free puddings and gelatins are important to many of my recipes, but if you prefer to avoid sugar substitutes, you could still prepare the recipes with regular puddings or gelatins. The calories will be higher, but you will still be cooking low-fat.

When a recipe calls for **chopped nuts** (and you only have whole ones), who wants to dirty the food processor just for a couple of tablespoons? You could try to chop them using your cutting board, but be prepared for bits and pieces to fly all over the kitchen. I use "Grandma's food processor." I take the biggest nuts I can find, put them in a small glass bowl, and chop them into chunks just the right size using a metal biscuit cutter.

If you have a **leftover muffin** and are looking for something a little different for breakfast, you can make a **"breakfast sundae."** Crumble the muffin into a cereal bowl. Sprinkle a serving of fresh fruit over it and top with a couple of tablespoons nonfat plain yogurt sweetened with sugar substitute and your choice of extract. The thought of it just might make you jump out of bed with a smile on your face. (Speaking of muffins, did you know that if you fill the unused muffin wells with water when baking muffins, you help ensure more even baking and protect the muffin pan at the same time?) Another muffin hint: lightly spray the inside of paper baking cups with butter-flavored cooking spray before spooning the muffin batter into them. Then you won't end up with paper clinging to your fresh-baked muffins.

The secret of making **good meringues** without sugar is to use 1 tablespoon of Sprinkle Sweet or Sugar Twin for every egg white, and a small amount of extract. Use ½ to 1 teaspoon for the batch. Almond, vanilla, and coconut are all good choices. Use the same amount of cream of tartar you usually do. Bake the meringue in the same old way. Don't think you can't have meringue pies because you can't eat sugar. You can, if you do it my way. (Remember that egg whites whip up best at room temperature.)

Homemade or Store-Bought?

I've been asked which is better for you, homemade from scratch or purchased foods. My answer is *both!* They each have a place in a healthy lifestyle, and what that place is has everything to do with you.

Take **piecrusts,** for instance. If you love spending your spare time in the kitchen preparing foods, and you're using low-fat, low-sugar, and reasonably low-sodium ingredients, go for it! But if, like so many people, your time is limited and you've learned to read labels, you could be better off using purchased foods.

I know that when I prepare a pie (and I experiment with a couple of pies each week, because this is Cliff's favorite dessert), I use a purchased crust. Why? Mainly because I can't make a good-tasting piecrust that is lower in fat than the brands I use. Also, purchased piecrusts fit my rule of "If it takes longer to fix than to eat, forget it!"

I've checked the nutrient information for the purchased piecrust against recipes for traditional and "diet" piecrusts, using my computer software program. The purchased crust calculated lower in both fat and calories! I have tried some low-fat and low-sugar recipes, but they just didn't spark my taste buds, or were so complicated you needed an engineering degree just to get the crust in the pie plate.

I'm very happy with the purchased piecrusts in my recipes, because the finished product rarely, if ever, has more than 30 percent of total calories coming from fat. I also believe that we have to prepare foods our families and friends will eat with us on a regular basis and not feel deprived, or we've wasted our time, energy, and money.

I could use a purchased "lite" **pie filling,** but instead I make my own. Here I can save both fat and sugar, and still make the filling almost as fast as opening a can. The bottom line: know what you have to spend when it comes to both time and fat/sugar calories, then make the best decision you can for you and your family. And don't go without an occasional piece of pie because you think it isn't *necessary.* A delicious pie prepared in a healthy way is one of the simple pleasures of life. It's a little thing, but it can make all the difference between just getting by with the bare minimum and living a full and healthy lifestyle.

Many people have experimented with my tip about **substituting applesauce and artificial sweetener for butter and sugar,** but what if you aren't satisfied with the result? One woman wrote to me about a recipe for her grandmother's cookies that called for 1 cup butter and 1½ cups sugar. Well, any recipe that depends on as much butter and sugar as this one does is generally not a good candidate for "healthy exchanges." The original recipe needed a large quantity of fat to produce the crisp cookies just like the ones Grandma made.

Unsweetened applesauce can be used to substitute for vegetable oil with varying degrees of success, but not to replace butter, lard, or margarine. If your recipe calls for ½ cup oil or less, and it's a quick bread, muffin, or bar cookie, replacing the oil with applesauce should work. If the recipe calls for more than ½ cup oil, then experiment with half oil, half applesauce. You've still made the recipe healthier, even if you haven't removed all the oil from it.

Another rule for healthy substitution: up to ½ cup sugar or less can be replaced by *an artificial sweetener* (like Sugar Twin or Sprinkle Sweet) *that can withstand the heat of baking.* If it requires more than ½ cup sugar, cut the amount needed by 75 percent and use ½ cup sugar substitute and sugar for the rest. Other options: reduce the butter and sugar by 25 percent and see if the finished product still satisfies you in taste and appearance. Or, make the cookies just like Grandma did, realizing they are part of your family's holiday tradition. Enjoy a moderate serving of a couple of cookies once or twice during the season, and just forget about them the rest of the year.

I'm sure you'll add to this list of cooking tips as you begin preparing Healthy Exchanges recipes and discover how easy it can be to adapt your own favorite recipes using these ideas and your own common sense.

A Peek into My Pantry and My Favorite Brands

--------■--------

Everyone asks me what foods I keep on hand and what brands I use. There are lots of good products on the grocery shelves today—many more than we dreamed about even a year or two ago. And I can't wait to see what's out there twelve months from now. The following are my staples and, where appropriate, my favorites *at this time*. I feel these products are healthier, tastier, easy to get—and deliver the most flavor for the least amount of fat, sugar, or calories. If you find others you like as well *or better,* please use them. This is only a guide to make your grocery shopping and cooking easier.

Fat-free plain yogurt *(Yoplait)*

Nonfat dry skim milk powder *(Carnation)*

Evaporated skim milk *(Carnation)*

Skim milk

Fat-free cottage cheese

Fat-free cream cheese *(Philadelphia)*

Fat-free mayonnaise *(Kraft)*

Fat-free salad dressings *(Kraft)*

Fat-free sour cream *(Land O Lakes)*

Reduced-calorie margarine *(Weight Watchers, Promise, or Smart Beat)*

Cooking spray:

> Olive oil–flavored and regular *(Pam)*
>
> Butter-flavored for sautéing *(Weight Watchers)*
>
> Butter-flavored for spritzing after cooking *(I Can't Believe It's Not Butter!)*

Vegetable oil *(Puritan Canola Oil)*

Reduced-calorie whipped topping *(Cool Whip Lite)*

Sugar Substitute:

> If no heating is involved *(Equal)*
>
> If heating is required:
>
> > white *(Sugar Twin or Sprinkle Sweet)*
> >
> > brown *(Brown Sugar Twin)*

Sugar-free gelatin and pudding mixes *(JELL-O)*

Baking mix *(Bisquick Reduced Fat)*

Pancake mix *(Aunt Jemima Reduced Calorie)*

Reduced-calorie pancake syrup *(Cary's Sugar Free)*

Parmesan cheese *(Kraft Fat-Free or Weight Watchers Fat Free)*

Reduced-fat cheese *(Kraft ⅓ Less Fat and Weight Watchers)*

Shredded frozen potatoes *(Mr. Dell's)*

Spreadable fruit spread *(Smucker's, Welch's, or Sorrell Ridge)*

Peanut butter *(Peter Pan Reduced Fat, Jif Reduced Fat, or Skippy Reduced Fat)*

Chicken broth *(Healthy Request)*

Beef broth *(Swanson)*

Tomato sauce *(Hunts—Chunky and Regular)*

Canned soups *(Healthy Request)*

Tomato juice *(Campbell's Reduced Sodium)*

Ketchup *(Heinz Light Harvest or Healthy Choice)*

Purchased piecrust:

    unbaked *(Pillsbury—from dairy case)*

    graham cracker, shortbread, or chocolate *(Keebler)*

Pastrami and corned beef *(Carl Buddig Lean)*

Luncheon meats *(Healthy Choice or Oscar Mayer)*

Ham *(Dubuque Extra-Lean Reduced Sodium or Healthy Choice)*

Frankfurters and Kielbasa sausage *(Healthy Choice)*

Canned white chicken, packed in water *(Swanson)*

Canned tuna, packed in water *(Starkist)*

90-percent-lean ground turkey and beef

Soda crackers *(Nabisco Fat Free)*

Reduced-calorie bread—*40 calories per slice or less*

Hamburger buns—*80 calories each (Colonial Old Fashion or Less)*

Rice—*instant, regular, brown, and wild*

Instant potato flakes *(Betty Crocker Potato Buds)*

Noodles, spaghetti, and macaroni

Salsa *(Chi-Chi's Mild)*

Pickle relish—dill, sweet, and hot dog

Mustard—Dijon, prepared, and spicy

Unsweetened apple juice

Unsweetened applesauce

Fruit—fresh, frozen (no sugar added) or canned in juice

Vegetables—*fresh, frozen, or canned*

Spices—*JO's Spices or any preferred brand*

Lemon and lime juice (in small plastic fruit-shaped bottles found in produce section)

Instant fruit beverage mixes *(Crystal Light)*

Dry dairy beverage mixes *(Nestlé's Quik and Swiss Miss)*

"Ice Cream" *(Well's Blue Bunny Health Beat Fat and Sugar Free or any fat- and sugar-free brand)*

The items on my shopping list are everyday foods found in just about any grocery store in America. But all are as low in fat, sugar, calories, and sodium that I can find—and that still taste good! I can make any recipe in my cookbooks and newsletters as long as I have my cupboards and refrigerator stocked with these items. Whenever I use the last of any one item, I just make sure I pick up another supply the next time I'm at the store.

If your grocer does not stock these items, why not ask if they can be ordered on a trial basis? If the store agrees to do so, be sure to tell your friends to stop by, so that sales are good enough to warrant restocking the new products. Competition for shelf space is fierce, so only products that sell well stay around.

Shopping the Healthy Exchanges Way

--------■--------

Sometimes, as part of a cooking demonstration, I take the group on a field trip to the nearest supermarket. There's no better place to share my discoveries about which healthy products taste best, which are best for you, and which healthy products don't deliver enough taste to include in my recipes.

While I'd certainly enjoy accompanying you to your neighborhood store, we'll have to settle for a field trip *on paper*. I've tasted and tried just about every fat- and sugar-free product on the market, but so many new ones keep coming out all the time, you're going to have to learn to play detective on your own. I've turned label reading into an art, but often the label doesn't tell me everything I need to know.

Sometimes you'll find, as I have, that the product with *no* fat doesn't provide the taste satisfaction you require; other times, a no-fat or low-fat product just doesn't cook up the same way as the original product. And some foods, including even the leanest meats, can't eliminate *all* the fat. That's okay, though—a healthy diet should include anywhere from 15 to 25 percent of total calories from fat on any given day.

Take my word for it—your supermarket is filled with lots of delicious foods that can and should be part of your healthy diet for life. Come, join me as we check it out on the way to the checkout!

First stop, the **salad dressing** aisle. Salad dressing is usually a high-fat food, but there are great alternatives available. Let's look first at the regular Ranch dressing—2 tablespoons have 170 calories and 18 grams of fat—and who can eat just 2 tablespoons? Already, that's about half the fat grams most people should consume in a day. Of course, it's the most flavorful too. Now let's look at the low-fat version. Two tablespoons have 110 calories and 11 grams of fat; they took about half of the fat out, but there's still a lot of sugar there. The fat-free version has 50 calories and zero grams of fat, but they also took most of the flavor out. Here's what you do to get it back: add a tablespoon of fat-free mayonnaise, a few more parsley flakes, and about a half teaspoon of sugar substitute to your two-tablespoon serving. That trick, with the fat-free mayo and sugar substitute, will work with just about any fat-free dressing and give it more of that full-bodied flavor of the high-fat version. Be careful not to add too much sugar substitute—you don't want it to become sickeningly sweet.

I even use Kraft fat-free **mayonnaise** at 10 calories per tablespoon to make scalloped potatoes. The Smart Beat brand is also a good one.

Before I buy anything at the store, I read the label carefully: the total fat plus the saturated fat; I look to see how many calories are in a realistic serving, and I say to myself, would I eat that much—or would I eat more? I look at the sodium and I look at the total carbohydrates. I like to check those ingredients because I'm cooking for diabetics and heart patients, too. And I check the total calories from fat.

Remember that 1 fat gram equals 9 calories, while 1 protein or 1 carbohydrate gram equals 4 calories.

A wonderful new product is I Can't Believe It's Not Butter spray, with zero calories and zero grams of fat in four squirts. It's great for your air-popped popcorn. As for **light margarine spread,** beware—most of the fat-free brands don't melt on toast, and they don't taste very good either, so I just leave them on the shelf. For the few times I do use a light margarine I tend to buy Smart Beat Ultra, Promise Ultra, or Weight Watchers Light Ultra. The number-one ingredient in them is water. I occasionally use the light margarine in cooking, but I don't really put margarine on my toast anymore. I use apple butter or make a spread with fat-free cream cheese mixed with a little spreadable fruit instead.

So far, Pillsbury hasn't released a reduced-fat **crescent roll,** so you'll only get one crescent roll per serving from me. I usually make eight of the rolls serve twelve by using them for a crust. The house brands may be lower in fat but they're usually not as good flavorwise—and don't quite cover the pan when you use them to make a crust. If you're going to use crescent rolls with lots of other stuff on top, then a house brand might be fine.

The Pillsbury French Loaf makes a wonderful **pizza crust** and fills a giant jelly roll pan. One-fifth of this package "costs" you only 1 gram of fat (and I don't even let you have that much!). Once you use this for your pizza crust, you will never go back to anything else instead. I use it to make calzones too.

I only use Philadelphia Fat Free **cream cheese** because it has the best consistency. I've tried other brands, but I wasn't happy with them. Healthy Choice makes lots of great products, but their cream cheese just doesn't work as well with my recipes.

Let's move to the **cheese** aisle. My preferred brand is Kraft reduced-fat shredded cheeses. I will not use the fat-free versions because *they don't melt.* I would gladly give up sugar and fat, but I will not give up flavor. This is a happy compromise. I use the reduced-fat version, I use less, and I use it where your eyes "eat" it, on top of the recipe. So you walk away satisfied and with a finished product that's very low in fat. If you want to make grilled-cheese sandwiches for your kids, use the Kraft ⅓ Less Fat cheese slices, and it'll taste exactly like the one they're used to. The fat-free will not.

Some brands have come out with a fat-free **hot dog,** but the ones we've tasted haven't been very good. So far, among the low-fat brands, I think Healthy Choice tastes the best. Did you know that regular hot dogs have as many as 15 grams of fat?

Dubuque's extra-lean reduced-sodium **ham** tastes wonderful, reduces the sodium as well as the fat, and gives you a larger serving. Don't be fooled by products called turkey ham; they may *not* be lower in fat than a very lean pork product. Here's one label as an example: I checked a brand of turkey ham called Genoa. It gives you a 2-ounce serving for 70 calories and 3½ grams of fat. The Dubuque extra-lean ham, made from pork, gives you a 3-ounce serving for 90 calories, but only 2½ grams of fat. *You get more food and less fat.*

The same can be true of packaged **ground turkey;** if you're not buying *fresh* ground turkey, you may be getting a product with turkey skin and lot of fat ground up in it. Look to be sure the package is labeled with the fat content; if it isn't, run the other way!

Your best bets in **snack foods** are pretzels, which are always low in fat, as well as the chips from the Guiltless Gourmet, which taste especially good with one of my dips.

Frozen dinners can be expensive and high in sodium, but it's smart to have two or three in the freezer as a backup when your best-laid plans go awry and you need to grab something on the run. It's not a good idea to rely on them too much—what if you can't get to the store to get them, or you're short on cash? The sodium can be high in some of them because they often replace the fat with salt, so do read the labels. Also ask yourself if the serving is enough to satisfy you; for many of us, it's not.

Egg substitute is expensive, and probably not necessary unless you're cooking for someone who has to worry about every bit of cholesterol in his or her diet. If you occasionally have a fried egg or an omelet, *use the real egg.* For cooking, you can usually substitute two egg whites for one whole egg. Most of the time it won't make any difference, but check your recipe carefully.

Frozen pizzas aren't particularly healthy, but used occasionally, in moderation, they're okay. Your best bet is to make your own using the Pillsbury French Loaf. Take a look at the frozen pizza package of your choice, though, because you may find that plain cheese pizza, which you might think would be the healthiest, might actually have the most fat. Since there's nothing else on there, they have to cover the crust with a heavy layer of high-fat cheese. A veggie pizza generally uses less cheese and more healthy, crunchy vegetables.

Healthy frozen desserts are hard to find except for the Weight Watchers brands. I've always felt that their portions are so small, and for their size still pretty high in fat and sugar. (This is one of the reasons I think I'll be successful marketing my frozen desserts someday. After Cliff tasted one of my earliest healthy pies—and licked the plate clean—he remarked that if I ever opened a restaurant, people would keep coming back for my desserts alone!) Keep an eye out for fat-free or very low-fat frozen yogurt or sorbet products. Even Häagen-Dazs, which makes some of the highest-fat-content ice cream, now has a fat-free fruit sorbet pop out that's pretty good. I'm sure there will be more before too long.

You have to be realistic: What are you willing to do, and what are you *not* willing to do? Let's take bread, for example. Some people just have to have the real thing—rye bread with caraway seeds or a whole-wheat version with bits of bran in it.

I prefer to use reduced-calorie **bread** because I like a *real* sandwich. This way, I can have two slices of bread and it counts as only one bread/starch exchange.

Do you love **croutons?** Forget the ones from the grocery store—they're extremely high in fat. Instead, take reduced-calorie bread, toast it, give it a quick spray of I Can't Believe It's Not Butter! spray, and let it dry a bit. Cut the bread in cubes. Then, for an extra-good flavor, put the pieces in a plastic bag with a couple of tablespoons of grated Kraft fat-free Parmesan cheese and shake them up. You might be surprised just how good they are! Here's another product that's really good for croutons—Corn Chex cereal. Sprinkle a few Chex on top of your salad, and I think you'll be pleasantly surprised. I've also found that Rice Chex, crushed up, with parsley flakes and a little bit of Parmesan cheese, makes a great topping for casseroles that you used to put potato chips on.

Salad toppers can make a lot of difference in how content you feel after you've eaten. Some low-fat cheese, some homemade croutons, and even some bacon bits on top of your greens deliver an abundance of tasty satisfaction. I always use the real Hormel **bacon bits** instead the imitation bacon-flavored bits. I only use a small amount, but you get that real bacon flavor—and less fat, too.

How I Shop for My Family

I always keep my kitchen stocked with my basic staples; that way, I can go to the cupboard and create new recipes anytime I'm inspired. I hope you will take the time (and allot the money) to stock your cupboards with items from the staples list, so you can enjoy developing your own healthy versions of family favorites without making extra trips to the market.

I'm always on the lookout for new products sitting on the grocery shelf. When I spot something I haven't seen before, I'll usually grab it, glance at the front, then turn it around and read the label carefully. I call it looking at the promises (the "come-on" on the front of the package) and then at the warranty (the ingredients list and the label on the back).

If it looks as good on the back as it does on the front, I'll say okay and either create a recipe on the spot or take it home for when I do think of something to do with it. Picking up a new product is just about the only time I buy something not on my list.

The items on my shopping list are normal, everyday foods, but as low-fat and low-sugar (*while still tasting good*) as I can find. I can make any recipe in this book as long as these staples are on my shelves. After using these products for a couple of weeks, you will find it becomes routine to have them on hand. And I promise you, I really don't spend any more at the store now than I did a few years ago when I told myself I couldn't afford some of these items. Back then, of course, plenty of unhealthy, high-priced snacks I really didn't need somehow made the magic leap from the grocery shelves into my cart. Who was I kidding?

Yes, you often have to pay a little more for fat-free or low-fat products, including meats. But since I frequently use a half pound of meat to serve four to six people, your cost per serving will be much lower.

Try adding up what you were spending before on chips and cookies, premium brand ice cream and fatty cuts of meat, and you'll soon see that we've *streamlined* your shopping cart—and taken the weight off your pocketbook as well as your hips!

Remember, your good health is *your* business—but it's big business, too. Write to the manufacturers of products you and your family enjoy but feel are just too high in fat, sugar, or sodium to be part of your new healthy lifestyle. Companies are spending millions of dollars to respond to consumers' concerns about food products, and I bet that in the next few years, you'll discover fat-free and low-fat versions of nearly every product piled high on your supermarket shelves!

The Man-Friendly Healthy Exchanges Kitchen

------∎------

You might be surprised to discover I still don't have a massive test kitchen stocked with every modern appliance and handy gadget ever made. The tiny galley kitchen where I first launched Healthy Exchanges has room for only one person at a time, but that never stopped me from feeling the sky's the limit when it comes to seeking out great healthy taste!

Because storage is at such a premium in my kitchen, I don't waste space with equipment I don't really need. Here's a list of what I consider worth having. If you notice serious gaps in your equipment, you can probably find most of what you need at a local discount store or garage sale. If your kitchen is equipped with more sophisticated appliances, don't feel guilty about using them. Enjoy every appliance you can find room for or that you can afford. Just be assured that healthy, quick, and delicious food can be prepared with the "basics."

A Healthy Exchanges Kitchen Equipment List

Good-quality nonstick skillets (medium, large)

Good-quality saucepans (small, medium, large)

Glass mixing bowls (small, medium, large)

Glass measures (1-cup, 2-cup, 4-cup, 8-cup)

Sharp knives (paring, chef, butcher)

Rubber spatulas

Wire whisks

Measuring spoons

Measuring cups

Large mixing spoons

Egg separator

Covered jar

Vegetable parer

Grater

Potato masher

Electric mixer

Electric blender

Electric skillet

Cooking timer

Slow cooker

Air popper for popcorn

Kitchen scales (unless you *always* use my recipes)

Wire racks for cooling baked goods

Electric toaster oven (to conserve energy for those times when only one item is being baked or for a recipe that calls for a short baking time)

4-inch round custard dishes

Glass pie plates

8-by-8-inch glass baking dishes

Cake pans (9-by-9-, 9-by-13-inch)

10¾-by-7-by-1½-inch biscuit pan

Cookie sheets (good nonstick ones)

Jelly roll pan

Muffin tins

5-by-9-inch bread pan

Plastic colander

Cutting board

Pie wedge server

Square-shaped server

Can opener (I prefer manual)

Rolling pin

How to Read a Healthy Exchanges® Recipe

--------■--------

The Healthy Exchanges Nutritional Analysis

Before using these recipes, you may wish to consult your physician or health-care provider to be sure they are appropriate for you. The information in this book is not intended to take the place of any medical advice. It reflects my experiences, studies, research, and opinions regarding healthy eating.

Each recipe includes nutritional information calculated in three ways:

Healthy Exchanges Weight-Loss Choices™ or Exchanges

Calories, fiber, and fat grams

Diabetic exchanges

In every Healthy Exchanges recipe, the diabetic exchanges have been calculated by a registered dietitian. All the other calculations were done by computer, using the Food Processor II software. When the ingredient listing gives more than one choice, the first ingredient listed is the one used in the recipe analysis. Due to inevitable variations in the ingredients you choose to use, the nutritional values should be considered approximate.

The annotation "(limited)" following Protein counts in some recipes indicates that consumption of whole eggs should be limited to four per week.

Please note the following symbols:

☆   This star means read the recipe's directions carefully for special instructions about **division** of ingredients.

❄   This symbol indicates **FREEZES WELL.**

A Few Cooking Terms to Ease the Way

---◼---

Everyone can learn to cook *The Healthy Exchanges Way.* It's simple, it's quick, and the results are delicious! If you've tended to avoid the kitchen because you find recipe instructions confusing or complicated, I hope I can help you feel more confident. I'm not offering a full cooking course here, just some terms I use often that I know you'll want to understand.

Bake: To cook food in the oven; sometimes called roasting

Beat: To mix very fast with a spoon, wire whisk, or electric mixer

Blend: To mix two or more ingredients together thoroughly so that the mixture is smooth

Boil: To cook in liquid until bubbles form

Brown: To cook at low to medium-low heat until ingredients turn brown

Chop: To cut food into small pieces with a knife, blender, or food processor

Cool: To let stand at room temperature until food is no longer hot to the touch

Combine: To mix ingredients together with a spoon

Dice: To chop into small, even-sized pieces

Drain: To pour off liquid; sometimes you will need to reserve the liquid to use in the recipe, so please read carefully.

Drizzle: To sprinkle drops of liquid (for example, chocolate syrup) lightly over top of food

Fold in: To combine delicate ingredients with other foods by using a gentle, circular motion. Example: adding Cool Whip Lite to an already stirred-up bowl of pudding

Preheat: To heat your oven to the desired temperature, usually about 10 minutes before you put your food in to bake

Sauté: To cook in skillet or frying pan until food is soft

Simmer: To cook in a small amount of liquid over low heat; this lets the flavors blend without too much liquid evaporating

Whisk: To beat with a wire whisk until mixture is well mixed; don't worry about finesse here, just use some elbow grease!

How to Measure

I try to make it as easy as possible by providing more than one measurement for many ingredients in my recipes—both the weight in ounces and the amount measured by a measuring cup, for example. Just remember:

- You measure **solids** (flour, Cool Whip Lite, yogurt, macaroni, nonfat dry milk powder) in your set of separate measuring cups (¼, ⅓, ½, 1 cup)

- You measure **liquids** (Diet Mountain Dew, water, tomato juice) in the clear glass or plastic measuring cups that measure ounces, cups, and pints. Set the cup on a level surface and pour the liquid into it.

- You can use your measuring spoon set for liquids or solids. **Note:** Don't pour a liquid like an extract into a measuring spoon held over the bowl and run the risk of overpouring; instead, do it over the sink.

Here are a few handy equivalents:

3 teaspoons	equals	**1 tablespoon**
4 tablespoons	equals	**¼ cup**
5⅓ tablespoons	equals	**⅓ cup**
8 tablespoons	equals	**½ cup**
10⅔ tablespoons	equals	**⅔ cup**
12 tablespoons	equals	**¾ cup**
16 tablespoons	equals	**1 cup**
2 cups	equals	**1 pint**
4 cups	equals	**1 quart**
8 ounces liquid	equals	**1 fluid cup**

That's it. Now, ready, set, cook!

THE RECIPES

Soups to Satisfy
a Hungry Man

------■------

When I cook soup, the wonderful aromas coming from my kitchen are as good as the loud clanging of a dinner bell to get my husband Cliff's attention. When winter comes to Iowa, it comes with more cold and snow than most of the country gets—and it stays and stays. So once there's a chill in the air, Cliff usually heads for the kitchen and starts lifting lids on my stove until he finds what he's been hoping for: a thick, substantial soup like Ranch Hand Corn Chowder that tastes as rich as if I'd mixed a whole container of cream into it. Packed in a thermos for him to take to work, or served up on a Sunday afternoon after hours spent digging out the car, soup warms a man's heart like almost nothing else!*

Remember those soup commercials that promised soups *hearty* enough for a man to enjoy? Full of big chunks of meat, potatoes, and vegetables? Rich with flavor, and so filling that a bowl of soup and a sandwich would satisfy a man's appetite?

They could have been talking about Healthy Exchanges soups, which are so intensely flavorful and delicious, so creamy and thick, you'll be surprised at how low in fat each one is. This section of the book includes chowders and cream soups, even some recipes so full of good things they're practically stews.

Soups

-----■-----

Tomato Rice Fagioli Soup

Quick Minestrone Soup

Mexican Cheese Soup

German Potato Soup

Cabbage Noodle Soup

Tuna Corn Chowder

Manhattan-Style
Clam Chowder

Mexican Chicken Soup

Iowa Chicken Noodle Soup

Italian Chicken
Spaghetti Soup

Creamy Vegetable Beef Soup

Ranch Hand Corn Chowder

Cabbage Patch Soup

Chili Veggie Soup

Blazing Glory Chili

Grandma's "Homemade"
Harvest Time Soup

Old-Fashioned Vegetable
Beef Soup

Frankfurter Vegetable Soup

Gringo Franks and Corn Soup

Chunky Corn-Ham Chowder

Garden Ham and Bean Soup

Cliff's Ham and Bean Soup

Chicken Noodle Vegetable Soup

Tomato Chicken Rice Soup

■

Tomato Rice Fagioli Soup

-------------------------- ❄ --------------------------

Here's a terrific rice and cheese combo—rich, fragrant, and oh-so-delicious, with the pleasant surprise of green beans to make it even more filling. It stirs up quickly and reheats well.

Serves 4

1 (10¾-ounce) can Healthy Request Tomato Soup
1⅓ cups skim milk
1 teaspoon Italian seasoning
2 teaspoons dried onion flakes
1 cup (one 8-ounce can) cut green beans, rinsed and drained

½ cup (2.5-ounce jar) sliced mushrooms, drained
⅔ cup (2 ounces) uncooked instant rice
¼ cup (¾ ounce) grated Kraft fat-free Parmesan cheese

In a large saucepan, combine tomato soup, skim milk, Italian seasoning, and onion flakes. Stir in green beans and mushrooms. Bring mixture to a boil. Stir in rice. Cover and remove from heat. Let set 5 minutes. For each serving, spoon 1 cup soup into a bowl and top with 1 tablespoon Parmesan cheese.

Each serving equals:

HE: ¾ Vegetable, ½ Bread, ⅓ Skim Milk, ¼ Protein, ½ Slider, 10 Optional Calories

153 Calories, 1 gm Fat, 7 gm Protein, 29 gm Carbohydrate, 486 mg Sodium, 5 gm Fiber

DIABETIC: 1½ Starch, 1 Vegetable

Quick Minestrone Soup

--------------------- ❄ ---------------------

When it comes to really hearty meatless soups, nothing is more tummy satisfying than this substantial bowl of goodness. Even meat-and-potato men don't miss the meat when they gobble down a big bowl of this homey favorite. Serve it with sandwiches—hot or cold—for a great comfort meal.

Serves 4 (1½ cups)

2 cups (one 16-ounce can) Healthy Request Chicken Broth
1 cup water
¾ cup frozen sliced carrots
1 cup frozen cut green beans
1 cup (one 8-ounce can) stewed tomatoes, coarsely chopped, undrained
½ teaspoon dried minced garlic
1 teaspoon Italian seasoning
⅔ cup (1½ ounces) uncooked pasta shells
6 ounces (one 8-ounce can) red kidney beans, rinsed and drained
1¼ cups diced zucchini

In a large saucepan, combine chicken broth, water, carrots, and green beans. Bring mixture to a boil. Stir in undrained tomatoes, minced garlic, and Italian seasoning. Add pasta shells, kidney beans, and zucchini. Mix well to combine. Lower heat. Simmer 10 minutes or until pasta shells and vegetables are tender. Continue simmering 10 minutes.

Each serving equals:

HE: 2 Vegetable, ¾ Protein, ½ Bread, 8 Optional Calories

116 Calories, 0 gm Fat, 6 gm Protein, 23 gm Carbohydrate, 425 mg Sodium, 5 gm Fiber

DIABETIC: 2 Vegetable, ½ Meat, ½ Starch

Mexican Cheese Soup

--------------------- ❋ ---------------------

Oh, how that crowd of men at my Healthy Man Taste-Testing Buffet went crazy over this one! I think it may have been the favorite choice among the six soups they sampled, probably because of my "secret ingredients"—the blend of spicy salsa and creamy cream of mushroom soup with the cheese. You may not believe how fast this tasty treat can be prepared. *Serves 4*

2 cups (one 16-ounce can) Healthy Request Chicken Broth
1 cup shredded carrots
1 cup finely chopped celery
½ cup chunky salsa (mild, medium, or hot)
1 (10¾-ounce) can Healthy Request Cream of Mushroom Soup

1 teaspoon Worcestershire sauce
1½ cups (6 ounces) shredded Kraft reduced-fat Cheddar cheese
⅔ cup Carnation Nonfat Dry Milk Powder
1 cup water
¼ cup chopped fresh parsley

In a medium saucepan, combine chicken broth, carrots, and celery. Cook over medium heat until vegetables are tender, about 10 minutes. Stir in salsa, mushroom soup, Worcestershire sauce, and Cheddar cheese. In a small bowl, combine dry milk powder and water. Stir milk mixture into soup. Continue cooking, stirring often, until cheese melts and mixture is heated through. For each serving, spoon 1¼ cups soup into a bowl and sprinkle 1 tablespoon chopped parsley evenly over top.

Each serving equals:

HE: 2 Protein, 1¼ Vegetable, ½ Skim Milk, ¼ Slider, 9 Optional Calories

195 Calories, 7 gm Fat, 17 gm Protein, 16 gm Carbohydrate, 971 mg Sodium, 1 gm Fiber

DIABETIC: 1½ Meat, 1 Vegetable, 1 Starch

German Potato Soup

-------------------------■-------------------------

If you like German potato salad, the kind that's served warm with vinegar, combining those great sweet-and-sour flavors, here's an irresistible soup that will serve up the flavors you love in a cozy, filling, quick-fix dish.   *Serves 4 (1 cup)*

½ cup chopped onion
1 cup diced celery
2 tablespoons Hormel Bacon Bits
1 (10¾-ounce) can Healthy Request Cream of Celery Soup or Mushroom Soup
2 tablespoons Sugar Twin or Sprinkle Sweet
2 tablespoons white vinegar
2⅔ cups skim milk
1½ cups (8 ounces) diced cooked potatoes

In a large saucepan sprayed with butter-flavored cooking spray, sauté onion and celery 10 minutes. Stir in bacon bits, celery soup, Sugar Twin, and vinegar. Add skim milk and potatoes. Mix well to combine. Lower heat and simmer 10 minutes or until mixture is heated through.

Each serving equals:

HE: ¾ Vegetable, ⅔ Skim Milk, ½ Bread, ½ Slider, 17 Optional Calories

178 Calories, 2 gm Fat, 9 gm Protein, 31 gm Carbohydrate, 498 mg Sodium, 2 gm Fiber

DIABETIC: 1 Skim Milk, 1 Starch

Cabbage Noodle Soup

-------------------- ❋ --------------------

I like to think of this as a "surprise" soup, because it may catch you off guard with its unexpected ingredients. Usually cabbage soups are combined with rice to make them into a hungry-man's main-dish meal, but I've created an even heartier version that adds noodles to the bowl. This one's a favorite with all the men in the family. **Serves 4 (1¼ cups)**

2 cups shredded cabbage	Request Cream of
1¾ cups (3 ounces) uncooked	Mushroom Soup
noodles	2 cups skim milk
2 cups water	⅛ teaspoon black pepper
2 teaspoons dried onion flakes	¼ cup (¾ ounce) grated
1 teaspoon dried parsley flakes	Kraft fat-free Parmesan
1 (10¾-ounce) can Healthy	cheese

In a medium saucepan, combine cabbage, noodles, water, onion flakes, and parsley flakes. Cook over medium heat, stirring occasionally, until cabbage and noodles are tender, about 10 minutes. Stir in mushroom soup, skim milk, and black pepper. Continue cooking, stirring often, until mixture is heated through, about 5 minutes. Add Parmesan cheese. Mix well to combine. Serve at once.

Each serving equals:

HE: 1 Vegetable, 1 Bread, ½ Skim Milk, ¼ Protein, ½ Slider, 1 Optional Calorie

219 Calories, 3 gm Fat, 11 gm Protein, 37 gm Carbohydrate, 461 mg Sodium, 2 gm Fiber

DIABETIC: 2 Starch, 1 Free Vegetable, ½ Skim Milk

Tuna Corn Chowder

My inspiration for this recipe was that delicious, easy-to-fix, and much-loved family favorite—tuna casserole! Did you ever think that you could savor those same flavors in a yummy soup? This was another big winner among the men who taste-tested a bundle of Healthy Exchanges recipes for me—and it got plenty of "yes" votes!

Serves 4 (1 cup)

1 (6-ounce) can white tuna, packed in water, drained and flaked
1 (10¾-ounce) can Healthy Request Cream of Mushroom Soup
1½ cups (one 12-fluid-ounce can) Carnation Evaporated Skim Milk
¾ cup (4 ounces) diced cooked potatoes
1½ cups frozen whole kernel corn
¼ cup (¾ ounce) grated Kraft fat-free Parmesan cheese
1 teaspoon dried onion flakes
1 teaspoon dried parsley flakes

In a large saucepan, combine tuna, mushroom soup, and evaporated skim milk. Stir in potatoes, corn, Parmesan cheese, onion flakes, and parsley flakes. Cook over low heat, stirring often, until mixture is heated through.

Each serving equals:

HE: 1 Bread, ¾ Protein, ¾ Skim Milk, ½ Slider, 1 Optional Calorie

150 Calories, 2 gm Fat, 15 gm Protein, 18 gm Carbohydrate, 543 mg Sodium, 1 gm Fiber

DIABETIC: 1½ Meat, 1 Skim Milk, ½ Starch

Manhattan-Style Clam Chowder

--------------------------------❋--------------------------------

I'll confess it: I don't like clams. But since both my husband, Cliff, and my son Tommy *love* them, I knew a thick and tasty clam chowder they both enjoyed belonged in this book. This dish is low in fat and high in protein, but best of all, it's truly high in tastiness! *Serves 2 (1½ cups)*

1 cup (5 ounces) diced raw potatoes	1¾ cups water
½ cup shredded carrots	1 cup (one 8-ounce can) stewed tomatoes, undrained
½ cup diced onion	
2 teaspoons dried parsley flakes	1 (6.5-ounce) can minced clams, undrained

In a medium saucepan, combine potatoes, carrots, onion, parsley flakes, and water. Cook over medium heat until vegetables are tender, about 20 minutes. Add undrained tomatoes and undrained clams. Mix well to combine. Continue cooking until heated through, about 5 minutes.

Each serving equals:

HE: 2 Vegetable, 1½ Protein, ½ Bread

----

183 Calories, 1 gm Fat, 16 gm Protein, 28 gm Carbohydrate, 453 mg Sodium, 3 gm Fiber

----

DIABETIC: 2 Vegetable, 2 Meat, 1 Starch

Mexican Chicken Soup

---------------------- ❋ ----------------------

For all the chicken soup fans in your house, here's a tangy version that is really substantial and will "fill 'em up"! The combination of corn and rice always wins men over, and it smells really "chicken-y" because you cook the chicken in the broth. I think anyone who likes to feel they're cooking "from scratch" will appreciate this recipe, too. Remember, it's okay to use one full cup diced cooked chicken breast or even cooked turkey if that's what you've got instead of the raw chicken.

Serves 4 (1½ cups)

2 cups (one 16-ounce can) Healthy Request Chicken Broth
2 cups water
8 ounces skinned and boned uncooked chicken breasts, cut into 16 pieces
1 (10¾-ounce) can Healthy Request Cream of Chicken Soup
1 cup chunky salsa (mild, medium, or hot)
1 cup hot cooked rice
1 cup frozen whole kernel corn
½ teaspoon dried minced garlic
1 teaspoon dried parsley flakes

In a large saucepan, combine chicken broth, water, and chicken pieces. Cook over medium heat until chicken is tender, about 10 minutes. Stir in chicken soup and salsa. Add rice, corn, garlic, and parsley flakes. Mix well to combine. Lower heat. Simmer 10 minutes, stirring occasionally.

HINT: ⅔ cup uncooked rice usually cooks to about 1 cup.

Each serving equals:

HE: 1½ Protein, 1 Bread, ½ Vegetable, ½ Slider, 13 Optional Calories

---

198 Calories, 2 gm Fat, 18 gm Protein, 27 gm Carbohydrate, 832 mg Sodium, 1 gm Fiber

---

DIABETIC: 1½ Meat, 1½ Starch, ½ Vegetable

Iowa Chicken Noodle Soup

------------------------------ ✳ ------------------------------

Here's a delicious combination of chicken, corn, and noodles that smells like Mom's home cooking! Maybe it's because corn is most men's favorite vegetable (and their favorite four-letter food word after "meat," too!), I always look for ways to incorporate it into recipes created for men's appetites.

Serves 4 (1½ cups)

4 cups (two 16-ounce cans)
   Healthy Request Chicken
   Broth
1 cup chopped celery
½ cup shredded carrots
½ cup chopped onion
1½ cups (8 ounces) diced
   cooked chicken breast

1 teaspoon dried parsley
   flakes
¼ teaspoon black pepper
1 cup frozen whole kernel
   corn
Scant 1 cup (1½ ounces)
   uncooked medium noodles

In a large saucepan, combine chicken broth, celery, carrots, and onion. Bring mixture to a boil. Stir in chicken, parsley flakes, and black pepper. Add corn and noodles. Mix well to combine. Bring mixture to a boil again. Lower heat. Cover and simmer 10 minutes or until noodles and vegetables are tender, stirring occasionally.

HINT: A 10-ounce can of Swanson White Chicken packed in water, drained and flaked is 8 ounces drained weight.

Each serving equals:

HE: 2 Protein, 1 Bread, 1 Vegetable, 16 Optional Calories

174 Calories, 2 gm Fat, 23 gm Protein, 16 gm Carbohydrate, 557 mg Sodium, 2 gm Fiber

DIABETIC: 2 Meat, 1 Starch, 1 Free Vegetable

Italian Chicken Spaghetti Soup

------------------------------ ❋ ------------------------------

Parmesan cheese gives you a lot of flavor for not a lot of calorie and fat grams, especially when you use the nonfat version. So make a small deduction from your daily food bank account and you'll yell, "Magnifico!" "Delicioso!" just like the men of Italy who always appreciate good food. To make for easier eating, and just because it's fun, break up the spaghetti in smaller pieces before dropping it into the pot.   *Serves 4*

2 cups (one 16-ounce can)
    Healthy Request Chicken
    Broth
2 cups water
1 (10¾-ounce) can Healthy
    Request Cream of Chicken
    Soup
1 cup finely chopped celery
½ chopped onion
½ cup (one 2.5-ounce jar)
    sliced mushrooms, drained

1½ cups (8 ounces) diced
    cooked chicken breast
1 teaspoon Italian seasoning
1 teaspoon dried parsley
    flakes
¾ cup (1½ ounces) uncooked
    broken spaghetti
¼ cup (¾ ounce) grated
    Kraft fat-free Parmesan
    cheese

In a large saucepan, combine chicken broth, water, and chicken soup. Stir in celery and onion. Bring mixture to a boil. Add mushrooms, chicken, Italian seasoning, parsley flakes, and spaghetti. Mix well to combine. Cover. Lower heat and simmer 30 minutes. For each serving, spoon 1½ cups soup into a bowl and top with 1 tablespoon Parmesan cheese.

Each serving equals:

HE: 2¼ Protein, 1 Vegetable, ½ Bread, ½ Slider, 13 Optional Calories

----

232 Calories, 4 gm Fat, 25 gm Protein, 24 gm Carbohydrate, 793 mg Sodium, 2 gm Fiber

----

DIABETIC: 2 Meat, 1½ Starch, ½ Vegetable

Creamy Vegetable Beef Soup

--------------------------- ❄ ---------------------------

Mmmm! Cliff thought this tasted almost like pot roast in a bowl. A bowl of it will stick to your ribs without padding them, and it'll fill you up without filling you out. You'll also get a little extra boost of calcium—and a lot of creamy flavor, which makes this recipe a winner on all counts!

Serves 4 (1⅓ cups)

8 ounces ground 90% lean
   turkey or beef
½ cup finely chopped onion
1¾ cups (one 15-ounce can)
   Swanson Beef Broth
Scant 1 cup (1½ ounces)
   uncooked noodles
1 cup (one 8-ounce can) sliced
   carrots, rinsed and drained

1 cup (one 8-ounce can) cut
   green beans, rinsed and
   drained
1 (10¾-ounce) can Healthy
   Request Cream of
   Mushroom Soup
⅓ cup Carnation Nonfat Dry
   Milk Powder
1 cup water

In a large saucepan sprayed with butter-flavored cooking spray, brown meat and onion. Stir in beef broth and noodles. Bring mixture to a boil. Add carrots and beans. Mix well to combine. Lower heat and simmer 10 minutes. In a small bowl, combine mushroom soup, dry milk powder, and water. Add soup mixture to meat mixture. Continue to simmer 5 minutes or until noodles are tender, stirring occasionally.

Each serving equals:

HE: 1½ Protein, ½ Bread, 1¼ Vegetable, ½ Slider, 10 Optional Calories

----

223 Calories, 7 gm Fat, 16 gm Protein, 24 gm Carbohydrate, 794 mg Sodium, 2 gm Fiber

----

DIABETIC: 1½ Meat, 1½ Starch, 1 Vegetable

Ranch Hand Corn Chowder

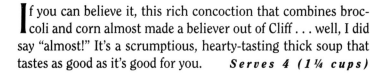

If you can believe it, this rich concoction that combines broccoli and corn almost made a believer out of Cliff . . . well, I did say "almost!" It's a scrumptious, hearty-tasting thick soup that tastes as good as it's good for you. *Serves 4 (1¼ cups)*

8 ounces ground 90% lean turkey or beef
½ cup chopped onion
1 (16-ounce) package frozen chopped broccoli
2 cups frozen whole kernel corn

1 (10¾-ounce) can Healthy Request Cream of Mushroom Soup
1⅓ cups skim milk
1 tablespoon Worcestershire sauce
1 teaspoon dried parsley flakes

In a large saucepan sprayed with butter-flavored cooking spray, brown meat and onion. Stir in broccoli and corn. Continue cooking, 5 minutes, stirring often. Add mushroom soup, skim milk, Worcestershire sauce, and parsley flakes. Mix well to combine. Lower heat. Cover and simmer 10 minutes, stirring occasionally.

Each serving equals:

HE: 1½ Protein, 1 Bread, ¾ Vegetable, ⅓ Skim Milk, ½ Slider, 1 Optional Calorie

254 Calories, 6 gm Fat, 18 gm Protein, 32 gm Carbohydrate, 448 mg Sodium, 4 gm Fiber

DIABETIC: 2 Starch, 1½ Meat, 1 Vegetable

Cabbage Patch Soup

-----------------❄-----------------

You know how much I believe in easy-to-fix recipes, right? Well, here's one of my time-saving secrets: coleslaw mix stirred into a tasty soup. It's not quite a chili, but it's more than a vegetable soup. Just think of it as two great flavors joining forces to become better together than either on its own.

Serves 4 (1½ cups)

8 ounces ground 90% lean
   turkey or beef
½ cup chopped onion
1 cup thinly sliced celery
1¾ cups (one 15-ounce can)
   Hunt's Chunky Tomato
   Sauce
2 cups water

10 ounces (one 16-ounce can)
   red kidney beans, rinsed
   and drained
2 teaspoons chili seasoning
¼ teaspoon black pepper
2½ cups purchased coleslaw
   mix
1 cup frozen whole kernel corn

In a large saucepan sprayed with butter-flavored cooking spray, brown meat, onion, and celery. Stir in tomato sauce, water, kidney beans, chili seasoning, and black pepper. Bring mixture to a boil. Stir in coleslaw mix and corn. Lower heat. Simmer until cabbage is tender, about 15 minutes, stirring occasionally.

HINT: 2 cups chopped cabbage and ½ cup shredded carrots may be used instead of purchased coleslaw mix.

Each serving equals:

HE: 3¾ Vegetable, 2¾ Protein, ½ Bread

----

233 Calories, 5 gm Fat, 17 gm Protein, 30 gm Carbohydrate,
288 mg Sodium, 8 gm Fiber

DIABETIC: 2 Vegetable, 2 Meat, 1 Starch

Chili Veggie Soup

--------------------■--------------------

This is a super-convenient chili that includes all the traditional vegetables men like best—and none of those "funny" ones! It's especially hearty, too, with the combination of beef broth and tomato sauce, plus just enough kidney beans to give it the "feel of a meal." Of course, not every man loves traditional chili. I remember when my son Tommy was six and got his foot caught in his bike and had to get it x-rayed. They asked me, Is he allergic to anything? Just kidney beans, he piped up. So if you have anyone in your family who is "allergic" to kidney beans, just leave them out.

Serves 6 (1½ cups)

8 ounces ground 90% lean turkey or beef
½ cup chopped onion
1¾ cups (one 15-ounce can) Hunt's Chunky Tomato Sauce
1¾ cups (one 15-ounce can) Swanson Beef Broth
1 cup water
2 teaspoons chili seasoning

½ cup chunky salsa (mild, medium, or hot)
1½ cups frozen cut green beans
1½ cups frozen cut carrots
1 cup frozen whole kernel corn
1 cup frozen peas
6 ounces (one 8-ounce can) red kidney beans, rinsed and drained

In a large skillet sprayed with butter-flavored cooking spray, brown meat and onion. In a crockpot container, combine browned meat mixture, tomato sauce, beef broth, water, chili seasoning, and salsa. Stir in green beans, carrots, corn, peas, and kidney beans. Cover. Cook on LOW 6 to 8 hours.

Each serving equals:

HE: 2½ Vegetable, 1½ Protein, ⅔ Bread, 5 Optional Calories

----
180 Calories, 4 gm Fat, 13 gm Protein, 23 gm Carbohydrate, 840 mg Sodium, 5 gm Fiber
----

DIABETIC: 2 Vegetable, 1½ Meat, 1 Starch

Blazing Glory Chili

------------ ❋ ------------

This time, instead of thickening up this recipe with beans, I added macaroni for more substance, and for a man-pleasing presentation. This dish is so good, you might try serving it up when you're hoping for a gift of jewelry—or just want the man in your life to promise to do those "honey-do" jobs without a single complaint.   *Serves 4 (1½ cups)*

8 ounces ground 90% lean
   turkey or beef
1 cup chopped onion
½ cup chopped green bell
   pepper
½ teaspoon dried minced
   garlic
1 (10¾-ounce) can
   Healthy Request
   Tomato Soup
2 cups (one 16-ounce can)
   tomatoes, coarsely
   chopped and
   undrained

6 ounces (one 8-ounce can)
   red kidney beans, rinsed
   and drained
2 teaspoons chili seasoning
⅛ teaspoon black pepper
1¾ cups (one 15-ounce can)
   Swanson Beef Broth
⅔ cup (1½ ounces) uncooked
   elbow macaroni
¼ cup Land O Lakes fat-free
   sour cream
⅓ cup (1½ ounces) shredded
   Kraft reduced-fat Cheddar
   cheese

In a large saucepan sprayed with olive-flavored cooking spray, brown meat, onion, and green pepper. Stir in garlic, tomato soup, and undrained tomatoes. Add kidney beans, chili seasoning, black pepper, and beef broth. Mix well to combine. Bring mixture to a boil. Stir in macaroni. Lower heat. Simmer 10 minutes or until macaroni is tender. When serving, top each bowl with 1 tablespoon sour cream and a scant 1½ tablespoons Cheddar cheese.

Each serving equals:

HE: 2¾ Protein, 1¾ Vegetable, ½ Bread, ¾ Slider, 9 Optional Calories

337 Calories, 9 gm Fat, 22 gm Protein, 42 gm Carbohydrate,
818 mg Sodium, 9 gm Fiber

DIABETIC: 2½ Meat, 2 Starch, 1½ Vegetable

Grandma's "Homemade" Harvest Time Soup

------------ ❄ ------------

You'll be amazed how homemade this tastes—and in just 15 minutes! Feel free to pretend you slaved hours over a hot stove to prepare this tummy-pleasing dish, knowing your secret is safe—a delicious sauce thickened with stewed tomatoes.

Serves 4 (1 ½ cups)

8 ounces ground 90% lean turkey or beef
¼ cup chopped onion
1 cup (one 8-ounce can) Hunt's Tomato Sauce
1¾ cups (one 14½-ounce can) stewed tomatoes, undrained
½ cup water
1 teaspoon dried parsley flakes
1 cup (one 8-ounce can) cut green beans, rinsed and drained
1 cup (one 8-ounce can) sliced carrots, rinsed and drained
½ cup frozen peas, rinsed and drained
½ cup frozen whole kernel corn

In a large saucepan sprayed with butter-flavored cooking spray, brown meat and onion. Add tomato sauce, undrained tomatoes, water, parsley flakes, green beans, and carrots. Mix well to combine. Bring mixture to a boil. Stir in peas and corn. Lower heat and simmer 10 minutes.

Each serving equals:

HE: 3 Vegetable, 1½ Protein, ½ Bread

----

225 Calories, 5 gm Fat, 16 gm Protein, 29 gm Carbohydrate, 989 mg Sodium, 5 gm Fiber

----

DIABETIC: 3 Vegetable, 1½ Meat, ½ Starch

Old-Fashioned Vegetable Beef Soup

T his is a real favorite served often to the guests who visit Jo's Kitchen Cafe, and it's a winner with the factory workers who line up to buy lunch from our catering truck. They don't care that it's healthy, they told me, just that it's *good*. But the men who've had to eat more carefully after a heart attack (or a warning from a doctor about cholesterol) love the fact that it's healthy *and* good!

Serves 4 (1 ½ cups)

2 cups (one 16-ounce can) tomatoes, undrained
1¾ cups (one 15-ounce can) Swanson Beef Broth
1 tablespoon lemon juice
2 teaspoons Sugar Twin or Sprinkle Sweet
1 teaspoon dried parsley flakes

2 cups coarsely chopped cabbage
1 cup chopped celery
1 cup chopped carrots
½ cup chopped onion
1 cup (5 ounces) diced lean cooked roast beef

In a blender container, combine undrained tomatoes and beef broth. Cover and process on CHOP for 10 seconds. Pour mixture into a large saucepan. Stir in lemon juice, Sugar Twin, and parsley flakes. Add cabbage, celery, carrots, onion, and roast beef. Mix well to combine. Bring mixture to a boil. Lower heat. Cover and simmer 30 minutes or until vegetables are tender, stirring occasionally.

Each serving equals:

HE: 3¼ Vegetable, 1¼ Protein, 10 Optional Calories

123 Calories, 3 gm Fat, 13 gm Protein, 11 gm Carbohydrate, 613 mg Sodium, 2 gm Fiber

DIABETIC: 2 Vegetable, 1 Meat

Frankfurter Vegetable Soup

---------------------------- ❈ ----------------------------

This is one for the kid in every man—and I know it's there, I've been feeding it for years! Tommy and Cliff both enjoyed this soup a lot and asked to have it again. When they vote with their taste buds, this one'll win by a landslide.

Serves 4 (1½ cups)

2 cups (one 16-ounce can)
    Healthy Request Chicken
    Broth
½ cup chopped onion
1 cup chopped celery
1¾ cups (one 15-ounce can)
    Hunt's Chunky Tomato
    Sauce

2 cups water
2 cups shredded cabbage
Scant 1 cup (1½ ounces)
    uncooked noodles
8 ounces diced Healthy
    Choice 97% fat free
    frankfurters
1 teaspoon chili seasoning

In a large saucepan, combine chicken broth, onion, and celery. Cook over medium heat until vegetables are crisp-tender, about 5 to 8 minutes. Stir in tomato sauce, water, cabbage, and noodles. Add frankfurters and chili seasoning. Mix well to combine. Lower heat. Simmer about 10 minutes or until cabbage and noodles are tender, stirring occasionally.

Each serving equals:

HE: 3½ Vegetable, 1½ Protein, ½ Bread, 8 Optional Calories

---

129 Calories, 1 gm Fat, 12 gm Protein, 18 gm Carbohydrate, 1,349 mg Sodium, 2 gm Fiber

---

DIABETIC: 1½ Meat, 1 Vegetable, 1 Free Vegetable, ½ Starch

Gringo Franks and Corn Soup

------------------------------- ✳ -------------------------------

This one is quick, spicy fun—faster than even a drive-up Mexican restaurant, and full of old-fashioned goodness that will make them cheer "Olé!" You choose how hot is hot enough for you and your family, but mild or wild, this soup is a real treat.

Serves 4 (1 ¼ cups)

1 (10¾-ounce) can Healthy
   Request Tomato Soup
8 ounces diced Healthy Choice
   97% fat free frankfurters
½ cup chunky salsa (mild,
   medium, or hot)

2 cups frozen whole kernel
   corn
1 cup skim milk
1 teaspoon dried parsley
   flakes

In a medium saucepan, combine tomato soup, frankfurters, salsa, and corn. Bring mixture to a boil. Lower heat. Simmer 5 minutes. Stir in skim milk and parsley flakes. Continue cooking, stirring often, until mixture is heated through. Serve at once.

Each serving equals:

HE: 1⅓ Protein, 1 Bread, ¼ Vegetable, ¼ Skim Milk, ½ Slider,
5 Optional Calories

----

218 Calories, 2 gm Fat, 13 gm Protein, 37 gm Carbohydrate,
911 mg Sodium, 5 gm Fiber

DIABETIC: 2 Starch, 1½ Meat

Chunky Corn-Ham Chowder

------------------------- ❄ -------------------------

James told me this was better than a ham-and-cheese on rye! He's Iowa born and bred, so of course he loves recipes that include a healthy helping of corn. He's not alone, either—most men tell me they just can't get enough corn, and that it makes just about everything but dessert better.   *Serves 4 (1 cup)*

1 full cup (6 ounces) diced
Dubuque 97% fat-free
ham or any extra-lean ham
½ cup diced onion
1 cup (5 ounces) diced raw
potatoes
1 cup water
1½ cups frozen whole kernel
corn

1½ cups (one 12-fluid-ounce
can) Carnation Evaporated
Skim Milk
2 teaspoons dried parsley
flakes
¾ cup (3 ounces) shredded
Kraft reduced-fat Cheddar
cheese
¼ teaspoon black pepper

In a large saucepan, combine ham, onion, potatoes, and water. Cook over medium heat until potatoes are tender, about 10 minutes. Stir in corn, evaporated skim milk, parsley flakes, Cheddar cheese, and black pepper. Continue cooking, stirring often, until mixture is heated through and cheese is melted.

Each serving equals:

HE: 2 Protein, 1 Bread, ¾ Skim Milk, ¼ Vegetable

----

269 Calories, 5 gm Fat, 23 gm Protein, 33 gm Carbohydrate,
641 mg Sodium, 2 gm Fiber

DIABETIC: 2 Meat, 1 Starch, 1 Skim Milk

Garden Ham and Bean Soup

---------------------------- ※ ----------------------------

Now that there are great low-fat ham choices, we can enjoy ham in many more dishes, secure in knowing that what tastes good is good for us too. Here's a rich and hearty soup that is almost a stew, with lots of satisfaction in the green beans, carrots, and great northern beans. If you're not sure which one they are, look for "cannellini" on the can. You'll be glad you did!

Serves 4 (1½ cups)

½ cup finely chopped onion
1½ cups (8 ounces) diced cooked potatoes
1 full cup (6 ounces) diced Dubuque 97% fat-free ham or any extra-lean ham
1 cup (one 8-ounce can) cut green beans, rinsed and drained
1 cup (one 8-ounce can) sliced carrots, rinsed and drained
10 ounces (one 16-ounce can) great northern beans, rinsed and drained
1 teaspoon dried parsley flakes
1 (10¾-ounce) can Healthy Request Tomato Soup
1 cup skim milk

In a medium saucepan sprayed with butter-flavored cooking spray, sauté onion until tender, about 5 minutes. Stir in potatoes, ham, green beans, carrots, and great northern beans. Add parsley flakes, tomato soup, and skim milk. Mix well to combine. Lower heat. Simmer 10 minutes or until heated through.

Each serving equals:

HD. 2¼ Protein, 1¼ Vegetable, ½ Bread, ¼ Skim Milk, ½ Slider, 5 Optional Calories

-----

283 Calories, 3 gm Fat, 17 gm Protein, 47 gm Carbohydrate, 702 mg Sodium, 9 gm Fiber

-----

DIABETIC: 2½ Starch, 2 Meat, 1 Vegetable

Cliff's Ham and Bean Soup

------------------------------ ❄ ------------------------------

You'll notice who inspired this particular thick and fragrant soup—the truck drivin' man who developed his taste buds in truck stops across the country. Cliff always looks forward to a new soup, especially when it comes with chunks of delicious ham. This dish is as pleasing to the nose as it is to the mouth, and you'll find that every man within "aroma distance" will soon find his way to the kitchen!   *Serves 4 (1 cup)*

20 ounces (two 16-ounce   *1 cup diced onion*
    cans) navy beans, rinsed   *1 cup diced celery*
    and drained   *1 cup shredded carrots*
½ cup (3 ounces) diced   *3 cups water*
    Dubuque 97% fat-free   *1 teaspoon dried parsley flakes*
    ham or any extra-lean ham   *¼ teaspoon black pepper*

In a large saucepan, combine navy beans, ham, onion, celery, and carrots. Add water, parsley flakes, and black pepper. Mix well to combine. Bring mixture to a boil. Lower heat. Cover and simmer 30 minutes or until vegetables are tender, stirring occasionally.

Each serving equals:

HE: 3 Protein, 1½ Vegetable

----

266 Calories, 2 gm Fat, 17 gm Protein, 45 gm Carbohydrate,
218 mg Sodium, 14 gm Fiber

DIABETIC: 2½ Starch, 2 Meat, 1 Vegetable

Chicken Noodle Vegetable Soup

------------------------------ ❄ ------------------------------

Yum, yum, yum. That's what I hear whenever this soup's on the menu, and I'll bet it's because the combination of chicken broth and old-fashioned noodles brings back wonderful memories of Sunday dinner at Grandma's house. Now you can enjoy that cozy goodness anytime, even if you live miles away.

Serves 6 (1½ cups)

4 cups (two 16-ounce cans)
    Healthy Request Chicken
    Broth
½ cup chopped onion
1 cup chopped celery
2 cups frozen cut green beans
2 cups frozen sliced carrots
1½ cups (8 ounces) diced
    cooked chicken breast

½ cup (one 2.5-ounce jar)
    sliced mushrooms,
    drained
1¾ cups (3 ounces) uncooked
    noodles
¼ teaspoon black pepper
1 teaspoon dried parsley
    flakes

In a large saucepan, combine broth, onion, celery, green beans, carrots, and chicken. Cover and cook over medium heat until vegetables are just tender, about 15 minutes. Add mushrooms, noodles, black pepper, and parsley flakes. Mix well to combine. Lower heat. Cover and simmer, about 15 minutes or until noodles are tender, stirring occasionally.

Each serving equals:

HE: 2 Vegetable, 1⅓ Protein, ¾ Bread, 11 Optional Calories

182 Calories, 2 gm Fat, 18 gm Protein, 23 gm Carbohydrate, 440 mg Sodium, 4 gm Fat

DIABETIC: 2 Vegetable, 1½ Meat, 1 Starch

Tomato Chicken Rice Soup

------------------------- ❄ -------------------------

You don't often get the combination of chicken and tomato in a soothing soup, but once you try this, you'll soon see that the unexpected is absolutely delicious! You don't have to choose between two favorite flavors, you can enjoy both at once. And if you want to use up some leftover cooked rice, you can stir in a cup of cooked cold rice. Waste not, want not . . .

Serves 4 (1½ cups)

2 cups (one 16-ounce can) Healthy Request Chicken Broth
¼ cup chopped onion
¾ cup chopped celery
1¾ cups (one 15-ounce can) Hunt's Chunky Tomato Sauce

1½ cups (8 ounces) diced cooked chicken breast
1 cup frozen peas
⅛ teaspoon black pepper
⅔ cup (2 ounces) uncooked instant rice

In a large saucepan, combine broth, onion, celery, tomato sauce, and chicken. Bring to a boil. Stir in peas, black pepper, and rice. Continue cooking 2 to 3 minutes. Remove from heat. Cover and let set 5 minutes.

Each serving equals:

HE: 2¼ Vegetable, 2 Protein, 1 Bread, 8 Optional Calories

194 Calories, 2 gm Fat, 23 gm Protein, 21 gm Carbohydrate, 805 mg Sodium, 1 gm Fiber

DIABETIC: 2 Meat, 1 Vegetable, 1 Starch

On the Run from Rabbit Food—Savory Salads He'll Enjoy

--------■--------

My father loved potato salad, especially the old-fashioned way Mom made it. It was a standard at every family picnic we ever had, and perfect for a summer potluck when the relatives gathered. When I decided to invent a special Father's Day menu for my newsletter, I knew potato salad had to be a featured dish.

As I combined flavors and textures in a much healthier version of this favorite, I kept thinking of Daddy. My version is just as delicious as that most traditional, frozen-in-time kind of recipe—and I think it's one that Mr. Cleaver, as well as his sons Wally and the Beaver, would eat and enjoy.

Because I invented Father's Classic Potato Salad to meet with a man's approval, I'm confident there isn't a man alive who won't give it his two-thumbs-up!

Most men turn their noses up at "rabbit food," but just watch them dig into a bowl of tangy coleslaw or a fruit-filled molded salad. Using the best available fresh vegetables, flavored with creamy (but low-fat) dressings and sauces, these recipes make healthy salad side dishes a pleasure instead of a duty, no longer to be eaten only because "it's good for you." You know that'll never be a "good-enough" reason for a man.

Savory Salads

■

Ham Pasta Salad with Maize
Dressing

Mexican Ham Macaroni Salad

Buffalo Chicken Macaroni Salad

Dilled Salmon-Pasta Salad

Cucumber Harvest Salad

Dilled Cucumber Salad

Potluck Sauerkraut Salad

Italian Green Bean Salad

English Pea Salad

Italian Pea Salad

Carrot French Pennies

Maple Nut Carrot Salad

Heavenly Carrot-Raisin Salad

Quick Corn Salad

Grande Corn and
Kidney Bean Salad

Celery Seed Coleslaw

Cabbage and Apple Slaw with
Walnuts

Father's Classic Potato Salad

Frankfurter Potato Salad

Layered BLT Salad

Tomato Rigatoni
Pasta Salad

Western Macaroni Salad

Ranch Pasta-Carrot Salad

Shrimp Cocktail Salad

Grande Potato Salad

Pizza Bacon-Lettuce-and-
Tomato Salad

■

Ham Pasta Salad with Maize Dressing

--------------------■--------------------

What inspired me to make a salad dressing with creamed corn I have no idea, but it seemed like it could work. Cliff really loves creamed corn—in fact, I haven't known a man who didn't—and this dish is a favorite of his.

Serves 4 (1¼ cups)

1½ full cups (9 ounces) diced Dubuque 97% fat-free ham or any extra-lean ham
1½ cups cold cooked rotini pasta, rinsed and drained
1 cup diced celery

1 cup (one 8-ounce can) cream-style corn
⅓ cup Kraft fat-free mayonnaise
2 teaspoons dried parsley flakes

In a large bowl, combine ham, rotini pasta, and celery. In a small bowl, combine corn, mayonnaise, and parsley flakes. Add corn mixture to pasta mixture. Mix well to combine. Cover and refrigerate at least 30 minutes. Gently stir again just before serving.

HINT: 1 cup uncooked rotini pasta usually cooks to about 1½ cups.

Each serving equals:

HE: 1½ Protein, 1¼ Bread, ½ Vegetable, 13 Optional Calories

207 Calories, 3 gm Fat, 14 gm Protein, 31 gm Carbohydrate, 789 mg Sodium, 2 gm Fiber

DIABETIC: 2 Meat, 2 Starch

Mexican Ham Macaroni Salad

---■---

Here's a true fiesta of flavors, with the ham, cheese, and macaroni giving this a hearty feel and a very tangy taste. I like it because it's so easy, but most of all because it's so good.

Serves 4 (1 cup)

2 cups cold cooked elbow macaroni, rinsed and drained

1 full cup (6 ounces) diced Dubuque 97% fat-free ham or any extra-lean ham

¾ cup (3 ounces) shredded Kraft reduced-fat Cheddar cheese

⅓ cup Kraft fat-free mayonnaise

2 tablespoons Kraft Fat Free Ranch Dressing

½ cup chunky salsa (mild, medium, or hot)

1 teaspoon dried parsley flakes

In a large bowl, combine macaroni, ham, and Cheddar cheese. In a small bowl, combine mayonnaise, Ranch dressing, salsa, and parsley flakes. Add mayonnaise mixture to macaroni mixture. Mix well to combine. Cover and refrigerate at least 1 hour. Gently stir again just before serving.

HINT: 1⅓ cups uncooked macaroni usually cooks to about 2 cups.

Each serving equals:

HE: 2 Protein, 1 Bread, ¼ Vegetable, ¼ Slider, 6 Optional Calories

221 Calories, 5 gm Fat, 16 gm Protein, 28 gm Carbohydrate, 852 mg Sodium, 1 gm Fiber

DIABETIC: 2 Meat, 1½ Starch

Buffalo Chicken Macaroni Salad

────────────────────■────────────────────

For all those men who enjoy buffalo chicken wings at their favorite sports bar, here's a delicious pasta salad that echoes those same flavors, but without the fat—*and* the sticky fingers. It's a real "go-for-the-gusto" dish.   *Serves 4 (1 full cup)*

*½ cup Kraft Fat Free Blue
  Cheese Dressing*
*¼ cup Kraft fat-free
  mayonnaise*
1 teaspoon Tabasco sauce
¼ teaspoon paprika
*1½ cups (8 ounces) diced
  cooked chicken breast*

½ cup chopped celery
*2 cups cold cooked elbow
  macaroni, rinsed and
  drained*
*1 cup diced fresh
  tomatoes*

In a large bowl, combine blue cheese dressing, mayonnaise, Tabasco sauce, and paprika. Add chicken, celery, and macaroni. Mix well to combine. Stir in tomatoes. Cover and refrigerate at least 30 minutes. Gently stir again just before serving.

HINT: 1⅓ cups uncooked elbow macaroni usually cooks to about 2 cups.

Each serving equals:

HE: 2 Protein, 1 Bread, ¾ Vegetable, ¼ Slider, 5 Optional Calories

222 Calories, 2 gm Fat, 21 gm Protein, 30 gm Carbohydrate,
401 mg Sodium, 1 gm Fiber

DIABETIC: 2 Meat, 1½ Starch, ½ Vegetable

Dilled Salmon-Pasta Salad

This makes a great-looking presentation, colorful and flavorful with the salmon and peas blended with a touch of dill. Served cold from the fridge, this makes a good choice for a men's buffet during football playoff season. Serving this will surely score a touchdown! *Serves 6 (⅔ cup)*

2 cups cold cooked rotini pasta, rinsed and drained

1 cup frozen peas

1 (14¾-ounce) can salmon, skinned, boned, and flaked

⅓ cup Land O Lakes fat-free sour cream

1 tablespoon skim milk

⅓ cup Kraft fat-free mayonnaise

2 teaspoons dried dill weed

1 teaspoon dried onion flakes

In a large bowl, combine rotini pasta, peas, and salmon. In a small bowl, combine sour cream, skim milk, mayonnaise, dill weed, and onion flakes. Add sour cream mixture to pasta mixture. Toss gently to combine. Cover and refrigerate at least 30 minutes. Toss gently again just before serving.

HINT: 1½ cups uncooked rotini pasta usually cooks to about 2 cups.

Each serving equals:

HE: 2 Protein, 1 Bread, ¼ Slider, 5 Optional Calories

188 Calories, 4 gm Fat, 18 gm Protein, 20 gm Carbohydrate, 436 mg Sodium, 2 gm Fiber

DIABETIC: 2 Meat, 1 Starch

Cucumber Harvest Salad

—————————————————— ■ ——————————————————

This is a nice end-of-the-summer seasonal salad. It's hearty and filled with so many flavors, men feel they're eating more than just a salad. If I were you, I'd add it to my menu for the Labor Day picnic or tailgate party, then just sit back and accept the compliments.

Serves 4 (¾ cup)

2¼ cups thinly sliced
    unpeeled cucumbers
¼ cup sliced green onion
1 cup diced fresh tomatoes
1 teaspoon dried parsley flakes

⅓ cup Kraft fat-free
    mayonnaise
Sugar substitute to equal 2
    teaspoons sugar
1 teaspoon lemon juice

In a large bowl, combine cucumbers, onion, and tomatoes. Add parsley flakes, mayonnaise, sugar substitute, and lemon juice. Mix gently to combine. Cover and refrigerate at least 30 minutes. Gently stir again just before serving.

Each serving equals:

HE: 1¾ Vegetable, 13 Optional Calories

———

32 Calories, 0 gm Fat, 1 gm Protein, 7 gm Carbohydrate, 145 mg Sodium, 1 gm Fiber

———

DIABETIC: 1 Vegetable

I have lost weight several times using many different diets, including low-carbohydrate and liquid diets. I was successful in losing the weight but not in keeping it off. Since beginning my low-fat lifestyle, I have lost over 80 pounds, walk an hour a day at least five days a week, and have been able to keep the weight off for over a year. It has become a "way of life," not a diet. I serve as the cook at our house, and my wife and I really enjoy the quick, easy recipes. Keep up the good work.

—J.C., IA

Dilled Cucumber Salad

——————————————◆——————————————

I bet there isn't a man alive who didn't look forward with glee to dining on cucumbers and cream at Grandma's! My extra little touches add punch without adding time to preparation. Enjoy!

Serves 4 (½ cup)

¼ cup Land O Lakes fat-free
   sour cream
2 teaspoons Sugar Twin or
   Sprinkle Sweet
¼ teaspoon dried minced
   garlic

2 tablespoons white
   vinegar
¼ teaspoon dried dill weed
2 cups sliced unpeeled
   cucumbers

In a medium bowl, combine sour cream, Sugar Twin, garlic, vinegar, and dill weed. Stir in cucumbers. Mix well to combine. Cover and refrigerate at least 30 minutes. Gently stir again just before serving.

Each serving equals:

HE: 1 Vegetable, 16 Optional Calories

24 Calories, 0 gm Fat, 1 gm Protein, 5 gm Carbohydrate, 22 mg Sodium, 1 gm Fiber

DIABETIC: 1 Vegetable

Potluck Sauerkraut Salad

--------------------------------■--------------------------------

I'll admit, this one is a little bit different—but in lots of great ways! The chili sauce definitely spices this up, but because there's no oil in it, everyone can dive in. I'd serve this at a family potluck along with roast pork, or at a cookout with grilled hot dogs. It's loads of fun and flavorful all at once.

Serves 6 (¾ cup)

*2 cups (one 16-ounce can)
    sauerkraut, well drained
1 cup chopped green bell
    pepper
½ cup chopped onion
1 cup chopped celery*

*¼ cup white vinegar
½ cup Sugar Twin or Sprinkle
    Sweet
2 tablespoons chili sauce
1 teaspoon dried parsley
    flakes*

In a large bowl, combine sauerkraut, green pepper, onion, and celery. In a small bowl, combine vinegar, Sugar Twin, chili sauce, and parsley flakes. Add vinegar mixture to sauerkraut mixture. Mix well to combine. Cover and refrigerate at least 1 hour. Gently stir again just before serving.

Each serving equals:

HE: 1½ Vegetable, 18 Optional Calories

52 Calories, 0 gm Fat, 1 gm Protein, 12 gm Carbohydrate,
519 mg Sodium, 3 gm Fiber

DIABETIC: 2 Vegetable

Italian Green Bean Salad

This is a really robust green bean salad. Cliff prefers his beans warm, but the men at our buffet gave high marks to this salad. Maybe it was the Parmesan cheese, or the olives, or the way the dressing pulled all the flavors together, but they kept coming back for more!   *Serves 4 (¾ cup)*

4 cups (two 16-ounce cans) cut green beans, rinsed and drained
½ cup cherry tomatoes, halved
¼ cup (1 ounce) sliced ripe olives

2 tablespoons Hormel Bacon Bits
¼ cup (¾ ounce) grated Kraft fat-free Parmesan cheese
⅓ cup Kraft Fat Free Italian Dressing

In a medium bowl, combine green beans, tomatoes, and olives. Stir in bacon bits and Parmesan cheese. Add Italian dressing. Mix well to combine. Cover and refrigerate at least 30 minutes. Gently stir again just before serving.

Each serving equals:

HE: 2¼ Vegetable, ¼ Fat, ¼ Protein, 18 Optional Calories

---

82 Calories, 2 gm Fat, 5 gm Protein, 11 gm Carbohydrate, 389 mg Sodium, 2 gm Fiber

---

DIABETIC: 1 Vegetable, ½ Starch

English Pea Salad

-----------------------------■-----------------------------

C liff is a real fan of peas and carrots, so he loved this spirited salad. The little peas give it a special pizazz, but if you can't find them, regular canned peas will do. This dish is full of surprises, which is why it's so much fun.

Serves 6 (full ½ cup)

½ cup Kraft fat-free
   mayonnaise
2 tablespoons sweet pickle
   relish
1 teaspoon dried onion flakes
¼ teaspoon black pepper
2 cups (one 16-ounce can)
   small English peas, rinsed
   and drained

1 cup (one 8-ounce can)
   sliced carrots, rinsed and
   drained
Full ½ cup (2¼ ounces)
   shredded Kraft reduced-fat
   Cheddar cheese
1 hard-boiled egg, chopped

In a large bowl, combine mayonnaise, pickle relish, onion flakes, and black pepper. Add peas and carrots. Mix well to combine. Stir in Cheddar cheese and egg. Cover and refrigerate at least 1 hour. Gently stir again just before serving.

HINT: If you want the look and feel of eggs without the cholesterol, toss out the yolk and dice the whites.

Each serving equals:

HE: ⅔ Bread, ⅔ Protein, ⅓ Vegetable, ¼ Slider

81 Calories, 1 gm Fat, 4 gm Protein, 14 gm Carbohydrate, 268 mg Sodium, 3 gm Fiber

DIABETIC: 1 Starch

Italian Pea Salad

-------------◆-------------

Another big winner at the taste-testing party, this salad uses common ingredients in uncommon ways, and the result really hits a home run! The peanuts and bacon join with the dressing to transform a basic idea into a side dish that stands proud!

Serves 6 (½ cup)

½ cup Kraft fat-free mayonnaise
¼ cup Kraft Fat Free Italian Dressing
3 cups frozen peas, thawed
¾ cup chopped celery

¼ cup chopped red onion
¼ cup (1 ounce) chopped dry-roasted peanuts
3 tablespoons Hormel Bacon Bits

In a large bowl, combine mayonnaise and Italian dressing. Stir in peas, celery, and onion. Add peanuts and bacon bits. Mix well to combine. Cover and refrigerate at least 30 minutes. Gently stir again just before serving.

HINT: Thaw peas by placing in a colander and rinsing under hot water for one minute.

Each serving equals:

HE: 1 Bread, ⅓ Vegetable, ⅓ Fat, ½ Slider, 1 Optional Calorie

123 Calories, 3 gm Fat, 7 gm Protein, 17 gm Carbohydrate, 318 mg Sodium, 4 gm Fiber

DIABETIC: 1 Starch, ½ Fat

Carrot French Pennies

---■---

This is another of my 1950s Midwestern classics, originally made using tomato soup. Here, the French dressing "dresses" it up in a way that makes it a perfect dinner party dish!

Serves 6 (⅔ cup)

¾ cup Kraft Fat Free French
    Dressing
1 teaspoon prepared mustard
½ teaspoon Worcestershire
    sauce
1 teaspoon dried parsley flakes

4 cups (two 16-ounce cans)
    sliced carrots, rinsed and
    drained
¼ cup chopped green bell
    pepper
¼ cup chopped onion

In a medium bowl, combine French dressing, mustard, Worcestershire sauce, and parsley flakes. Add carrots, green pepper, and onion. Mix well to combine. Cover and refrigerate at least 2 hours. Gently stir again just before serving.

Each serving equals:

HE: 1½ Vegetable, ¼ Slider, 10 Optional Calories

60 Calories, 0 gm Fat, 1 gm Protein, 14 gm Carbohydrate,
297 mg Sodium, 2 gm Fiber

DIABETIC: 1½ Vegetable, ½ Starch

A while back, my mother-in-law subscribed to your newsletter, and
after a while my wife started to look at it too. Just as we started
using your recipes, I became sick and had to have open-heart surgery.
I had six bypasses done on my heart. I have recovered and I feel great.
Your recipes are fantastic for meals and out of this world for desserts.

—R.L., FL

Maple Nut Carrot Salad

--------------------------------■--------------------------------

Ican imagine your doubts about the combination of maple
syrup and mayonnaise, but you'll be amazed to see and taste
just how well it works! It's creamy, sweet, and crunchy all at
once—and surprisingly scrumptious!   *Serves 6 (½ cup)*

> **3 cups shredded carrots**
> **½ cup raisins**
> **1 cup chopped celery**
> **2 tablespoons (½ ounce)**
> **chopped pecans**
>
> **½ cup Kraft fat-free**
> **mayonnaise**
> **¼ cup Cary's Sugar Free**
> **Maple Syrup**

In a large bowl, combine carrots, raisins, celery, and pecans. In a
small bowl, combine mayonnaise and maple syrup. Add mayonnaise mixture to carrot mixture. Mix gently to combine. Cover
and refrigerate until ready to serve. Gently stir again just before
serving.

HINT: To plump up raisins without "cooking," place in a glass
measuring cup and microwave on HIGH for 20 seconds.

Each serving equals:

HE: 1⅓ Vegetable, ⅔ Fruit, ⅓ Fat, ¼ Slider

----

94 Calories, 2 gm Fat, 1 gm Protein, 18 gm Carbohydrate,
185 mg Sodium, 2 gm Fiber

DIABETIC: 1 Vegetable, 1 Fruit

Heavenly Carrot-Raisin Salad

---■---

Here's a true down-home recipe taken "uptown," in a way. Combining the carrots with the pineapple and Cool Whip is also a great way to get men to eat their vegetables.

Serves 6 (⅔ cup)

3 cups shredded carrots
1 cup (one 8-ounce can)
   pineapple tidbits, packed
   in fruit juice, drained,
   and 2 tablespoons liquid
   reserved ☆
½ cup raisins
½ cup (1 ounce) miniature
   marshmallows

½ cup Kraft fat-free
   mayonnaise
½ cup Cool Whip Lite
1 teaspoon coconut extract
6 lettuce leaves
2 tablespoons flaked
   coconut

In a large bowl, combine carrots, pineapple, raisins, and marshmallows. In a small bowl, combine mayonnaise, Cool Whip Lite, reserved 2 tablespoons pineapple juice, and coconut extract. Add mayonnaise mixture to carrot mixture. Cover and refrigerate until ready to serve. For each serving, place lettuce leaf on plate and spoon salad over lettuce. Top each salad with 1 teaspoon flaked coconut.

HINTS: 1. If you can't find tidbits, use chunk pineapple and coarsely chop.
2. To plump up raisins without "cooking," place in a glass measuring cup and microwave on HIGH for 20 seconds.

Each serving equals:

HE: 1 Vegetable, 1 Fruit, ½ Slider, 1 Optional Calorie

---

133 Calories, 1 gm Fat, 1 gm Protein, 30 gm Carbohydrate, 167 mg Sodium, 2 gm Fiber

---

DIABETIC: 1 Vegetable, 1 Fruit, ½ Starch

Quick Corn Salad

----------------■----------------

I took a basic corn salad, then added basil and tomatoes to make it spectacular. It's so colorful, it'll call to you from your plate!

Serves 6 (½ cup)

*3 cups frozen whole kernel
  corn, thawed*
*1½ cups chopped fresh
  tomatoes*
½ cup chopped onion
*⅔ cup Kraft fat-free
  mayonnaise*

*¼ teaspoon black
  pepper*
1 teaspoon dried basil
*Sugar substitute to
  equal 2 teaspoons
  sugar*

In a large bowl, combine corn, tomatoes, and onion. In a small bowl, combine mayonnaise, black pepper, basil, and sugar substitute. Add mayonnaise mixture to corn mixture. Mix gently to combine. Cover and refrigerate at least 1 hour. Gently stir again just before serving.

HINT: Thaw corn by placing in a colander and rinsing under hot water for one minute.

Each serving equals:

HE: 1 Bread, ⅔ Vegetable, 18 Optional Calories

108 Calories, 0 gm Fat, 3 gm Protein, 24 gm Carbohydrate,
219 mg Sodium, 3 gm Fiber

DIABETIC: 1 Starch, 1 Vegetable

Grande Corn and Kidney Bean Salad

Brimming with crunch and substance, rich in flavor and color, this hearty concoction became a blockbuster success at the tasting buffet. It's a great dish to mix up for a crowd, and so quick to prepare, you can have it on the table only a half hour after you return from a fishing trip (along with those grilled bass)! *Serves 6 (⅔ cup)*

2 cups (one 16-ounce can)
whole kernel corn, rinsed
and drained
10 ounces (one 16-ounce can)
red kidney beans, rinsed
and drained
¼ cup finely chopped onion
½ cup finely chopped green
bell pepper

¾ cup (3 ounces) shredded
Kraft reduced-fat Cheddar
cheese
¾ cup Kraft fat-free
mayonnaise
Sugar substitute to equal 2
teaspoons sugar
1 teaspoon dried parsley
flakes

In a large bowl, combine corn, kidney beans, onion, green pepper, and Cheddar cheese. Add mayonnaise, sugar substitute, and parsley flakes. Mix well to combine. Cover and refrigerate at least 30 minutes. Gently stir again just before serving.

Each serving equals:

HE: 1½ Protein, ⅔ Bread, ¼ Vegetable, ¼ Slider

146 Calories, 2 gm Fat, 8 gm Protein, 24 gm Carbohydrate, 324 mg Sodium, 4 gm Fiber

DIABETIC: 1½ Starch, 1 Meat

Celery Seed Coleslaw

----------------■----------------

This is an old standby I created for my son James. Ever since he started talking at the age of two, *coleslaw* became his favorite food, but because he was still learning to talk at the time, he used to call it "cold-slop"! (I didn't take it personally, of course. I knew he loved it.)　　　*Serves 4 (½ cup)*

½ cup Kraft fat-free
　mayonnaise
1 tablespoon skim milk
1 teaspoon prepared mustard
Sugar substitute to equal 2
　teaspoons sugar

1 teaspoon dried parsley
　flakes
1 teaspoon celery seed
3 cups purchased coleslaw
　mix

In a medium bowl, combine mayonnaise, skim milk, mustard, sugar substitute, parsley flakes, and celery seed. Add coleslaw mix. Stir well to combine. Cover and refrigerate at least 30 minutes. Gently stir again just before serving.

HINT: 2½ cups shredded cabbage and ¼ cup shredded carrots may be used in place of purchased coleslaw mix.

Each serving equals:

HE: 1½ Vegetable, ¼ Slider, 3 Optional Calories

36 Calories, 0 gm Fat, 1 gm Protein, 8 gm Carbohydrate, 242 mg Sodium, 1 gm Fiber

DIABETIC: 1½ Vegetable

Cabbage and Apple Slaw
with Walnuts

---■---

Apples and walnuts go together like rhythm and blues, but the cabbage is a delectable and unexpected touch here. You'll be a hit at any fall party if you serve this creamy, crunchy, cold salad that satisfies three palate senses at once. This will provide an unexpected pleasure for a early fall cookout—or with meat loaf anytime at all.

Serves 4 (¾ cup)

3 cups shredded cabbage
1 cup (2 small) cored,
    unpeeled, finely chopped
    Red Delicious apples
2 tablespoons (½ ounce)
    chopped walnuts

½ cup Kraft fat-free
    mayonnaise
1 tablespoon skim milk
1 teaspoon lemon juice
Sugar substitute to equal 1
    tablespoon sugar

In a large bowl, combine cabbage, apples, and walnuts. In a small bowl, combine mayonnaise, skim milk, lemon juice, and sugar substitute. Add mayonnaise mixture to cabbage mixture. Mix well to combine. Cover and refrigerate at least 30 minutes. Gently stir again just before serving.

Each serving equals:

HE: 1½ Vegetable, ½ Fruit, ¼ Fat, ¼ Slider, 4 Optional Calories

62 Calories, 2 gm Fat, 1 gm Protein, 10 gm Carbohydrate, 148 mg Sodium, 2 gm Fiber

DIABETIC: ½ Fruit, 1 Free Vegetable

Father's Classic Potato Salad

------------------------------■------------------------------

I've always found you can't have enough potato salad recipes to satisfy men—they could eat it every single day! In fact, we offer this dish daily in JO's Kitchen Cafe, where it's won our male customers' seal of approval again and again! By the way, I call this "classic" because it's prepared the old-fashioned way, with a hard-boiled egg, just the way Daddy liked it.

Serves 6 (½ cup)

⅔ cup Kraft fat-free
   mayonnaise
1 tablespoon white vinegar
Sugar substitute to equal 1
   teaspoon sugar
¼ teaspoon black pepper

3 cups (16-ounces) diced
   cooked potatoes
1 cup sliced celery
½ cup chopped onion
1 hard-boiled egg,
   chopped

In a large bowl, combine mayonnaise, vinegar, sugar substitute, and black pepper. Add potatoes, celery, and onion. Mix well to combine. Fold in egg. Cover and refrigerate at least 30 minutes. Gently stir again just before serving.

HINT: If you want the look and feel of eggs without the cholesterol, toss out the yolk and dice the whites.

Each serving equals:

HE: ⅔ Bread, ½ Vegetable, ¼ Slider, 4 Optional Calories

101 Calories, 1 gm Fat, 3 gm Protein, 20 gm Carbohydrate,
172 mg Sodium, 2 gm Fiber

DIABETIC: 1 Starch

Frankfurter Potato Salad

T his puts a different spin on a traditional side dish by turning
it into a one-bowl entree salad stirred up in a hurry! On a
hot July night, it'd be just right, served with a vegetable, roll,
and of course, one of my luscious desserts!

Serves 6 (¾ cup)

**8 ounces Healthy Choice
97% fat-free frankfurters,
cooked, cooled, and
diced
3 cups (16 ounces) diced
cooked potatoes
¾ cup sliced celery
¼ cup chopped onion**

**¾ cup Kraft fat-free
mayonnaise
2 tablespoons skim milk
1 teaspoon prepared mustard
¼ teaspoon black pepper
½ teaspoon celery seed
(optional)
2 hard-boiled eggs, chopped**

In a large bowl, combine frankfurters, potatoes, celery, and
onion. In a small bowl, combine mayonnaise, skim milk, mustard, black pepper, and celery seed. Add mayonnaise mixture to
potato mixture. Mix gently to combine. Gently fold in eggs.
Cover and refrigerate at least 30 minutes. Gently stir again just
before serving.

HINT: If you want the look and feel of eggs without the cholesterol, toss out the yolk and dice the whites.

Each serving equals:

HE: 1¼ Protein (⅓ limited), ⅔ Bread, ⅓ Vegetable, ¼ Slider,
2 Optional Calories

159 Calories, 3 gm Fat, 9 gm Protein, 24 gm Carbohydrate,
644 mg Sodium, 2 gm Fiber

DIABETIC: 1½ Starch, 1 Meat

Layered BLT Salad

---■---

I can still hear the comments men made after discovering this treat at the tasting buffet. It was simple, really—I just took most men's much-loved sandwich, the BLT, and transformed it into something that tasted great but didn't come between two or three slices of bread! *Serves 4*

4 cups finely shredded lettuce
1½ cups chopped fresh tomatoes
¼ cup Hormel Bacon Bits
4 slices reduced-calorie white bread, toasted and cubed

⅓ cup (1½ ounces) shredded Kraft reduced-fat Cheddar cheese
½ cup Kraft Fat Free Thousand Island Dressing
¼ cup Kraft fat-free mayonnaise
1 teaspoon dried parsley flakes

In an 8-by-8-inch dish, layer lettuce, tomatoes, bacon bits, toast cubes, and Cheddar cheese. In a medium bowl, combine Thousand Island dressing, mayonnaise, and parsley flakes. Spread dressing mixture evenly over top. Cover and refrigerate at least 30 minutes. Divide into 4 servings.

HINT: Lightly spray toast with I Can't Believe It's Not Butter Spray before cubing.

Each serving equals:

HE: 2¾ Vegetable, ½ Bread, ½ Protein, 1 Slider, 5 Optional Calories

175 Calories, 3 gm Fat, 10 gm Protein, 27 gm Carbohydrate, 684 gm Sodium, 2 gm Fiber

DIABETIC: 1½ Starch, 1 Vegetable, 1 Free Vegetable, ½ Meat

Tomato Rigatoni Pasta Salad

■

This mixture has a kind of masculine taste with its hearty combination of two cheeses, olives, and the crunch of red onion to add eye appeal. Make this when your tomato plants are covered with ripe, red beauties, and you're sure to satisfy the hungry men at your table.   *Serves 4 (1½ cups)*

2 cups cold cooked rigatoni pasta, rinsed and drained
2 cups diced fresh tomatoes
¼ cup diced red onion
¼ cup chopped green bell pepper
¼ cup (1 ounce) sliced ripe olives

¾ cup (3 ounces) shredded Kraft reduced-fat mozzarella cheese
½ cup Kraft Fat Free Italian Dressing
¼ cup (¾ ounce) grated Kraft fat-free Parmesan cheese

In a large bowl, combine pasta, tomatoes, onion, green pepper and olives. Add mozzarella cheese. Mix gently to combine. Stir in Italian dressing and Parmesan cheese. Cover and refrigerate at least 30 minutes. Gently stir again just before serving.

HINT: 1. Rotini pasta is a good substitute for rigatoni pasta.
2. 1½ cups uncooked rigatoni pasta usually cooks to about 2 cups.

Each serving equals:

HE: 1¼ Protein, 1 Bread, 1 Vegetable, ¼ Fat, 8 Optional Calories

196 Calories, 4 gm Fat, 12 gm Protein, 28 gm Carbohydrate, 637 mg Sodium, 2 gm Fiber

DIABETIC: 1½ Starch, 1 Meat, ½ Vegetable

Western Macaroni Salad

----------------------------■----------------------------

This brings together the two M's—macaroni and men—in an easy-to-fix, tangy, and pleasing dish that won the heart of Cliff's dad, Cleland. He thinks the combination of macaroni and tomatoes makes a perfect pair! *Serves 4 (¾ cup)*

½ cup Kraft Fat Free Catalina or French Dressing
1 teaspoon chili seasoning
½ cup chopped green bell pepper
½ cup chopped red onion

¼ cup (1 ounce) sliced ripe olives
2 cups cold cooked macaroni, rinsed and drained
1 cup chopped fresh tomatoes

In a large bowl, combine Catalina dressing and chili seasoning. Stir in green pepper, onion, and olives. Add macaroni and tomatoes. Mix well to combine. Cover and refrigerate at least 30 minutes. Gently stir again just before serving.

HINT: 1⅓ cups uncooked macaroni usually cooks to about 2 cups.

Each serving equals:
HE: 1 Bread, ¾ Vegetable, ¼ Fat, ½ Slider, 10 Optional Calories

149 Calories, 1 gm Fat, 3 gm Protein, 32 gm Carbohydrate, 363 mg Sodium, 2 gm Fiber

DIABETIC: 1½ Starch, ½ Vegetable

Ranch Pasta-Carrot Salad

———

Those pretty and colorful carrots peeping out from a bowl of pasta help create an appealing and filling lunch. Because every now and then men need a change, offer this creative combo as a delectable surprise that is as soothing and comforting as it is G-O-O-D!   *Serves 6 (½ cup)*

2 cups water
1¼ cups (3¾ ounces)
    uncooked tiny shell
    macaroni
¾ cup shredded carrots
½ cup frozen peas
½ cup Kraft fat-free
    mayonnaise

¼ cup Kraft Fat Free Ranch
    Dressing
1 teaspoon dried parsley
    flakes
1 teaspoon dried onion flakes
¼ teaspoon black pepper
3 tablespoons Hormel Bacon
    Bits

In a medium saucepan, bring water to a boil. Stir in uncooked shell macaroni and carrots. Cook until macaroni is almost tender, about 15 minutes. Stir in frozen peas. Continue cooking 2 to 3 minutes. Drain and rinse under cold water in a colander until mixture is cooled. In a large bowl, combine mayonnaise, Ranch dressing, parsley flakes, onion flakes, and black pepper. Add bacon bits. Mix well to combine. Stir in macaroni mixture. Cover and refrigerate at least 30 minutes. Gently stir again just before serving.

Each serving equals:

HE: 1 Bread, ¼ Vegetable, ½ Slider, 3 Optional Calories

———

121 Calories, 1 gm Fat, 4 gm Protein, 24 gm Carbohydrate,
318 mg Sodium, 1 gm Fiber

———

DIABETIC: 1½ Starch

Shrimp Cocktail Salad

M en, especially my son Tommy, love to order shrimp cocktail at restaurants but they usually aren't offered this treat at home. Because Tommy liked to slather lots of sauce on his, and always finished up the lettuce, too, I was inspired to create a salad based on his favorite appetizer! *Serves 4 (1 cup)*

⅓ cup Heinz Cocktail Sauce
¼ cup Kraft fat-free
   mayonnaise
1 teaspoon lemon juice

4 cups thinly shredded lettuce
1 (4.5-ounce drained weight)
   can small shrimp, rinsed
   and drained

In a medium bowl, combine cocktail sauce, mayonnaise, and lemon juice. Add lettuce and shrimp. Mix gently to combine. Serve at once or cover and refrigerate until ready to serve. If refrigerated, gently toss again just before serving.

Each serving equals:

HE: 2 Vegetable, 1 Protein, ¼ Slider, 10 Optional Calories

77 Calories, 1 gm Fat, 8 gm Protein, 9 gm Carbohydrate, 465 mg Sodium, 1 gm Fiber

DIABETIC: 1 Meat, 1 Free Vegetable, ½ Starch

Grande Potato Salad

––––––––––––––––––– ∎ –––––––––––––––––––

Here's an intriguing Mexican version of the family favorite that tickles your taste buds and conjures up all those sunny flavors in each mouthful. Make it spicy or make it mild, it'll make you smile!   *Serves 4 (1 cup)*

*3 full cups (16 ounces) diced
    cooked potatoes*
¾ cup diced celery
¼ cup diced red onion
*¾ cup (3 ounces) shredded
    Kraft reduced-fat Cheddar
    cheese*
*⅔ cup Kraft fat-free
    mayonnaise*

*¼ cup Land O Lakes fat-free
    sour cream*
*2 teaspoons dried parsley
    flakes*
*½ cup chunky salsa (mild,
    medium, or hot)*
*⅓ cup (1½ ounces) chopped
    ripe olives*

In a large bowl, combine potatoes, celery, and onion. Stir in Cheddar cheese. In a medium bowl, combine mayonnaise, sour cream, parsley flakes, and salsa. Add mayonnaise mixture to potato mixture. Mix well to combine. Gently stir in olives. Cover and refrigerate at least 30 minutes. Gently stir again just before serving.

Each serving equals:

HE: ⅔ Bread, ⅔ Protein, ½ Vegetable, ¼ Fat, ¼ Slider, 8 Optional Calories

138 Calories, 2 gm Fat, 6 gm Protein, 24 gm Carbohydrate,
476 mg Sodium, 1 gm Fiber

DIABETIC: 1½ Starch, ½ Meat

Pizza Bacon-Lettuce-and-Tomato Salad

-----------------◼-----------------

What if, I asked myself, you took the flavors of a BLT and joined them to that other irresistible favorite, pizza, with its blend of cheeses? Why, you'd get this surprising salad, chock full of color and crunch. Think of it as a BLT pizza in a bowl!

Serves 4 (2 cups)

⅔ cup Kraft fat-free mayonnaise

¼ cup (¾ ounce) grated Kraft fat-free Parmesan cheese

1½ teaspoons pizza seasoning

1½ cups chopped fresh tomato

¾ cup chopped green bell pepper

¾ cup sliced fresh mushrooms

½ cup chopped red onion

¾ cup (3 ounces) shredded Kraft reduced-fat mozzarella cheese

¾ cup (3 ounces) shredded Kraft reduced-fat Cheddar cheese

¼ cup Hormel Bacon Bits

4 cups shredded lettuce

1 cup (1½ ounces) Pepperidge Farm Dried Bread Cubes

In a large bowl, combine mayonnaise, Parmesan cheese, and pizza seasoning. Add tomato, green pepper, mushrooms, onion, mozzarella cheese, Cheddar cheese, and bacon bits. Mix well to combine. Stir in lettuce. Cover and refrigerate at least 15 minutes. Just before serving, stir in bread cubes.

Each serving equals:

HE: 3¾ Vegetable, 2 Protein, ½ Bread, ½ Slider, 12 Optional Calories

273 Calories, 9 gm Fat, 20 gm Protein, 28 gm Carbohydrate, 932 mg Sodium, 2 gm Fiber

DIABETIC: 2 Vegetable, 2 Meat, 1 Starch, 1 Free Vegetable

Sweet Salads—
Or, JELL-O Every Day
If You Want It . . .

———■———

Sweet salads are a wonderful Midwestern tradition,
and you won't find a truck stop buffet with fewer
than half a dozen choices that are deliciously creamy and
filled with fruit. And no self-respecting family gathering
would be complete without a selection of everyone's best-
loved favorites.

My son James wasn't interested in variety, however.
What he always wanted was a salad that starred cherries,
and I've done my best to satisfy his passion for this ruby
red fruit. My Heavenly Cherry Salad got its name when
James took a bite, got up from his chair, and hugged me.
"I'm in heaven," he said.

Well, ever since George Washington, men have been
willing to do just about anything for cherries! See what
the men in your family might do for you if you serve
them this gorgeous treat.

If you've been raised to eat these luscious gelatin
dishes only for dessert, I hope you'll decide to give our

beloved heartland custom a try. You may be amazed to discover that a spoonful or two of a deliciously decadent sweet salad may satisfy your tummy as fully as a fat-and-sugar-laden dessert! And knowing it's healthy will just make it taste even sweeter.

Sweet Salads

Heavenly Cherry Salad

Jewel Box Salad

Fruit Cloud Salad

Basic Waldorf Salad

Apple Sunshine Salad

New England Apple Salad

Pistachio Apple Cream Salad

Banana Rice Salad

Key West Raspberry Salad

Refreshing Pear-Mint Salad

Pistachio Creme Fruit Salad

Creamy Strawberry Fruit Salad

Orange-Pecan Tapioca Salad

Southern Blueberry Fruit Salad

Citrus Cinnamon Salad

Decadent "Candy Bar" Salad

Cherry-Chocolate
Cloud Salad

Strawberry-Pineapple
Fluff Salad

Carrot Marshmallow Salad

Heavenly Cherry Salad

-------------------■-------------------

H ere's a terrific way to win a man's heart! You've got all the ingredients for a party of flavors, and the rosy color makes it look extra-delicious!   *Serves 6*

1 (4-serving) package JELL-O sugar-free vanilla cook-and-serve pudding mix	*2 cups (one 16-ounce can) tart red cherries, packed in water, undrained*
1 (4-serving) package JELL-O sugar-free cherry gelatin	*1 teaspoon coconut extract*
¼ cup water	*¾ cup Cool Whip Lite*
1 cup (one 8-ounce can) crushed pineapple, packed in fruit juice, undrained	*3 tablespoons (¾ ounce) chopped pecans*
	½ cup (1 ounce) miniature marshmallows
	2 tablespoons flaked coconut

In a medium saucepan, combine dry pudding mix, dry gelatin, water, and undrained pineapple. Stir in undrained cherries. Cook over medium heat, stirring often, until mixture thickens and starts to boil, being careful not to crush cherries. Remove from heat. Stir in coconut extract. Place pan on a wire rack and let set 20 minutes. Spoon cherry mixture into a large bowl. Add Cool Whip Lite, pecans, marshmallows, and coconut. Mix gently to combine. Spread mixture into an 8-by-8-inch dish. Cover and refrigerate at least 1 hour. Divide into 6 servings.

Each serving equals:

HE: 1 Fruit, ½ Fat, ½ Slider, 13 Optional Calories

----
144 Calories, 4 gm Fat, 2 gm Protein, 25 gm Carbohydrate,
125 mg Sodium, 1 gm Fiber

DIABETIC: 1 Fruit, ½ Fat, ½ Starch

Jewel Box Salad

--------------■--------------

When I was creating this salad, the bowl looked like a jewelry box full of sparkling gems. If you serve this to the man in your house, you may end up with beautiful jewelry all over your hands and wrists. Do men like kiwi fruit? If they've never tried it, they may be surprised to discover it's a kind of banana-strawberry combo in a little round fruit. Men may resist trying something new, but if they like it, they'll keep coming back for more. *Serves 4 (⅔ cup)*

*1 cup (1 medium) diced
    banana*
1 cup sliced fresh strawberries
*½ cup (1 medium) diced kiwi
    fruit*

*1 cup Yoplait fat-free and
    sugar-free strawberry
    yogurt*

In a medium bowl, combine banana, strawberries, and kiwi fruit. Add strawberry yogurt. Mix gently to combine. Cover and refrigerate at least 15 minutes. Gently stir again just before serving.

HINT: To prevent bananas from turning brown, mix with 1 teaspoon lemon juice or sprinkle with Fruit Fresh.

Each serving equals:

HE: 1 Fruit, ¼ Skim Milk

----

96 Calories, 0 gm Fat, 4 gm Protein, 20 gm Carbohydrate, 46 mg Sodium, 2 gm Fiber

----

DIABETIC: 1 Fruit, ½ Skim Milk

Fruit Cloud Salad

-----------------◼-----------------

T he cottage cheese takes on a really creamy taste instead of a diet taste. Men have always liked fruit cocktail, so that just adds to the pleasure in this pretty dish that resembles a cloud.

Serves 6

1 (4-serving) package JELL-O
    sugar-free orange gelatin
1 cup boiling water
2 cups (one 16-ounce can)
    fruit cocktail, packed in
    fruit juice, drained, and ½
    cup juice reserved ☆

¾ cup Cool Whip Lite
1 cup (one 11-ounce can)
    mandarin oranges, rinsed
    and drained
1 cup fat-free cottage
    cheese

In a large bowl, combine dry gelatin and boiling water. Mix well to dissolve gelatin. Stir in reserved fruit cocktail juice. Refrigerate 15 minutes. Stir in Cool Whip Lite. Add fruit cocktail, mandarin oranges, and cottage cheese. Mix gently to combine. Pour mixture into an 8-by-8-inch dish. Refrigerate until firm, about 2 hours. Cut into 6 servings.

Each serving equals:

HE: 1 Fruit, ⅓ Protein, ¼ Slider, 7 Optional Calories

----

101 Calories, 1 gm Fat, 6 gm Protein, 17 gm Carbohydrate,
182 mg Sodium, 1 gm Fiber

DIABETIC: 1 Fruit, ½ Meat

Basic Waldorf Salad

-------------------■-------------------

I haven't met a man yet who doesn't love Waldorf salad. Their moms used to bring it out only on special occasions, so they equate it with times to celebrate. This version will surely get cheers! *Serves 4 (⅔ cup)*

½ cup Kraft fat-free
  mayonnaise
1 teaspoon lemon juice
Sugar substitute to equal
  2 teaspoons sugar
2 cups (4 small) cored,
  unpeeled, chopped
  Red Delicious apples

½ cup chopped celery
½ cup (1 ounce) miniature
  marshmallows
¼ cup (1 ounce) chopped
  walnuts

In a medium bowl, combine mayonnaise, lemon juice, and sugar substitute. Add apples, celery, marshmallows, and walnuts. Mix gently to combine. Cover and refrigerate at least 30 minutes. Gently stir again just before serving.

Each serving equals:

HE: 1 Fruit, ½ Fat, ¼ Vegetable, ¼ Protein, ¼ Slider, 12 Optional Calories

116 Calories, 4 gm Fat, 1 gm Protein, 19 gm Carbohydrate,
227 mg Sodium, 1 gm Fiber

DIABETIC: 1 Fruit, ½ Fat, ½ Starch

Apple Sunshine Salad

-----------------■-----------------

The name says it right—this looks just like a bowl of sunshine! My grandbaby Zach loved it the very first time he tasted it, so I guess you could say that this nutty, fruity dish will please men from 4 to 94.

Serves 6 (1 cup)

¾ cup Yoplait plain fat-free
    yogurt
⅓ cup Carnation Nonfat Dry
    Milk Powder
1 (4-serving) package JELL-O
    sugar-free orange gelatin
¾ cup Cool Whip Lite

3 cups (6 small) cored,
    unpeeled, diced Red
    Delicious apples
3 tablespoons (¾ ounce)
    chopped pecans
½ cup (1 ounce) miniature
    marshmallows

In a large bowl, combine yogurt and dry milk powder. Add dry gelatin. Mix well to combine. Fold in Cool Whip Lite. Stir in apples, pecans, and marshmallows. Cover and refrigerate at least 30 minutes. Gently stir again just before serving.

Each serving equals:

HE: 1 Fruit, ½ Fat, ⅓ Skim Milk, ½ Slider, 12 Optional Calories

----

128 Calories, 4 gm Fat, 4 gm Protein, 19 gm Carbohydrate,
80 mg Sodium, 1 gm Fiber

DIABETIC: 1 Fruit, ½ Fat, ½ Starch

New England Apple Salad

T he combination of maple syrup and apples is downright irresistible to men. It's substantial, unusual, and really palate pleasing. For me, the pleasure is in the sweet and crunchy texture.

Serves 6 (full ½ cup)

1 (4-serving) package JELL-O
    sugar-free instant vanilla
    pudding mix
⅔ cup Carnation Nonfat Dry
    Milk Powder
½ cup Cary's Sugar Free
    Maple Syrup
1 cup water

½ cup Cool Whip Lite
2 cups (4 small) cored,
    unpeeled, diced Red
    Delicious apples
¼ cup raisins
3 tablespoons (¾ ounce)
    chopped pecans

In a large bowl, combine dry pudding mix and dry milk powder. Add maple syrup and water. Mix well using a wire whisk. Blend in Cool Whip Lite. Add apples, raisins, and pecans. Mix gently to combine. Cover and refrigerate at least 30 minutes. Gently stir again just before serving.

HINT: To plump up raisins without "cooking," place in a glass measuring cup and microwave on HIGH for 15 seconds.

Each serving equals:

HE: 1 Fruit, ½ Fat, ⅓ Skim Milk, ¼ Slider, 12 Optional Calories

131 Calories, 3 gm Fat, 3 gm Protein, 23 gm Carbohydrate, 288 mg Sodium, 1 gm Fiber

DIABETIC: 1 Fruit, ½ Fat, ½ Starch

Pistachio Apple Cream Salad

---■---

I admit this is an unusual combination, but blending the pistachio pudding and the apple produces such a pretty mix of colors. Men may not admit they want things to look attractive but they definitely do, from this appetizing apple salad to the apples of their eyes!

Serves 6 (⅔ cup)

1 (4-serving) package JELL-O
    sugar-free instant
    pistachio pudding mix
⅔ cup Carnation Nonfat Dry
    Milk Powder
¾ cup water
1 cup (one 8-ounce can)
    pineapple tidbits, packed
    in fruit juice, undrained

⅓ cup Cool Whip Lite
2 cups (4 small) cored,
    unpeeled, diced Red
    Delicious apples
½ cup (1 ounce) miniature
    marshmallows
2 tablespoons (½ ounce)
    chopped pecans

In a large bowl, combine dry pudding mix and dry milk powder. Add water and undrained pineapple. Mix well using a wire whisk. Blend in Cool Whip Lite. Add apples, marshmallows, and pecans. Mix well to combine. Cover and refrigerate at least 30 minutes. Gently stir again just before serving.

Each serving equals:

HE: 1 Fruit, ⅓ Skim Milk, ⅓ Fat, ¼ Slider, 14 Optional Calories

---

130 Calories, 2 gm Fat, 3 gm Protein, 25 gm Carbohydrate, 257 mg Sodium, 1 gm Fiber

---

DIABETIC: 1 Fruit, ½ Fat, ½ Starch

Banana Rice Salad

-----------------∎-----------------

I know they say necessity is the mother of invention, but for me it's often leftovers that inspire a new recipe. I invented this one on the spot at the Healthy Man Taste-Testing Buffet so we could handle the hungry crowds that were much larger than we had expected. With everyone working to feed the multitudes, I was "slinging" rice and bananas and came up with this winner.

Serves 4 (¾ cup)

*1 cup (1 medium) diced
banana*
2 teaspoons lemon juice
*2 tablespoons Kraft fat-free
mayonnaise*
2 tablespoons Cool Whip Lite

*¼ cup Cary's Sugar Free
Maple Syrup*
1½ cups cold cooked rice
¼ cup raisins
*2 tablespoons (½ ounce)
chopped pecans*

In a small bowl, combine banana and lemon juice. In a medium bowl, combine mayonnaise, Cool Whip Lite, and syrup. Add rice, raisins, and pecans. Toss gently to combine. Refrigerate at least 30 minutes. Gently stir again just before serving.

HINTS: 1. 1 cup uncooked rice usually cooks to about 1½ cups.
      2. To plump up raisins without "cooking," place in a glass measuring cup and microwave on HIGH for 15 seconds.

Each serving equals:
HE: 1 Fruit, ¾ Bread, ½ Fat, ¼ Slider

167 Calories, 3 gm Fat, 2 gm Protein, 33 gm Carbohydrate,
152 mg Sodium, 2 gm Fiber

DIABETIC: 1 Fruit, 1 Starch, ½ Fat

Key West Raspberry Salad

------------------------------■------------------------------

Inspired by a Key West sundae I saw served in a restaurant, this salad is a true delight. When I started dreaming about it in my mind, I decided to toss in the raspberries as a kind of shock flavor, just to see what would happen, and it worked. Ever taste a tropical sunset before? You'll love this one!

Serves 6 (½ cup)

1 (4-serving) package JELL-O
    sugar-free instant vanilla
    pudding mix
1 (4-serving) package
    JELL-O sugar-free lime
    gelatin
⅔ cup Carnation Dry Milk
    Powder

1 cup (one 8-ounce can)
    crushed pineapple, packed
    in fruit juice, undrained
¾ cup water
¾ cup Cool Whip Lite
1½ cups fresh red raspberries
½ cup (1 ounce) miniature
    marshmallows

In a large bowl, combine dry pudding mix, dry gelatin, and dry milk powder. Add undrained pineapple and water. Mix well using a wire whisk. Blend in Cool Whip Lite. Add raspberries and marshmallows. Mix gently to combine. Cover and refrigerate at least 30 minutes. Gently stir again just before serving.

Each serving equals:

HE: ⅔ Fruit, ⅓ Skim Milk, ½ Slider, 5 Optional Calories

----

125 Calories, 1 gm Fat, 4 gm Protein, 25 gm Carbohydrate,
300 mg Sodium, 1 gm Fiber

DIABETIC: 1 Fruit, ½ Starch

Refreshing Pear-Mint Salad

--------------------------■--------------------------

A dding mint extract and green food coloring to this simple
blend made it anything but plain, don't you agree? The
canned pears make it easy to stir up any time of the year.

Serves 6 (full ½ cup)

*2 cups (one 16-ounce can)
pear halves, packed in
fruit juice, drained and
liquid reserved ☆
1 (4-serving) package JELL-O
sugar-free instant vanilla
pudding mix
⅓ cup Carnation Nonfat Dry
Milk Powder*

*¾ cup Yoplait plain fat-free
yogurt
¾ cup Cool Whip Lite
½ teaspoon mint extract
6 to 8 drops green food
coloring
½ cup (1 ounce) miniature
marshmallows*

Coarsely chop pear halves. Set aside. Add enough water to reserved pear juice to make 1 cup liquid. In a large bowl, combine
dry pudding mix, dry milk powder, liquid, and yogurt. Mix well
using a wire whisk. Blend in Cool Whip Lite, mint extract, and
green food coloring. Add marshmallows and chopped pears. Mix
gently to combine. Cover and refrigerate at least 30 minutes.
Gently stir again just before serving.

Each serving equals:

HE: ⅔ Fruit, ⅓ Skim Milk, ½ Slider, 5 Optional Calories

----

117 Calories, 1 gm Fat, 3 gm Protein, 24 gm Carbohydrate,
267 mg Sodium, 1 gm Fiber

DIABETIC: 1 Fruit, ½ Starch

Pistachio Creme Fruit Salad

---■---

S ometimes I believe in going back to basics when preparing food for the men in my life. In this case, I mixed up a fun-flavor pudding with man-pleasing pineapple, then added bananas and marshmallows to boost the playful quotient. Men are like kids in a candy store when they see those marshmallows peeping out!

Serves 6 (⅔ cup)

1 (4-serving) package JELL-O sugar-free instant pistachio pudding mix
⅓ cup Carnation Nonfat Dry Milk Powder
¾ cup Yoplait plain fat-free yogurt

1 cup (one 8-ounce can) crushed pineapple, packed in fruit juice, undrained
¾ cup Cool Whip Lite
½ cup (1 ounce) miniature marshmallows
1 cup (1 medium) diced banana

In a large bowl, combine dry pudding mix and dry milk powder. Add yogurt and undrained pineapple. Mix gently to combine. Stir in Cool Whip Lite. Add marshmallows and bananas. Mix gently to combine. Cover and refrigerate at least 15 minutes. Gently stir again just before serving.

Each serving equals:

HE: ⅔ Fruit, ⅓ Skim Milk, ½ Slider, 5 Optional Calories

125 Calories, 1 gm Fat, 3 gm Protein, 20 gm Carbohydrate, 258 mg Sodium, 1 gm Fiber

DIABETIC: 1 Fruit, ½ Starch

Creamy Strawberry Fruit Salad

W hen the recipe stars strawberries, you can usually be sure I created it to please me, but in this recipe my favorite fruit also delighted Cliff and my grandson Zach. When I served it for lunch on a recent Sunday, both asked for more!

Serves 6

1 (4-serving) package JELL-O
    sugar-free strawberry
    gelatin
¾ cup boiling water
1 (8-ounce) package
    Philadelphia fat-free
    cream cheese

1 cup (one 8-ounce can)
    crushed pineapple, packed
    in fruit juice, undrained
2 cups diced fresh
    strawberries
1 cup (1 medium) diced
    banana

In a blender container, combine dry gelatin and boiling water. Cover and process on BLEND 10 seconds. Add cream cheese. Process on BLEND 20 seconds or until mixture is smooth. Pour into a large bowl. Stir in undrained pineapple. Add strawberries and banana. Mix gently to combine. Pour mixture into an 8-by-8-inch dish. Refrigerate until firm, about 3 hours. Cut into 6 servings.

Each serving equals:

HE: 1 Fruit, ⅔ Protein, 6 Optional Calories

96 Calories, 0 gm Fat, 7 gm Protein, 17 gm Carbohydrate,
264 mg Sodium, 1 gm Fiber

DIABETIC: 1 Fruit, 1 Meat

Orange-Pecan Tapioca Salad

D o the men you know love tapioca as much as Cliff does? I think it's such a popular food because of those cozy memories it brings back, of meals with the family gathered around, and afternoons at Grandma's. This is a special mix of tastes I stirred up to please my "truck-drivin' man"—and it really did!

Serves 6 (½ cup)

1 (4-serving) package JELL-O
   sugar-free vanilla cook-
   and-serve pudding mix
3 tablespoons Quick Cooking
   Minute Tapioca
2 cups skim milk
1 (4-serving) package JELL-O
   sugar-free orange gelatin

¾ cup Cool Whip Lite
1 cup (one 11-ounce can)
   mandarin oranges, rinsed
   and drained
3 tablespoons (¾ ounce)
   chopped pecans

In a large saucepan, combine dry pudding mix, tapioca, skim milk, and dry gelatin. Mix well using a wire whisk. Let set 5 minutes. Cook over medium heat, stirring constantly until mixture thickens and starts to boil. Remove from heat. Pour mixture into a large bowl and place bowl on wire rack. Cool 30 minutes. Add Cool Whip Lite, mandarin oranges, and pecans. Mix gently to combine. Cover and refrigerate at least 15 minutes or until ready to serve. Gently stir again just before serving.

Each serving equals:

HE: ½ Fat, ⅓ Skim Milk, ⅓ Fruit, ½ Slider, 2 Optional Calories

119 Calories, 3 gm Fat, 4 gm Protein, 19 gm Carbohydrate, 157 mg Sodium, 0 gm Fiber

DIABETIC: 1 Starch, ½ Fat

Southern Blueberry Fruit Salad

---------------------------------■---------------------------------

Let's celebrate the wonderful tastes of the old South together in this delectable dish. The peaches and blueberries are beautifully juicy and the pecans give it such a nice crunch, you'll want to serve this at every family party during the months fresh fruit is available at roadside stands and in your market. You could use frozen blueberries, but it won't be as "magical," and you could use canned peaches, but only in an emergency in the dead of winter when you're craving this unique combination of flavors.   *Serves 6 (⅔ cup)*

¾ cup Yoplait plain fat-free yogurt
⅓ cup Carnation Nonfat Dry Milk Powder
1 (4-serving) package JELL-O sugar-free lemon gelatin
¾ cup Cool Whip Lite
2 cups (4 medium) peeled and diced fresh peaches
1½ cups fresh blueberries
2 tablespoons (½ ounce) chopped pecans

In a medium bowl, combine yogurt and dry milk powder. Stir in dry gelatin. Add Cool Whip Lite. Mix gently to combine. Fold in peaches, blueberries, and pecans. Cover and refrigerate at least 30 minutes. Gently stir again just before serving.

Each serving equals:

HE: 1 Fruit, ⅓ Skim Milk, ¼ Slider, 7 Optional Calories

119 Calories, 3 gm Fat, 5 gm Protein, 18 gm Carbohydrate, 80 mg Sodium, 2 gm Fiber

DIABETIC: 1 Fruit, ½ Fat

Citrus Cinnamon Salad

---■---

This is one dish the folks on both coasts would definitely call dessert, but my heartland heritage justifies calling this tangy-sweet blend a salad! It certainly pleases all the men in my life whenever it's served. If you've never bought cinnamon graham crackers before, you're in for a real treat.

Serves 8 (full ½ cup)

1 (4-serving) package JELL-O sugar-free instant vanilla pudding mix

1 (4-serving) package JELL-O sugar-free orange gelatin

⅓ cup Carnation Nonfat Dry Milk Powder

1 cup unsweetened orange juice

¾ cup Yoplait plain fat-free yogurt

¾ cup Cool Whip Lite

1 cup (one 11-ounce can) mandarin oranges, rinsed and drained

½ cup raisins

¼ cup (1 ounce) chopped pecans

12 (2½-inch) Nabisco Honey Maid Cinnamon Graham Crackers, coarsely crushed

In a large bowl, combine dry pudding mix, dry gelatin, and dry milk powder. Add orange juice. Mix well using a wire whisk. Blend in yogurt and Cool Whip Lite. Add mandarin oranges, raisins, and pecans. Mix gently to combine. Fold in crushed cinnamon graham crackers. Cover and refrigerate at least 30 minutes. Gently stir again just before serving.

HINT: To plump up raisins without "cooking," place in a glass measuring cup and microwave on High for 20 seconds.

Each serving equals:

HE: 1 Fruit, ½ Fat, ½ Bread, ¼ Skim Milk, ¼ Slider, 13 Optional Calories

---

139 Calories, 3 gm Fat, 4 gm Protein, 24 gm Carbohydrate, 243 mg Sodium, 1 gm Fiber

---

DIABETIC: 1 Fruit, ½ Fat, ½ Starch

Decadent "Candy Bar" Salad

—————————————————————■—————————————————————

Can a recipe be called "too good," I wonder? This sweet concoction would make a satisfying dessert, and the mix of
goodies that are blended together in its creaminess may remind
you of German chocolate cake topping. It's okay to run a little
wild occasionally and enjoy these luscious flavors, especially
when they're combined in a healthy salad.

Serves 6 (¾ cup)

*1 (4-serving) package JELL-O
   sugar-free instant
   butterscotch pudding mix
⅔ cup Carnation Nonfat Dry
   Milk Powder
1½ cups water
1 teaspoon coconut extract
¾ cup Yoplait plain fat-free
   yogurt*

*½ cup Cool Whip Lite
12 (2½-inch) chocolate-
   flavored graham crackers,
   coarsely crushed
2 tablespoons (½ ounce)
   chopped pecans
2 tablespoons flaked coconut*

In a large bowl, combine dry pudding mix, dry milk powder, and
water. Mix well using a wire whisk. Blend in coconut extract, yogurt, and Cool Whip Lite. Add graham cracker crumbs, pecans,
and coconut. Mix gently to combine. Cover and refrigerate at
least 15 minutes. Gently stir again just before serving.

Each serving equals:

HE: ⅔ Bread, ½ Skim Milk, ⅓ Fat, ¼ Slider, 15 Optional Calories

———

148 Calories, 4 gm Fat, 5 gm Protein, 23 gm Carbohydrate,
383 mg Sodium, 0 gm Fiber

———

DIABETIC: 1 Starch, ½ Skim Milk, ½ Fat

Cherry-Chocolate Cloud Salad

M y father just loved chocolate-covered cherries, and tasting this dish took me back to my days as a little girl when he brought a box home at Christmastime! Again, this straddles the line between sweet salads and desserts, but I haven't known a man yet who couldn't make room for a little chocolate-cherry magic. *Serves 6 (⅔ cup)*

1 (4-serving) package JELL-O sugar-free vanilla cook-and-serve pudding mix
1 (4-serving) package JELL-O sugar-free cherry gelatin
¾ cup water

2 cups (one 16-ounce can) tart red cherries, packed in water, undrained
¾ cup Cool Whip Lite
9 (2½-inch) chocolate graham crackers
½ cup (1 ounce) miniature marshmallows

In a medium saucepan, combine dry pudding mix, dry gelatin, and water. Stir in undrained cherries. Cook over medium heat, stirring often, until mixture thickens and starts to boil, being sure not to crush cherries. Spoon mixture into a large bowl. Place bowl on a wire rack and let set 45 minutes. Stir in Cool Whip Lite. Refrigerate at least 10 minutes. Break chocolate graham crackers into large pieces. Just before serving, stir in cracker pieces and marshmallows.

Each serving equals:

HE: ⅔ Fruit, ½ Bread, ½ Slider, 8 Optional Calories

126 Calories, 2 gm Fat, 2 gm Protein, 25 gm Carbohydrate, 188 mg Sodium, 1 gm Fiber

DIABETIC: 1 Fruit, ½ Starch

Strawberry-Pineapple Fluff Salad

This is so luscious and smooth, and the fruit flavors so intense, silence will fall upon your table while everyone devours this treat with speed! The marshmallows make it fun, but the real star of the party is the berries. Since I consider strawberries the queen of fruits, it seems only fair to share their goodness with the king of the household, don't you think?

Serves 6 (full ½ cup)

1 (4-serving) package JELL-O sugar-free vanilla cook-and-serve pudding mix
1 (4-serving) package JELL-O sugar-free strawberry gelatin
1 cup (one 8-ounce can) crushed pineapple, packed in fruit juice, undrained

1 cup water
2 cups frozen unsweetened strawberries
¾ cup Cool Whip Lite
½ cup (1 ounce) miniature marshmallows

In a large saucepan, combine dry pudding mix, dry gelatin, undrained pineapple, and water. Cook over medium heat, stirring often, until mixture thickens and starts to boil. Remove from heat. Stir in frozen strawberries. Place pan on a wire rack and let cool 30 minutes. Whip mixture, using an electric mixer on HIGH, until mixture is fluffy. Stir in Cool Whip Lite and marshmallows. Spoon into serving bowl. Cover and refrigerate at least 10 minutes. Gently stir again just before serving.

Each serving equals:

HE: ⅔ Fruit, ½ Slider, 8 Optional Calories

89 Calories, 1 gm Fat, 1 gm Protein, 19 gm Carbohydrate, 116 mg Sodium, 1 gm Fiber

DIABETIC: 1 Fruit

Carrot Marshmallow Salad

———————————————■———————————————

This is one of Tommy's favorites, created for my youngest and newest college grad because he likes carrots and orange flavor, and has since he was a little boy. It's fun, fruity, and it's full of vitamin A, so you can feel good about treating yourself so well.

Serves 6

1 (4-serving) package JELL-O
   sugar-free lemon gelatin
1 cup boiling water
1 cup (one 8-ounce can)
   crushed pineapple, packed
   in fruit juice, undrained

2 cups shredded carrots
½ cup (1 ounce) miniature
   marshmallows
¾ cup Cool Whip Lite
2 tablespoons Kraft fat-free
   mayonnaise

In a large bowl, combine dry gelatin and boiling water. Mix well using a wire whisk. Stir in undrained pineapple. Cover and refrigerate 15 minutes. Add carrots and marshmallows. Mix well to combine. Pour mixture into an 8-by-8-inch dish. Cover and refrigerate at least 2 hours. Just before serving, in a small bowl, combine Cool Whip Lite and mayonnaise. Evenly spread mixture over top. Cut into 6 servings.

Each serving equals:

HE: ⅔ Vegetable, ⅓ Fruit, ¼ Slider, 14 Optional Calories

81 Calories, 1 gm Fat, 1 gm Protein, 17 gm Carbohydrate, 88 mg Sodium, 1 gm Fiber

DIABETIC: 1 Starch

---■---

Last year my husband, Travis, was told he was diabetic and MUST change his diet. Ha! After reading every can and box in the store as to its content, buying books that cooked for the diabetic and getting a thumbs-down (and nose-up) reaction after hours of research and preparation, I was about to cry!

Then I bought your book. I was much impressed that lean beef could be used instead of ground turkey. Although Travis is an avid fisherman, he doesn't eat anything with fins or feathers. And only 8 ounces for most dishes—I could actually defend the cost of 91% lean. The first recipe I tried was the Salisbury Steak—it sounded like "closest to home." And he liked it! Travis even said, "You can fix the hamburger like this when you cook just plain hamburger." I was cautiously excited . . . but let's wait until I try something more exotic. The next night I tried Tamale Pie. Not only was it the best Tamale Pie I've ever eaten, but Travis gave it TWO THUMBS UP! . . . You've made a big hit in our household.

—G.A., CA

---■---

Vegetables for Men Who "Never Touch 'em!"

--------■--------

Everyone has a growing-up story about being forced to eat a hated food—and for most of the men I've talked to, it was vegetables. But for every memory of sitting at the table for hours facing a mound of bright red beets or a pile of Brussels sprouts, there's another one, of remembered pleasure in devouring a dish that Mom made just for us, full of the tastes of childhood and home.

My recipe for Dixieland Green Beans was like a time machine for a friend of ours who lives in California now but who grew up in the South. He told me they tasted just like the beans his mother fixed when he was young, and that every single bite took him back to those carefree days.

I think that's the secret with getting most men to eat vegetables. Figuring out what they loved when they were little, and preparing healthy but still tasty versions to serve them now, is the key to making these nourishing foods a welcome part of a man's menu.

Do you live with a man who insists he only likes peas and carrots, creamed corn, and string beans from a can? Is his idea of potatoes those deep-fried sticks at the local fast-food place? Well, Healthy Exchanges vegetable recipes are just the thing to change his mind—and fast! These recipes include some of his favorites, prepared in fresh new ways, but they'll also introduce him to foods he's often avoided (even—yes!—broccoli!) that may change the way he views vegetables . . . forever.

Vegetables

German Green Beans

Green Bean Mushroom Casserole

Spanish Green Beans

Dixieland Green Beans

Carrots with Mushrooms

Polynesian Carrots

Carrot-Cabbage Casserole

Mustard Cauliflower and Broccoli

Easy Marinated Mushrooms

Corn and Onion au Gratin

Cheesy Broccoli and Corn Casserole

French Squaw Corn

Potluck Corn

Potato Corn Bake

Country Scalloped Tomatoes

German Green Beans

-------------------■-------------------

Cliff loves canned green beans, so anytime I want to win favor with him, I stir up some new way to serve his favorite vegetable. You can also prepare this dish with fresh or frozen beans if you prefer. I think you'll agree that the combination of almonds and bacon bits is a true man-pleaser, especially when added to this dish's sweet-and-sour flavor. (The secret's in the combo of vinegar and Sugar Twin or Sprinkle Sweet!)

Serves 6 (⅔ cup)

½ cup chopped onion
¼ cup (1 ounce) slivered
   almonds
2 tablespoons Hormel Bacon
   Bits
4 cups (two 16-ounce cans)
   cut green beans, rinsed
   and drained

¼ cup white vinegar
¼ cup Sugar Twin or Sprinkle
   Sweet

In a large skillet sprayed with butter-flavored cooking spray, sauté onion until tender, about 5 minutes. Stir in almonds and bacon bits. Add green beans. Mix well to combine. In a small bowl, combine vinegar and Sugar Twin. Stir vinegar mixture into green bean mixture. Lower heat. Simmer 5 minutes or until most of the liquid evaporates, stirring occasionally.

Each serving equals:

HE: 1½ Vegetable, ⅓ Fat, ¼ Slider, 4 Optional Calories

----

75 Calories, 3 gm Fat, 3 gm Protein, 9 gm Carbohydrate, 50 mg Sodium, 2 gm Fiber

----

DIABETIC: 1½ Vegetable, ½ Fat

Green Bean Mushroom Casserole

<hr>

This is real 1950s-style, Grandma-made comfort food. It's great served steaming from the oven or warmed in the microwave as leftovers. I can just imagine how your mouth will water over this one. *Serves 6*

4 cups frozen cut green beans
1 cup (two 2.5-ounce jars) sliced mushrooms, drained
1 (10¾-ounce) can Healthy Request Cream of Mushroom Soup
¼ cup diced pimiento
¼ cup (1 ounce) chopped almonds

6 tablespoons Bisquick Reduced Fat Baking Mix
¼ cup (¾ ounce) grated Kraft fat-free Parmesan cheese
1 teaspoon dried parsley flakes
1 teaspoon dried onion flakes
1 tablespoon + 1 teaspoon reduced-calorie margarine

Preheat oven to 350 degrees. Spray an 8-by-8-inch baking dish with butter-flavored cooking spray. In a large saucepan, cook green beans with water until tender. Drain. Return beans to saucepan. Stir in mushrooms, mushroom soup, pimiento, and almonds. Pour mixture into prepared baking dish. In a small bowl, combine Bisquick, Parmesan cheese, parsley flakes, onion flakes, and margarine. Mix together with fork until mixture is crumbly. Sprinkle crumb mixture evenly over top. Bake 45 minutes. Place baking dish on a wire rack and let set 5 minutes. Divide into 6 servings.

HINT: If you can get your hands on fresh green beans, use them!

Each serving equals:

HE: 1⅔ Vegetable, ½ Fat, ⅓ Protein, ⅓ Bread, ¼ Slider, 8 Optional Calories

<hr>

137 Calories, 5 gm Fat, 5 gm Protein, 18 gm Carbohydrate, 467 mg Sodium, 4 gm Fiber

<hr>

DIABETIC: 2 Vegetable, ½ Fat, ½ Starch

Spanish Green Beans

---■---

You know how I pride myself on dishes that stir and cook up quickly. Well, this one takes a few more minutes than some of my recipes, but you'll soon see it's worth it. The stewed tomatoes need to cook a little longer for all the flavors to shake hands and say howdy. Besides, the dish requires only about five minutes of "baby-sitting" and no more than a half hour to reach perfection!   *Serves 6 (1 cup)*

¾ cup chopped onion
5½ cups frozen cut green beans
1 cup water
½ teaspoon dried minced garlic
1¾ cups (one 14½-ounce can)
    stewed tomatoes, undrained
⅓ cup Heinz Light Harvest
    or Healthy Choice
    ketchup
2 tablespoons Hormel
    Bacon Bits
¼ teaspoon black pepper

In a large skillet sprayed with butter-flavored cooking spray, sauté onion until tender, about 5 minutes. Add green beans, water, and garlic. Mix well to combine. Lower heat. Cover and simmer 20 minutes or until green beans are tender. Add undrained tomatoes, ketchup, bacon bits, and black pepper. Mix well to combine. Continue cooking 10 minutes, stirring occasionally.

Each serving equals:

HE: 2⅔ Vegetable, 17 Optional Calories

---

97 Calories, 1 gm Fat, 4 gm Protein, 18 gm Carbohydrate,
264 mg Sodium, 4 gm Fiber

DIABETIC: 3 Vegetable

Dixieland Green Beans

----------------------■----------------------

One of those delicious southern food traditions surfaces in this old-fashioned dish that recalls lusciously laden buffet tables on summer nights. Can't you just imagine the sweet perfume of magnolias as you enjoy this tasty dish?

Serves 4 (¾ cup)

4 cups frozen or fresh green beans
1 cup water
½ cup chopped onion
2 teaspoons Sugar Twin or Sprinkle Sweet

3 ounces (⅓) finely chopped Dubuque 97% lean fat-free ham
¼ teaspoon black pepper

Place green beans and water in large saucepan. Add onion, Sugar Twin, ham, and pepper. Bring to a boil. Cover. Lower heat and simmer 45 minutes.

Each serving equals:

HE: 2¼ Vegetable, ½ Protein, 1 Optional Calorie

----

65 Calories, 1 gm Fat, 6 gm Protein, 10 gm Carbohydrate,
188 mg Sodium, 2 gm Fiber

DIABETIC: 2 Vegetable, ½ Meat

Carrots with Mushrooms

———————————————■———————————————

L ots of people are nervous about cooking with herbs, concerned they don't know which ones to use and in what
amounts. I used basil here for an especially nice touch in this
easy-to-fix dish, and you'll think it must be magic when the
calcium-rich sauce thickens up so nicely with just a little flour.

Serves 4 (½ cup)

1 tablespoon + 1 teaspoon
  reduced-calorie
  margarine
3 cups shredded carrots
½ cup finely chopped onion
½ cup (one 2.5-ounce jar)
  sliced mushrooms,
  undrained

¼ teaspoon dried minced
  garlic
½ teaspoon basil
⅛ teaspoon black pepper
1 tablespoon all-purpose flour
⅓ cup Carnation Nonfat Dry
  Milk Powder
⅔ cup water

In a large skillet, melt reduced-calorie margarine. Add carrots
and onion. Mix well to combine. Stir in mushrooms, minced
garlic, basil, and black pepper. Cover and cook over low heat 10
to 15 minutes or until tender. In a covered jar, combine flour,
dry milk powder, and water. Shake well to blend. Add milk mixture to carrot mixture. Continue cooking 3 to 4 minutes or until
mixture thickens.

Each serving equals:

HE: 2 Vegetable, ½ Fat, ¼ Skim Milk, 8 Optional Calories

73 Calories, 1 gm Fat, 3 gm Protein, 13 gm Carbohydrate,
150 mg Sodium, 2 gm Fiber

DIABETIC: 2 Vegetable, ½ Fat

Polynesian Carrots

————————————■————————————

Here's a great dish to serve with grilled burgers or grilled extra-lean pork chops—or even baked chicken breasts. The variety of textures and tastes will appeal to every member of the family, and it smells so good. I invented this "hot carrot salad" because I know how men love pineapple. . . .

Serves 4 (¾ cup)

1 cup (one 8-ounce can)
   crushed pineapple, packed
   in fruit juice, drained, and
   ¼ cup liquid reserved ☆
½ cup water

½ teaspoon apple pie spice
3 cups shredded carrots
¼ cup raisins
2 tablespoons (½ ounce)
   chopped pecans

In a large skillet, combine pineapple juice, water, and apple pie spice. Add carrots. Mix well to combine. Cover. Cook over medium heat, stirring occasionally until tender, about 8 to 10 minutes. Stir in raisins, pineapple, and pecans. Lower heat. Continue cooking until mixture is heated through, about 5 minutes, stirring often.

Each serving equals:

HE: 1½ Vegetable, 1 Fruit, ½ Fat

130 Calories, 2 gm Fat, 2 gm Protein, 26 gm Carbohydrate,
31 mg Sodium, 3 gm Fiber

DIABETIC: 1 Vegetable, 1 Fruit, ½ Fat

Carrot-Cabbage Casserole

---■---

This bubbles over with so much old-time cozy goodness, you'll want to serve it any time of year. Baked to a golden delight, topped with cracker crumbs and cheese, it'll definitely make the year's Top Ten List.   *Serves 4*

1½ cups shredded carrots
3 cups coarsely shredded
  cabbage
2 cups water
½ cup chopped onion
1 (10¾-ounce) can Healthy
  Request Cream of Celery
  Soup

⅓ cup skim milk
¾ cup (3 ounces) shredded
  Kraft reduced-fat
  Cheddar cheese
1 teaspoon dried parsley
  flakes
10 Ritz Reduced Fat Crackers,
  made into crumbs

Preheat oven to 350 degrees. Spray an 8-by-8-inch baking dish with butter-flavored cooking spray. In a large saucepan, combine carrots, cabbage, and water. Cook over medium heat until vegetables are tender, about 10 minutes. Drain. Meanwhile, in a large skillet sprayed with butter-flavored cooking spray, sauté onion until tender. Stir in celery soup, skim milk, Cheddar cheese, and parsley flakes. Continue cooking until cheese melts, stirring often. Stir in drained carrots and cabbage mixture. Mix well to combine. Pour mixture into prepared baking dish. Evenly sprinkle Ritz cracker crumbs over top. Bake 30 minutes. Place baking dish on a wire rack and let set 5 minutes. Divide into 4 servings.

Each serving equals:

HE: 2½ Vegetable, 1 Protein, ¼ Bread, ½ Slider, 9 Optional Calories

---

178 Calories, 6 gm Fat, 9 gm Protein, 22 gm Carbohydrate, 584 mg Sodium, 2 gm Fiber

---

DIABETIC: 1½ Vegetable, 1 Meat, 1 Starch

Mustard Cauliflower and Broccoli

A very popular special at Jo's Kitchen Cafe, this recipe overflows with flavors men like, especially mustard and cheese—and its creamy tanginess will get them to eat their veggies, just wait and see! The mayonnaise delivers such creaminess, and because you cook it in the microwave, the vegetables soften and the flavors blend quickly. **Serves 6 (⅔ cup)**

3 cups chopped cauliflower	*1 teaspoon dried onion flakes*
2 cups chopped broccoli	*1 teaspoon prepared mustard*
¼ cup water	*¾ cup (3 ounces) shredded*
½ cup Kraft fat-free	*Kraft reduced-fat Cheddar*
mayonnaise	*cheese*

In an 8-cup glass measuring bowl, combine cauliflower, broccoli, and water. Cover. Microwave on HIGH for 6 minutes. Drain. In the same bowl, combine mayonnaise, onion flakes, mustard, and Cheddar cheese. Stir in drained vegetables. Cover and microwave on HIGH for 2 minutes or until cheese starts to melt. Let set 2 minutes. Gently stir again just before serving.

Each serving equals:

HE: 1⅔ Vegetable, ⅔ Protein, 13 Optional Calories

70 Calories, 2 gm Fat, 6 gm Protein, 7 gm Carbohydrate, 284 mg Sodium, 2 gm Fiber

DIABETIC: 1½ Vegetable, ½ Meat

Easy Marinated Mushrooms

------------------------■------------------------

The sweet-and-sour taste of this simply scrumptious dish will win you lots of fans. The dressing makes a good marinade on its own, but I like to add a few additional flavors to smooth it out and sparkle it up. *Serves 6 (½ cup)*

*1 cup Kraft Fat Free Italian
   Dressing*
*1 tablespoon Sugar Twin or
   Sprinkle Sweet*
1 tablespoon white vinegar
2 teaspoons dried parsley flakes

*1 cup coarsely chopped
   onion*
*2 cups fresh sliced
   mushrooms, cleaned and
   ends trimmed*

In a large bowl, combine Italian dressing, Sugar Twin, vinegar, and parsley flakes. Stir in onion. Add mushrooms. Mix gently to coat. Cover and refrigerate at least 4 hours or overnight.

Each serving equals:

HE: 1 Vegetable, 13 Optional Calories

----

32 Calories, 0 gm Fat, 1 gm Protein, 7 gm Carbohydrate, 376 mg Sodium, 1 gm Fiber

----

DIABETIC: 1 Vegetable

Corn and Onion au Gratin

------------------------------■------------------------------

Just reading the list of ingredients is enough to start your appetite asking "What time is dinner?" If you like onions and you like corn, you're guaranteed to love this.   *Serves 6*

2 cups chopped onion	2 tablespoons canned chopped
1 (10¾-ounce) can	pimiento
Healthy Request	1 teaspoon dried parsley flakes
Cream of Mushroom	¼ teaspoon black pepper
Soup	2½ cups frozen whole kernel
¾ cup (3 ounces) shredded	corn
Kraft reduced-fat Cheddar	5 Ritz Reduced Fat Crackers,
cheese	made into crumbs

Preheat oven to 350 degrees. Spray an 8-by-8-inch baking dish with butter-flavored cooking spray. In a large skillet sprayed with butter-flavored cooking spray, sauté onion until tender. Stir in mushroom soup and Cheddar cheese. Add pimiento, parsley flakes, and black pepper. Mix well to combine. Cook over medium heat, stirring often until cheese melts. Stir in corn. Spread mixture into prepared baking dish. Evenly sprinkle cracker crumbs over top. Bake 60 minutes. Place baking dish on a wire rack and let set 5 minutes. Divide into 6 servings.

Each serving equals:

HE: 1 Bread, ⅔ Vegetable, ⅔ Protein, ¼ Slider, 8 Optional Calories

----
155 Calories, 3 gm Fat, 7 gm Protein, 25 gm Carbohydrate,
349 mg Sodium, 3 gm Fiber

DIABETIC: 1½ Starch, ½ Vegetable, ½ Meat

Cheesy Broccoli and Corn Casserole

C an you tell I'm a real fan of cheddar cheese soup? I love it so much, I just had to figure out how to make it into a terrific casserole that will remind you of rich and hearty broccoli cheese soup you've enjoyed at country restaurants. One little secret I'll share with you: to thaw your frozen broccoli, just leave it in the refrigerator in the morning, and when evening comes it'll be just right.

Serves 6

2 cups (one 16-ounce can) cream-style corn

1 egg or equivalent in egg substitute

2 teaspoons dried onion flakes

⅓ cup (1½ ounces) shredded Kraft reduced-fat Cheddar cheese

3 cups frozen chopped broccoli, thawed

10 Ritz Reduced Fat Crackers, made into crumbs

Preheat oven to 350 degrees. Spray an 8-by-8-inch baking dish with butter-flavored cooking spray. In a large bowl, combine corn, egg, onion flakes, and Cheddar cheese. Stir in broccoli. Pour mixture into prepared baking dish. Evenly sprinkle cracker crumbs over top. Bake 35 to 40 minutes. Place baking dish on a wire rack and let set 5 minutes. Divide into 6 servings.

Each serving equals:

HE: 1 Vegetable, 1 Bread, ½ Protein

139 Calories, 3 gm Fat, 6 gm Protein, 22 gm Carbohydrate, 366 mg Sodium, 2 gm Fiber

DIABETIC: 1 Vegetable, 1 Starch, ½ Meat

French Squaw Corn

-----------------■-----------------

S quaw corn is a real old-timey Midwest recipe, and over the years I've stirred up several different versions. It smells amazingly good when you start cooking the dressing. This is probably Tommy's favorite, but I like it too for its rainbow of colors—yellow and green and red plus the coral-colored dressing. What a beautiful and satisfying dish! *Serves 4 (½ cup)*

¼ cup diced green bell pepper
¾ cup diced onion
2 cups frozen whole kernel
  corn
¼ cup diced canned pimiento
¼ teaspoon black pepper

1 teaspoon dried parsley
  flakes
1 tablespoon Sugar Twin or
  Sprinkle Sweet
¼ cup Kraft Fat Free French
  Dressing

In a large skillet sprayed with butter-flavored cooking spray, sauté green pepper and onion until tender. Stir in corn. Continue cooking 5 minutes, stirring constantly. Add pimiento, black pepper, parsley flakes, Sugar Twin, and French dressing. Mix well to combine. Lower heat. Simmer 5 minutes.

Each serving equals:

HE: 1 Bread, ½ Vegetable, ¼ Slider, 5 Optional Calories

108 Calories, 0 gm Fat, 3 gm Protein, 24 gm Carbohydrate,
126 mg Sodium, 3 gm Fiber

DIABETIC: 1½ Starch

Potluck Corn

---■---

Here's a clear favorite of my "truck-drivin' man"! Cliff couldn't stop telling people for days on end about this corn pudding. He just went bananas over it. He can be selective about eating mushrooms, but this time he licked his platter clean.

Serves 6

2 cups (one 16-ounce can) cream-style corn
⅔ cup Carnation Dry Milk Powder
½ cup water
¼ cup finely chopped onion
½ cup (2.5-ounce jar) sliced mushrooms, drained
¾ cup (3 ounces) shredded Kraft reduced-fat Cheddar cheese
4 slices day-old reduced-calorie white bread, made into crumbs
1 teaspoon dried parsley flakes
¼ teaspoon black pepper

Preheat oven to 350 degrees. Spray an 8-by-8-inch baking dish with butter-flavored cooking spray. In a large bowl, combine corn, dry milk powder, and water. Stir in onion, mushrooms, Cheddar cheese, and bread crumbs. Add parsley flakes and black pepper. Mix well to combine. Pour mixture into prepared baking dish. Bake 45 to 50 minutes or until center is firm. Place baking dish on a wire rack and let set 5 minutes. Cut into 6 servings.

Each serving equals:

HE: 1 Bread, ⅔ Protein, ⅓ Skim Milk, ¼ Vegetable

162 Calories, 2 gm Fat, 10 gm Protein, 26 gm Carbohydrate, 510 mg Sodium, 1 gm Fiber

DIABETIC: 1½ Starch, ½ Meat

Potato Corn Bake

-----------------■-----------------

This is a cross between scalloped corn and scalloped potatoes, but celebrating the best of both! I left out some of the traditional ingredients like eggs, so you can enjoy this dish with meat loaf or roast beef, even with burgers on a Sunday night. If you've got some leftover ham, dice that up and throw it in if you like—just remember to count the exchanges. And be glad if you've got leftovers, because they taste even better than on the first day.

Serves 8

⅔ cup Carnation Nonfat Dry Milk Powder

½ cup water

2 cups (one 16-ounce can) cream-style corn

2 teaspoons dried onion flakes

1 teaspoon dried parsley flakes

¼ cup (one 2-ounce jar) diced pimiento

¼ teaspoon black pepper

½ cup frozen whole kernel corn

6 cups (15 ounces) frozen Mr. Dell's Loose Hash Browns or any frozen loose hash browns

Preheat oven to 375 degrees. Spray a 9-by-13-inch baking dish with butter-flavored cooking spray. In a large bowl, combine dry milk powder and water. Stir in cream-style corn, onion flakes, parsley flakes, pimiento, and black pepper. Add frozen corn and potatoes. Mix well to combine. Pour mixture into prepared baking dish. Bake 40 to 45 minutes. Divide into 8 servings. Serve at once.

Each serving equals:

HE: 1 Bread, ¼ Skim Milk

----

137 Calories, 1 gm Fat, 4 gm Protein, 28 gm Carbohydrate, 230 mg Sodium, 2 gm Fiber

----

DIABETIC: 1½ Starch

Country Scalloped Tomatoes

------------------------------■------------------------------

I admit it, I like tomatoes in any way, shape, or form, so I really created this one for me. Thank heavens Cliff liked it, too—probably because of the cornbread stuffing!   *Serves 4*

¾ cup chopped onion
¼ cup chopped green bell
* pepper*
¾ cup water
1 cup (3 ounces) Stovetop
* Cornbread Stuffing Mix*
* with 1½ tablespoons dry*
* vegetable seasoning packet*

3 cups thinly sliced fresh
* tomatoes*
⅓ cup (1½ ounces) shredded
* Kraft reduced-fat*
* Cheddar cheese*

Preheat oven to 350 degrees. Spray an 8-by-8-inch baking dish with butter-flavored cooking spray. In a large skillet sprayed with butter-flavored cooking spray, sauté onion and green pepper until vegetables are tender, about 5 minutes. Remove from heat. Stir in water and dry vegetable seasoning. Add dry cornbread stuffing mix. Mix well to combine. Spread half of stuffing mixture into prepared baking dish. Evenly arrange tomato slices over top. Stir Cheddar cheese into remaining stuffing mixture. Evenly spoon stuffing mixture over tomatoes. Bake 45 to 50 minutes or until top is golden brown. Place baking dish on a wire rack and let set 5 minutes. Cut into 4 servings.

Each serving equals:

HE: 2 Vegetable, 1 Bread, ½ Protein

----

159 Calories, 3 gm Fat, 7 gm Protein, 26 gm Carbohydrate, 369 mg Sodium, 2 gm Fiber

----

DIABETIC: 2 Vegetable, 1 Starch, ½ Meat

--------■--------

*I have used your cookbooks and newsletter recipes EVERY SINGLE
DAY. Besides having to continually fight the battle of the bulge
myself, my husband discovered he had a potentially life-threatening
high blood cholesterol at his annual checkup last November. Since
using Healthy Exchanges recipes almost exclusively since then, he
has shed 30 pounds and is looking forward to a new cholesterol check
later this month. I feel confident that he will show a marked
improvement from last time.*

—N.B., NH

--------■--------

Man-Sized
Main Dishes

-------■-------

My son Tommy simply loves cheeseburgers.
He loves them every bit as much as a 25-year-
old graduate student as he did when he was ten and managed to con Cliff into pulling into McDonald's for
cheeseburgers when he was trucking with him during
the summers.

I've created several recipes that deliver the taste he
loves, particularly Fast Food Cheeseburger Skillet and
Tommy's Cheeseburger Turnovers. When he tasted my
skillet version, he told me it was as close to his favorite
flavors in a casserole as you could get without going to
the Golden Arches for the real thing.

In fact, when he took a bite of my turnovers, he went
ballistic, he was so excited. He kept saying to me, "Are
you sure, Mom? Are you sure? Are you conning people,
fixing this the old traditional way and telling people it's
not?" When I told him that yes, they really were healthy,
he smiled and took another big bite. "Boy, are they
good!" he told me, finishing one turnover and reaching
for another!

We know that daily platters of 22-ounce steaks and fried potatoes aren't what a man needs to live happily and healthily for a long time. But men want meat and potatoes. Switching over to chicken and fish just doesn't sit well with most men. Sure, they'll eat these foods occasionally, but they don't want that to be all they ever get.

Many of my main-dish recipes can be prepared with either ground turkey or lean beef, and some of my poultry recipes may surprise the man in your life. I prepare my Party Turkey Tetrazzini in many cooking demonstrations attended by men. Lots of them have told me "I don't really care for turkey except at Thanksgiving time, but this is outstanding." It's a good example of how often men think they don't like something, but if it's prepared in a tasty, eye-pleasing way, they eat it with relish.

The recipes in this section include spicy Mexican favorites, Italian pasta dishes, meaty casseroles topped with melted cheese, and much, much more—all served in genuinely satisfying portions: a quarter of an 8-by-8-inch casserole dish looks substantial, even to a man's "suspicious" eye.

Main Dishes

Three Cheeses and
Rice Bake

Eggs Creole

Skillet Tomato
Mac 'n' Cheese

Golden Onion Pie

Oven-Fried Fish

Salsa-Topped Baked Fish

Tuna Tetrazzini

Tuna-Plus Casserole

Tuna Almondine

Cajun Country
Shrimp and Rice

Salmon Cheese Loaf

Turkey-Stuffed Peppers

Turkey Club Casserole

Turkey Biscuit Stew

Creamy Turkey Skillet

Macho Burritos

Hamburger Potato
Casserole

Ruby Rio Stroganoff

Texas Lasagna

Texas Jo Casserole

California Beef Bake

Cabbage Patch Meat Loaf

Salisbury Noodle Skillet

Bavarian Meat Loaf

Magic Meat Loaf

Pizza Skillet

Pizza Muffins

Fast-Food
Cheeseburger Skillet

Tommy's Cheeseburger
Turnovers

He-Man's
Gravy and Biscuits

"Pot Roast" Stroganoff over
Noodles

Easy Salisbury Steak

Coney Island
Pasta Casserole

Meatballs in Sour Cream
Onion-Mushroom Sauce

Mex-Italian-Style
Minute Steaks

Bar-B-Que Beef Strips

Steak Pizzaola

Swiss Steak Ultra

Luau Pork

Creamy "Pork and Beans"

Bohemian Goulash

Cowpoke Pork Tenders

Ham Lasagna Toss

Ham and Corn Scallop

Mexicalli Ham-Rice Dish

Creole Ham Skillet

Grande Macaroni and
Ham Bake

Heartland Macaroni and Cheese

Taco Chicken Bake

Cabbage Patch Chicken and
Noodles

Layered Chicken Dinner

Chicken Lovers'
Pizza Casserole

Italian Chicken
Noodle Skillet

Grande Chicken-Rice Olé!

"French" Chicken and Noodles

Italian Grilled Chicken

Ham and Chicken Skillet

Chuck Wagon
Franks and Beans

Bavarian Hash

Veggie Hot Dog Skillet

Corned Beef
and Cabbage Quiche

Corned Beef Pasta Bake

■

Three Cheeses and Rice Bake

If one is good, I figured that three delicious flavors of cheese would be even better! This substantial rice dish is rich in flavor and hearty enough to make any man feel truly satisfied.

Serves 4

1 (10¾-ounce) can Healthy
    Request Cream of
    Mushroom Soup
¼ cup skim milk
1 (8-ounce) package
    Philadelphia fat-free
    cream cheese
¾ cup (3 ounces) Kraft
    reduced-fat Cheddar cheese

2 teaspoons dried parsley
    flakes ☆
¼ cup (¾ ounce) grated Kraft
    fat-free Parmesan cheese
½ cup (2.5-ounce jar) sliced
    mushrooms, drained
2 cups hot cooked rice
½ teaspoon paprika

Preheat oven to 350 degrees. Spray an 8-by-8-inch baking dish with butter-flavored cooking spray. In a large skillet, combine mushroom soup, skim milk, cream cheese, and Cheddar cheese. Cook over medium heat, stirring constantly, until mixture is smooth and cheeses are melted. Stir in 1 teaspoon parsley flakes and Parmesan cheese. Add mushrooms and rice. Mix well to combine. Pour mixture into prepared baking dish. Evenly sprinkle remaining 1 teaspoon parsley flakes and paprika over top. Bake 25 to 30 minutes. Place baking dish on a wire rack and let set 2 to 3 minutes before serving. Cut into 4 servings.

HINT: 1⅓ cups uncooked rice usually cooks to about 2 cups.

Each serving equals:

HE: 2¼ Protein, 1 Bread, ½ Slider, 7 Optional Calories

241 Calories, 5 gm Fat, 19 gm Protein, 30 gm Carbohydrate, 883 mg Sodium, 1 gm Fiber

DIABETIC: 2 Meat, 2 Starch

Eggs Creole

-------- ■ --------

I've combined eggs with a spicy sauce and the goodness of rice to make any mealtime a flavor celebration. This is a great choice for a weekend brunch when it's just the family or for a crowd.

Serves 4

½ cup finely chopped celery
½ cup finely diced onion
½ cup chopped green bell pepper
1 (10¾-ounce) can Healthy Request Tomato Soup
¼ cup water

1 teaspoon Worcestershire sauce
1 teaspoon dried parsley flakes
¼ teaspoon black pepper
2 cups hot cooked rice
4 hard-boiled eggs

In a large skillet sprayed with butter-flavored cooking spray, sauté celery, onion, and green pepper until tender, about 5 minutes. Stir in tomato soup, water, Worcestershire sauce, parsley flakes, and black pepper. Lower heat and simmer 5 minutes, stirring occasionally. For each serving, place ½ cup rice on plate, slice 1 egg over rice and spoon about ¼ cup hot sauce over top.

Each serving equals:

HE: 1 Bread, 1 Protein (limited), ¾ Vegetable, ½ Slider, 5 Optional Calories

231 Calories, 7 gm Fat, 9 gm Protein, 33 gm Carbohydrate, 382 mg Sodium, 4 gm Fiber

DIABETIC: 2 Starch, 1 Meat

Skillet Tomato Mac 'n' Cheese

----------------------■----------------------

This blend of tomato-y goodness and a traditional, creamy macaroni-and-cheese casserole is something different yet still familiar—a new classic you'll want to enjoy often. I think you'll discover it appeals to the boy in every man.

Serves 6 (1 cup)

1¾ cups (one 15-ounce can)
   Hunt's Chunky Tomato
   Sauce
1 (10¾-ounce) can Healthy
   Request Cream of
   Mushroom Soup
1 tablespoon dried onion
   flakes
½ cup (2.5-ounce jar) sliced
   mushrooms, drained

1½ cups (6 ounces) shredded
   Kraft reduced-fat Cheddar
   cheese
2 teaspoons dried parsley
   flakes
¼ teaspoon black pepper
3 cups hot cooked elbow
   macaroni, rinsed and
   drained

In a large skillet, combine tomato sauce, mushroom soup, onion flakes, and mushrooms. Stir in Cheddar cheese, parsley flakes, and black pepper. Cook over medium heat, stirring often, until cheese melts. Add macaroni. Mix well to combine. Lower heat. Cover and simmer 10 minutes, stirring occasionally.

HINT: 2 cups uncooked macaroni usually cooks to about 3 cups.

Each serving equals:

HE: 1⅓ Vegetable, 1⅓ Protein, 1 Bread, ½ Slider, 1 Optional Calorie

213 Calories, 5 gm Fat, 13 gm Protein, 29 gm Carbohydrate,
853 mg Sodium, 1 gm Fiber

DIABETIC: 1½ Starch, 1 Vegetable, 1 Meat

Golden Onion Pie

----------------■----------------

Maybe real men don't eat "quiche," but a crusty, cheesy bacon- and onion-flavored pie in a flaky crust wins the vote of hungry men everywhere. Prepared the usual way, this dish would be overflowing with butter, but I'll bet you'll find that this healthy version is just as big a hit.   *Serves 8*

3 cups sliced onion

2½ cups water ☆

1 refrigerated unbaked 9-inch Pillsbury piecrust

⅔ cup Carnation Nonfat Dry Milk Powder

3 tablespoons all-purpose flour

1½ cups (6 ounces) shredded Kraft reduced-fat Cheddar cheese ☆

1 teaspoon dried parsley flakes

2 tablespoons Hormel Bacon Bits

¼ cup dried fine bread crumbs

Preheat oven to 375 degrees. In a medium saucepan, cook onion in 1 cup water just until tender, about 10 minutes. Drain. Meanwhile, place piecrust in a 9-inch pie plate and flute edges. In a large saucepan, combine remaining 1½ cups water, dry milk powder, and flour. Mix well using a wire whisk. Stir in 1 cup Cheddar cheese, parsley flakes, and bacon bits. Cook over medium heat, stirring often, until mixture thickens and starts to boil. Arrange onion in piecrust. Evenly spoon sauce mixture over onion. In a small bowl, combine remaining ½ cup Cheddar cheese and bread crumbs. Evenly sprinkle cheese mixture over top. Bake 35 to 40 minutes or until crust is golden brown and filling is bubbly. Place pie plate on a wire rack and let set 10 minutes. Cut into 8 servings.

Each serving equals:

HE: 1 Protein, ¾ Vegetable, ⅔ Bread, ¼ Skim Milk

----

230 Calories, 10 gm Fat, 10 gm Protein, 25 gm Carbohydrate, 364 mg Sodium, 1 gm Fiber

----

DIABETIC: 1 Meat, 1 Vegetable, 1 Starch, 1 Fat

Oven-Fried Fish

Better than any old bread crumbs is the crunchy crust that only cornflakes can deliver! The flavor is so good, you'll find it easy to persuade your family to skip the fast-food fried fish for better and nearly as fast at home.   *Serves 4*

¾ cup (1½ ounces) crushed
  corn flakes
⅓ cup Carnation Nonfat Dry
  Milk Powder
¼ cup water
1 teaspoon dried parsley flakes

1 teaspoon lemon pepper
16 ounces white fish, cut into
  4 pieces
4 teaspoons reduced-calorie
  margarine

Preheat oven to 400 degrees. Spray a cookie sheet with butter-flavored cooking spray. Place corn flake crumbs on waxed paper. In a small flat bowl, combine dry milk powder, water, parsley flakes, and lemon pepper. Dip fish in milk mixture then into corn flake crumbs. Arrange fish on prepared cookie sheet. Dot each piece with 1 teaspoon margarine. Bake 15 minutes or until fish flakes easily.

Each serving equals:

HE: 1½ Protein, ½ Bread, ½ Fat, ¼ Skim Milk

162 Calories, 2 gm Fat, 24 gm Protein, 12 gm Carbohydrate,
233 mg Sodium, 0 gm Fiber

DIABETIC: 3 Meat, 1 Starch, ½ Fat

Salsa-Topped Baked Fish
--------------------------- ❈ ---------------------------

This spicy, creamy, oven-baked fish is so easy to fix and so
tangy, it appeals to the fussiest appetites. If combining sour
cream and salsa seems surprising, just remember how great it
tastes on a burrito!   *Serves 4*

16 ounces white fish, cut into   *½ cup chunky salsa (mild,*
4 pieces   *medium, or hot)*
2 teaspoons dried parsley   *¼ cup Land O Lakes fat-free*
flakes   *sour cream*

Preheat oven to 350 degrees. Spray an 8-by-8-inch baking dish
with butter-flavored cooking spray. Rinse fish pieces in cold
water and pat dry. Place fish pieces in prepared baking dish.
Lightly spray with butter-flavored cooking spray. Evenly sprinkle parsley flakes over top. Bake 20 minutes. In a small bowl,
combine salsa and sour cream. Evenly spoon about 3 tablespoons salsa mixture over top of each piece of fish. Continue
baking 10 minutes or until fish flakes easily. Serve at once.

Each serving equals:

HE: 1½ Protein, ¼ Vegetable, 15 Optional Calories

113 Calories, 1 gm Fat, 22 gm Protein, 4 gm Carbohydrate,
208 mg Sodium, 0 gm Fiber

DIABETIC: 3 Meat

Tuna Tetrazzini

One of my most popular dishes has been my Party Turkey Tetrazzini, which appeared in my first cookbook. Here's a kissing cousin of that well-loved dish, a yummy tuna casserole that's creamy, cheesy, and filling—and always a favorite with men.

Serves 4 (1 full cup)

¾ cup finely chopped celery
¼ cup finely chopped onion
2 (6-ounce) cans white tuna, packed in water, drained and flaked
1 (10¾-ounce) can Healthy Request Cream of Mushroom Soup
¾ cup (3 ounces) shredded Kraft reduced-fat Cheddar cheese

¼ cup skim milk
¼ cup chopped pimiento
¼ teaspoon black pepper
1 tablespoon chopped fresh parsley or 1 teaspoon dried parsley flakes
2 cups hot cooked spaghetti, rinsed and drained

In a large skillet sprayed with butter-flavored cooking spray, sauté celery and onion until vegetables are tender, about 7 to 8 minutes. Stir in tuna, mushroom soup, Cheddar cheese, and skim milk. Continue cooking, stirring often, until cheese melts. Add pimiento, black pepper, and parsley. Mix well to combine. Stir in spaghetti. Continue cooking, stirring occasionally, until mixture is heated through, about 3 minutes.

HINTS: 1. 1½ cups uncooked spaghetti usually cooks to about 2 cups.
2. Break the spaghetti into about four-inch pieces before cooking.

Each serving equals:

HE: 2½ Protein, 1 Bread, ½ Vegetable, ½ Slider, 7 Optional Calories

297 Calories, 5 gm Fat, 33 gm Protein, 30 gm Carbohydrate, 800 mg Sodium, 2 gm Fiber

DIABETIC: 3 Meat, 2 Starch

Tuna-Plus Casserole

D are I say it? Better than the old-fashioned tuna casserole you enjoyed at Grandma's house, this version adds an amazing amount of good flavor and crunch—not to mention nutrition—with the delicious surprise of a few veggies.

Serves 4

½ cup chopped onion
¼ cup chopped green bell
  pepper
1 (10¾-ounce) can Healthy
  Request Cream of Celery
  or Mushroom Soup
⅓ cup skim milk
¾ cup (3 ounces) shredded
  Kraft reduced-fat Cheddar
  cheese

½ cup (2.5-ounce jar) sliced
  mushrooms, drained
¼ cup canned chopped
  pimiento
1 (6-ounce) can white tuna,
  packed in water, drained
  and flaked
2 cups hot cooked elbow
  macaroni, rinsed and
  drained

Preheat oven to 350 degrees. Spray an 8-by-8-inch baking dish with butter-flavored cooking spray. In a large skillet sprayed with butter-flavored cooking spray, sauté onion and green pepper 8 to 10 minutes or just until tender. Stir in celery soup, skim milk, and Cheddar cheese. Continue cooking, stirring often, until cheese melts. Add mushrooms, pimiento, and tuna. Mix well to combine. Stir in macaroni. Spread mixture into prepared baking dish. Bake 20 to 25 minutes. Place baking dish on a wire rack and let set 5 minutes. Divide into 4 servings.

HINT: 1⅓ cups uncooked macaroni usually cooks to about 2 cups.

Each serving equals:

HE: 1¾ Protein, 1 Bread, ¾ Vegetable, ½ Slider, 1 Optional Calorie

257 Calories, 5 gm Fat, 22 gm Protein, 31 gm Carbohydrate, 721 mg Sodium, 2 gm Fiber

DIABETIC: 2 Meat, 1½ Starch, ½ Vegetable

Tuna Almondine

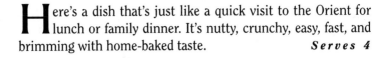

Here's a dish that's just like a quick visit to the Orient for lunch or family dinner. It's nutty, crunchy, easy, fast, and brimming with home-baked taste.   *Serves 4*

1 cup sliced celery
½ cup chopped onion
¼ cup (1 ounce) slivered almonds
½ cup (2.5-ounce jar) sliced mushrooms, drained
1 (10¾-ounce) can Healthy Request Cream of Mushroom Soup

1 tablespoon reduced-sodium soy sauce
1 (6-ounce) can white tuna, packed in water, drained and flaked
2 cups hot cooked rice

In a large skillet sprayed with butter-flavored cooking spray, sauté celery, onion, and almonds until vegetables are tender, about 10 to 15 minutes. Stir in mushrooms, mushroom soup, and soy sauce. Add tuna. Mix well to combine. Lower heat. Simmer 5 minutes, stirring occasionally. For each serving, place ½ cup rice on a plate and spoon about ½ cup tuna mixture over top.

HINT: 1⅓ cups uncooked rice usually cooks to about 2 cups.

Each serving equals:

HE: 1 Vegetable, 1 Protein, 1 Bread, ½ Fat, ½ Slider, 1 Optional Calorie

221 Calories, 5 gm Fat, 15 gm Protein, 29 gm Carbohydrate, 583 mg Sodium, 2 gm Fiber

DIABETIC: 1½ Meat, 1½ Starch, ½ Vegetable, ½ Fat

Cajun Country Shrimp and Rice

----------------------------∎----------------------------

Here's my version of a simple jambalaya, stirred up in just minutes. If you like walking on the wild side when it comes to spicy food (Cliff does!), this is the flavorful dish for you.

Serves 4

1 cup chopped onion
½ cup chopped green bell pepper
1¾ cups (one 15-ounce can) Hunt's Chunky Tomato Sauce
1 (10¾-ounce) can Healthy Request Cream of Mushroom Soup

1 teaspoon Sugar Twin or Sprinkle Sweet
2 to 3 drops Tabasco sauce
1 (4.5-ounce drained weight) can small shrimp, rinsed and drained
2 cups hot cooked rice

In a large skillet sprayed with butter-flavored cooking spray, sauté onion and green pepper until tender. Stir in tomato sauce, mushroom soup, Sugar Twin, and Tabasco sauce. Add shrimp. Mix well to combine. Cover. Lower heat. Simmer 10 minutes. For each serving, place ½ cup rice on a plate and spoon a full ¾ cup shrimp sauce over top.

HINT: 1⅓ cups uncooked rice usually cooks to about 2 cups.

Each serving equals:

HE: 2½ Vegetable, 1 Bread, 1 Protein, ½ Slider, 2 Optional Calories

202 Calories, 2 gm Fat, 12 gm Protein, 34 gm Carbohydrate, 974 mg Sodium, 1 gm Fiber

DIABETIC: 2 Vegetable, 1½ Starch, 1 Meat

Salmon Cheese Loaf

T his seafood and cheese dish is a wonderful way to enjoy the
rich taste of salmon in an easy-to-fix loaf that also makes a
great sandwich filling. This is a classic '50s dish beloved by men
and kids, but I gave it an up-to-date dimension by adding the
cheese.   *Serves 6*

*1 (14.5-ounce) can salmon,
    drained and flaked*
*¾ cup (3 ounces) shredded
    Kraft reduced-fat Cheddar
    cheese*
¼ cup finely chopped onion
½ cup finely chopped celery

*6 slices reduced-calorie white
    bread, made into crumbs*
*1 egg, beaten, or equivalent in
    egg substitute*
2 teaspoons lemon juice
⅓ cup skim milk

Preheat oven to 350 degrees. Spray a 9-by-5-inch loaf pan with
butter-flavored cooking spray. Remove skin and bones from
salmon, if desired. In a large bowl, combine salmon, Cheddar
cheese, onion, celery, and bread crumbs. Add egg, lemon juice,
and skim milk. Mix well to combine. Pat mixture into prepared
loaf pan. Bake 55 to 60 minutes. Place loaf pan on a wire rack
and let set 2 to 3 minutes before serving. Cut into 6 servings.

Each serving equals:

HE: 3¼ Protein, ½ Bread ¼ Vegetable, 5 Optional Calories

187 Calories, 7 gm Fat, 22 gm Protein, 9 gm Carbohydrate,
606 mg Sodium, 0 gm Fiber

DIABETIC: 3 Meat, ½ Starch

Turkey-Stuffed Peppers

-------------------- ❄ --------------------

H ere's one of the stars on my Healthy Exchanges "Comfort Foods Hit Parade," an old-time dish that's brought deliciously into the present by the combination of rice and diced turkey. This went over big-time with our 20-year-old male chef, Jerry, at JO's Kitchen Cafe. Why not give it a try at your house?

Serves 4

4 medium green bell peppers
½ cup finely chopped onion
1½ cups hot cooked rice
½ cup (2.5-ounce jar) sliced mushrooms, drained
1 cup (one 8-ounce can) Hunt's Tomato Sauce

1 full cup (6 ounces) diced cooked turkey breast
1 teaspoon dried parsley flakes
½ teaspoon Worcestershire sauce
¼ cup (¾ ounce) grated Kraft fat-free Parmesan cheese

Preheat oven to 350 degrees. Cut tops off green peppers. Remove seeds and membranes. Place in large saucepan. Cover with water. Bring to a boil. Cook about 3 to 4 minutes. Drain peppers. In a large skillet sprayed with butter-flavored cooking spray, sauté onion until tender. Add rice, mushrooms, tomato sauce, turkey, parsley flakes, and Worcestershire sauce. Continue cooking 2 to 3 minutes. Fill peppers with mixture. Place peppers in an 8-by-8-inch baking dish. Sprinkle 1 tablespoon Parmesan cheese over top of each. Bake uncovered 30 minutes.

HINT: 1 cup uncooked rice usually cooks to about 1½ cups.

Each serving equals:

HE: 2½ Vegetable, 1¾ Protein, ¾ Bread

169 Calories, 1 gm Fat, 12 gm Protein, 28 gm Carbohydrate, 643 mg Sodium, 3 gm Fiber

DIABETIC: 2 Vegetable, 2 Meat, 1 Starch

Turkey Club Casserole

————————————————■————————————————

This dish was almost as much fun to create as it is to eat! Cliff loved the idea of enjoying the great flavors of a traditional club sandwich in a good-tasting and good-for-you casserole. I invented this to please my husband, but Cliff is glad to share one of his special dishes with men everywhere!

Serves 6

1½ cups (8 ounces) diced cooked turkey breast
2 tablespoons Hormel Bacon Bits
¾ cup peeled, diced fresh tomato
½ cup Kraft fat-free mayonnaise

¾ cup (3 ounces) shredded Kraft reduced-fat Cheddar cheese
1 teaspoon dried basil
1 (7.5-ounce) can Pillsbury refrigerated buttermilk biscuits

Preheat oven to 375 degrees. In an 8-by-8-inch baking dish sprayed with butter-flavored cooking spray, layer turkey, bacon bits, and tomato. In a medium bowl, combine mayonnaise, Cheddar cheese, and basil. Evenly spread mixture over tomato layer. Separate biscuits and cut each into 4 pieces. Sprinkle biscuit pieces evenly over top. Bake 18 to 20 minutes or until biscuit pieces are golden brown. Lightly spray top with butter-flavored cooking spray. Place baking dish on a wire rack and let set 5 minutes. Cut into 6 servings.

Each serving equals:

HE: 2 Protein, 1¼ Bread, ¼ Vegetable, 13 Optional Calories

209 Calories, 5 gm Fat, 19 gm Protein, 22 gm Carbohydrate, 629 mg Sodium, 2 gm Fiber

DIABETIC: 2 Meat, 1½ Starch

Turkey Biscuit Stew

------------------◼------------------

I f you looked forward all week long to Sunday chicken and biscuits, here's a simple and simply scrumptious creamy stew
that delivers even more flavor than the list of ingredients
promises. One of our most popular specials at the cafe, this feast
of flavors appeals because it's as homey tasting as a classic
pot pie. *Serves 6*

1 (10¾-ounce) can Healthy
    Request Cream of Chicken
    Soup
¼ cup Land O Lakes fat-free
    sour cream
1 teaspoon dried parsley flakes
2 teaspoons dried onion flakes
1½ cups (8 ounces) diced
    cooked turkey breast

¾ cup frozen peas
1 cup (one 8-ounce can)
    sliced carrots, rinsed and
    drained
1 (7.5-ounce) can Pillsbury
    refrigerated flaky
    buttermilk biscuits

Preheat oven to 375 degrees. Spray an 8-by-8-inch baking dish
with butter-flavored cooking spray. In a large skillet, combine
chicken soup, sour cream, parsley flakes, and onion flakes. Cook
over medium heat, stirring often, until mixture is hot and bubbly. Add turkey, peas, and carrots. Mix well to combine. Spread
mixture into prepared baking dish. Separate biscuits and cut
each biscuit into 4 pieces. Evenly sprinkle pieces over top.
Lightly spray top with butter-flavored cooking spray. Bake 20 to
25 minutes or until top is golden brown. Lightly spray top with
butter-flavored cooking spray. Place baking dish on a wire rack
and let set 5 minutes. Divide into 6 servings.

Each serving equals:

HE: 1½ Bread, 1⅓ Protein, ⅓ Vegetable, ½ Slider

----
216 Calories, 4 gm Fat, 17 gm Protein, 28 gm Carbohydrate,
577 mg Sodium, 3 gm Fiber

DIABETIC: 2 Starch, 1½ Meat

Creamy Turkey Skillet

------------------ ❄ ------------------

S killet suppers are some of Cliff's favorite and fastest meals. He really likes this dish's creamy and cheesy goodness, and he always asks for seconds.   *Serves 4 (1 cup)*

½ cup chopped onion
1½ cups (8 ounces) diced cooked turkey breast
1 (10¾-ounce) can Healthy Request Cream of Chicken Soup
½ cup Land O Lakes fat-free sour cream
¼ cup (¾ ounce) grated Kraft fat-free Parmesan cheese

½ cup (2.5-ounce jar) sliced mushrooms, drained
2 teaspoons dried parsley flakes
¼ teaspoon black pepper
2 cups hot cooked rotini pasta, rinsed and drained

In a large skillet sprayed with butter-flavored cooking spray, sauté onion and turkey until onion is tender, about 5 minutes. Stir in chicken soup, sour cream, and Parmesan cheese. Add mushrooms, parsley flakes, and black pepper. Mix well to combine. Stir in rotini pasta. Lower heat, simmer 5 minutes or until mixture is heated through, stirring occasionally. Divide into 4 servings.

HINT: 1½ cups uncooked rotini pasta usually cooks to about 2 cups.

Each serving equals:

HE: 2¼ Protein, 1 Bread, ½ Vegetable, 1 Slider

----

292 Calories, 4 gm Fat, 27 gm Protein, 37 gm Carbohydrate, 568 mg Sodium, 2 gm Fiber

----

DIABETIC: 2 Meat, 2 Starch, ½ Vegetable

Macho Burritos

----------------■----------------

The name says it all—meaty and spicy, hearty and hot as you like it! I could serve this three times a week and still win Cliff's lip-smacking approval. Good garnished with fat-free sour cream, but remember to count optional calories accordingly. Olé!

Serves 4

8 ounces ground 90% lean
   turkey or beef
½ cup chopped onion
2 teaspoons chili seasoning
1¾ cups (one 15-ounce can)
   Hunt's Chunky Tomato
   Sauce ☆

4 (6-inch) tortillas
½ cup chunky salsa (mild,
   medium, or hot)
1 teaspoon dried parsley flakes
⅓ cup (1½ ounces) shredded
   Kraft reduced-fat Cheddar
   cheese

Preheat oven to 350 degrees. In a large skillet sprayed with olive oil–flavored cooking spray, brown meat and onion. Add chili seasoning and 1 cup tomato sauce. Bring mixture to a boil. Cover and simmer 5 minutes. Spoon about 3 tablespoons of the mixture on each tortilla. Roll up tortillas. Place tortillas on a cookie sheet, seam sides down. Lightly spray tops with olive oil–flavored cooking spray. In a medium bowl, combine salsa, parsley flakes, and remaining ¾ cup tomato sauce. Evenly spoon mixture over tortillas. Bake 10 minutes. Sprinkle 2 teaspoons Cheddar cheese over top of each. Continue baking until cheese starts to melt, about 3 minutes.

Each serving equals:

HE: 2 Protein, 1¼ Vegetable, 1 Bread

----

232 Calories, 8 gm Fat, 17 mg Protein, 23 gm Carbohydrate, 944 mg Sodium, 2 gm Fiber

----

DIABETIC: 2 Meat, 1 Vegetable, 1 Starch

Hamburger-Potato Casserole

------------------------------ ❄ ------------------------------

This fresh take on classic shepherd's pie tastes just enough like a cheeseburger to get my son Tommy's vote.

Serves 4

8 ounces ground 90% lean turkey or beef
½ cup chopped onion
2 cups (one 16-ounce can) cut green beans, rinsed and drained
1 (10¾-ounce) can Healthy Request Cream of Mushroom Soup
¾ cup frozen whole kernel corn, thawed
¼ teaspoon black pepper
2 cups water
1⅓ cups (3 ounces) instant potato flakes
⅓ cup Carnation Nonfat Dry Milk Powder
⅓ cup (1½ ounces) shredded Kraft reduced-fat Cheddar cheese

Preheat oven to 350 degrees. Spray an 8-by-8-inch baking dish with butter-flavored cooking spray. In a large skillet sprayed with butter-flavored cooking spray, brown meat and onion. Add green beans, mushroom soup, corn, and black pepper. Mix well to combine. Pour into prepared baking dish. Bake 20 minutes. Place baking dish on a wire rack while preparing potato mixture. Cook water until boiling. Remove from heat. Stir in potato flakes and dry milk powder. Mix gently until blended. Layer potato mixture on top of meat mixture. Lightly spray potatoes with butter-flavored cooking spray. Sprinkle Cheddar cheese on top. Bake an additional 10 minutes. Place baking dish on a wire rack and let set 5 minutes. Cut into 4 servings.

Each serving equals:

HE: 2 Protein, 1¼ Vegetable, 1 Bread

----

300 Calories, 8 gm Fat, 19 gm Protein, 38 gm Carbohydrate, 509 mg Sodium, 3 gm Fiber

----

DIABETIC: 2 Meat, 2 Starch, 1 Vegetable

Ruby Rio Stroganoff

------------------ ❊ ------------------

T his is a truly rich and savory noodle dish, with extra tangy
taste provided by the blend of salsa and tomato soup. It's fit
to please the appetite of the Tsar!   *Serves 4*

*8 ounces ground 90% lean
turkey or beef*
*1 (10¾-ounce) can Healthy
Request Tomato Soup*
*¼ cup Land O Lakes fat-free
sour cream*
*½ cup (2.5-ounce jar) sliced
mushrooms, drained*

*½ cup chunky salsa (mild,
medium, or hot)*
*1 teaspoon dried parsley
flakes*
*2 cups hot cooked noodles,
rinsed and drained*

In a large skillet sprayed with olive oil–flavored cooking spray,
brown meat. Stir in tomato soup and sour cream. Add mushrooms, salsa, and parsley flakes. Mix well to combine. Lower
heat. Simmer 5 minutes or until mixture is heated through, stirring occasionally. For each serving, place ½ cup noodles on plate
and spoon about ¾ cup meat mixture over top.

HINT: 1¾ cups uncooked noodles usually cooks to about 2 cups.

Each serving equals:

HE: 1½ Protein, 1 Bread, ½ Vegetable, ¾ Slider

271 Calories, 7 gm Fat, 16 gm Protein, 36 gm Carbohydrate,
562 mg Sodium, 5 gm Fiber

DIABETIC: 2 Starch, 1½ Meat, ½ Vegetable

Texas Lasagna

----------- ❋ -----------

Know how they say that everything is big in Texas? This dish is no exception. It's big on flavor, big on eye appeal, and just plain big on the plate! (Think of it—one quarter of a 9-by-9-inch pan is a hearty serving!) *Serves 4*

8 ounces ground 90% lean
   turkey or beef
½ cup chopped onion
1¾ cups (one 15-ounce can)
   Hunt's Chunky Tomato
   Sauce
1 teaspoon chili seasoning
¼ teaspoon black pepper
1 teaspoon dried parsley flakes
½ cup (4 ounces) Philadelphia
   fat-free cream cheese

½ cup Land O Lakes fat-free
   sour cream
½ cup (2.5-ounce jar) sliced
   mushrooms, drained
2 cups hot cooked noodles,
   rinsed and drained
¾ cup (3 ounces) shredded
   Kraft reduced-fat Cheddar
   cheese

Preheat oven to 350 degrees. Spray a 9-by-9-inch cake pan with butter-flavored cooking spray. In a large skillet sprayed with butter-flavored cooking spray, brown meat and onion. Stir in tomato sauce, chili seasoning, black pepper, and parsley flakes. Lower heat and simmer. Meanwhile, in a medium bowl, stir cream cheese with a spoon until soft. Add sour cream and mushrooms. Mix well to combine. Layer half of noodles in prepared pan. Spoon half of meat sauce over noodles. Drop cream cheese mixture evenly over sauce. Repeat layers with noodles and meat sauce. Evenly sprinkle Cheddar cheese over top. Bake 45 minutes. Place pan on a wire rack and let set 5 minutes. Cut into 4 servings.

HINT: 1¾ cups uncooked noodles usually cooks to about 2 cups. (These are regular noodles, not lasagna noodles.)

Each serving equals:

HE: 3 Protein, 2¼ Vegetable, 1 Bread, ¼ Slider, 10 Optional Calories

349 Calories, 9 gm Fat, 32 gm Protein, 35 gm Carbohydrate, 1,088 mg Sodium, 2 gm Fiber

DIABETIC: 3 Meat, 2 Vegetable, 1½ Starch

Texas Jo Casserole

-------------------- ❄ --------------------

Here's a cousin of my classic Healthy JO's, a lively, meaty festival of flavors perfect for fall football potlucks and full of cozy warmth. When it comes bubbling and brown from the oven, your taste buds are sure to sizzle! *Serves 4*

8 ounces ground 90% lean turkey or beef
½ cup chopped onion
½ cup frozen whole kernel corn
½ cup (2.5-ounce jar) sliced mushrooms, drained
¼ cup (1 ounce) sliced ripe olives
1½ cups hot cooked rotini pasta, rinsed and drained

1 (10¾-ounce) can Healthy Request Tomato Soup
½ cup chunky salsa (mild, medium, or hot)
1 tablespoon Brown Sugar Twin
⅓ cup (1½ ounces) shredded Kraft reduced-fat Cheddar cheese

Preheat oven to 350 degrees. Spray an 8-by-8-inch baking dish with butter-flavored cooking spray. In a large skillet sprayed with butter-flavored cooking spray, brown meat and onion. Stir in corn, mushrooms, olives, and rotini pasta. Add tomato soup, salsa, Brown Sugar Twin, and Cheddar cheese. Mix well to combine. Spread mixture into prepared baking dish. Bake 30 minutes. Place baking dish on a wire rack and let set 5 minutes. Cut into 4 servings.

HINTS: 1. 1 cup uncooked rotini pasta usually cooks to about 1½ cups.

2. Also good topped with 1 tablespoon fat-free sour cream.

Each serving equals:

HE: 2 Protein, 1 Bread, ¾ Vegetable, ¼ Fat, ½ Slider, 6 Optional Calories

293 Calories, 9 gm Fat, 18 gm Protein, 35 gm Carbohydrate, 698 mg Sodium, 5 gm Fiber

DIABETIC: 2 Meat, 2 Starch, 1 Vegetable

California Beef Bake

T his is a great way to enjoy the crunchy blend of good-for-you veggies combined with tummy-satisfying noodles in a creamy cheese sauce that tastes too good to be healthy but is!

Serves 6

8 ounces ground 90% lean turkey or beef
½ cup chopped onion
1 (16-ounce) package frozen carrot, broccoli, and cauliflower blend, cooked and drained
1½ cups hot cooked noodles, rinsed and drained

3 tablespoons all-purpose flour
1½ cups (one 12-fluid-ounce can) Carnation Evaporated Skim Milk
½ cup (2¼ ounces) shredded Kraft reduced-fat Cheddar cheese
⅛ teaspoon black pepper
½ teaspoon pizza seasoning

Preheat oven to 350 degrees. Spray an 8-by-8-inch baking dish with butter-flavored cooking spray. In a large skillet sprayed with butter-flavored cooking spray, brown meat and onion. Add vegetables and noodles. Lower heat. Simmer 5 minutes. Meanwhile, in a covered jar, combine flour and evaporated skim milk. Shake well to combine. Spray a medium saucepan with butter-flavored cooking spray. Pour milk mixture into saucepan. Cook until mixture starts to thicken. Add Cheddar cheese, black pepper, and pizza seasoning. Continue cooking until Cheddar cheese melts. Add cheese mixture to meat mixture. Mix well to combine. Pour mixture into prepared baking dish. Bake 20 to 25 minutes. Place baking dish on a wire rack and let set 5 minutes. Cut into 6 servings.

HINT: 1¼ cups uncooked noodles usually cooks to 1½ cups.

Each serving equals:

HE: 1½ Protein, 1½ Vegetable, ¾ Bread, ½ Skim Milk

217 Calories, 5 gm Fat, 17 gm Protein, 26 gm Carbohydrate, 188 mg Sodium, 2 gm Fiber

DIABETIC: 1½ Meat, 1½ Vegetable, 1 Starch, ½ Skim Milk

Cabbage Patch Meat Loaf

F or men who wouldn't mind meat loaf on the menu every day of the week, here's another surprising but satisfying crunchy version of the truck stop classic. My boys think it's a winner!

Serves 6

16 ounces ground 90% lean turkey or beef

6 tablespoons (1½ ounces) dried fine bread crumbs

1½ cups purchased coleslaw mix

¼ cup finely chopped onion

¼ cup finely chopped green bell pepper

¼ teaspoon dried minced garlic

⅔ cup Heinz Light Harvest or Healthy Choice ketchup ☆

Preheat oven to 350 degrees. Spray a 9-by-5-inch loaf pan with butter-flavored cooking spray. In a large bowl, combine meat, bread crumbs, coleslaw mix, onion, green pepper, garlic, and ⅓ cup ketchup. Mix well using hands. Pat mixture into prepared loaf pan. Bake 45 minutes. Spread remaining ⅓ cup ketchup over top and continue baking 15 minutes. Place loaf pan on a wire rack and let set 5 minutes. Cut into 6 servings.

HINT: 1¼ cups shredded cabbage and ¼ cup shredded carrots may be substituted for purchased coleslaw mix.

Each serving equals:

HE: 2 Protein, ⅔ Vegetable, ⅓ Bread, 18 Optional Calories

150 Calories, 6 gm Fat, 14 gm Protein, 10 gm Carbohydrate, 332 mg Sodium, 1 gm Fiber

DIABETIC: 2 Meat, ½ Starch

Salisbury Noodle Skillet

-------------------- ❈ --------------------

When you've got only minutes to make and eat dinner before heading out to a movie or a game, give this speedy, tasty dish a try. One man told me at a cooking demonstration that when his wife fixed my Salisbury steak for him, he'd still be raving about it two hours later—and wanting to know when she'd fix it again! I wanted to bring back those flavors in another way so he wouldn't get tired of the same old thing.

Serves 4 (1 full cup)

8 ounces ground 90% lean
    turkey or beef
½ cup finely chopped onion
1 (10¾-ounce) can Healthy
    Request Cream of
    Mushroom Soup
⅓ cup Carnation Nonfat Dry
    Milk Powder
½ cup water

1 teaspoon dried parsley flakes
3 tablespoons Heinz Light
    Harvest or Healthy Choice
    ketchup
2 tablespoons Worcestershire
    sauce
2 cups hot cooked noodles,
    rinsed and drained

In a large skillet sprayed with butter-flavored cooking spray, brown meat and onion. In a medium bowl, combine mushroom soup, dry milk powder, and water. Add parsley flakes, ketchup, and Worcestershire sauce. Mix well to combine. Stir soup mixture into meat mixture. Add noodles. Mix well to combine. Lower heat. Simmer 5 minutes, stirring occasionally.

HINT: 1¾ cups uncooked noodles usually cooks to about 2 cups.

Each serving equals:

HE: 1½ Protein, 1 Bread, ¼ Vegetable, ¼ Skim Milk, ½ Slider, 1 Optional Calorie

263 Calories, 7 gm Fat, 16 gm Protein, 34 gm Carbohydrate, 576 mg Sodium, 1 gm Fiber

DIABETIC: 2 Starch, 1½ Meat

Bavarian Meat Loaf

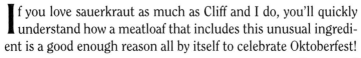

If you love sauerkraut as much as Cliff and I do, you'll quickly understand how a meatloaf that includes this unusual ingredient is a good enough reason all by itself to celebrate Oktoberfest!

Serves 6

16 ounces ground 90% lean turkey or beef
1¾ cups (one 14½-ounce can) Frank's Bavarian-style sauerkraut, well drained
¾ cup finely chopped onion
6 tablespoons (1½ ounces) dried fine bread crumbs

1¾ cups (one 15-ounce can) Hunt's Chunky Tomato Sauce ☆
4 (¾-ounce) slices Kraft reduced-fat Swiss cheese
1 tablespoon Brown Sugar Twin
1 teaspoon dried parsley flakes

Preheat oven to 350 degrees. Spray an 8-by-8-inch baking dish with butter-flavored cooking spray. In a large bowl, combine meat, sauerkraut, onion, bread crumbs, and ¼ cup tomato sauce. Mix well with hands. Pat mixture into prepared baking dish. Bake 35 minutes. Place Swiss cheese slices evenly over top. Continue baking 5 minutes. Place baking dish on a wire rack while preparing sauce. In a medium saucepan, combine remaining 1½ cups tomato sauce, Brown Sugar Twin, and parsley flakes. Cook over medium heat, stirring often, until heated through, about 5 minutes. Cut loaf into 6 servings. For each serving, place a piece of meatloaf on a plate and spoon about ¼ cup tomato sauce over top.

HINT: If you can't find Bavarian sauerkraut, use regular sauerkraut, ½ teaspoon caraway seeds, and 1 teaspoon Brown Sugar Twin.

Each serving equals:

HE: 2⅔ Protein, 2 Vegetable, ⅓ Bread, 1 Optional Calorie

195 Calories, 7 gm Fat, 19 gm Protein, 14 gm Carbohydrate, 613 mg Sodium, 2 gm Fiber

DIABETIC: 2½ Meat, 2 Vegetable

Magic Meat Loaf

-------------- ❄ --------------

When I asked the men who raved about this dish to guess the secret ingredient that made it so very good, they were stumped. They tasted the tomato soup but never guessed that healthy oats made this favorite dish even more delicious.

Serves 6

16 ounces ground 90% lean turkey or beef
1 cup (3 ounces) quick oats
¾ cup finely chopped onion
1 teaspoon dried parsley flakes
¼ teaspoon black pepper

1 teaspoon prepared mustard
1 tablespoon Brown Sugar Twin
1 (10¾-ounce) can Healthy Request Tomato Soup

Preheat oven to 350 degrees. Spray a 9-by-5-inch loaf pan with butter-flavored cooking spray. In a large bowl, combine meat, oats, onion, parsley flakes, black pepper, mustard, Brown Sugar Twin, and tomato soup. Mix well with hands to combine. Pat mixture into prepared loaf pan. Bake 1 hour. Place loaf pan on a wire rack and let set 5 minutes. Cut into 6 servings.

Each serving equals:

HE: 2 Protein, ⅔ Bread, ¼ Vegetable, ½ Slider, 6 Optional Calories

----

212 Calories, 8 gm Fat, 16 gm Protein, 19 gm Carbohydrate, 266 mg Sodium, 4 gm Fiber

----

DIABETIC: 2 Meat, 1½ Starch

Pizza Skillet

----------❄----------

E ven a fast delivery man couldn't supply the ease and taste of this simple skillet supper. With so much flavor, it's ready fast enough to please the hungriest men in the house.

Serves 6

16 ounces ground 90% lean turkey or beef
½ cup chopped onion
½ cup chopped green bell pepper
1¾ cups (one 15-ounce can) Hunt's Chunky Tomato Sauce
⅓ cup (1½ ounces) sliced ripe olives

½ cup (2.5-ounce jar) sliced mushrooms, drained
1½ teaspoons pizza or Italian seasoning
¾ cup (3 ounces) shredded Kraft reduced-fat mozzarella cheese
3 cups hot cooked elbow macaroni, rinsed and drained

In a large skillet sprayed with olive oil–flavored cooking spray, brown meat, onion, and green pepper. Stir in tomato sauce, olives, mushrooms, and pizza seasoning. Add mozzarella cheese and macaroni. Mix well to combine. Lower heat. Cover. Simmer 10 minutes. Mix well just before serving.

HINT: 2 cups uncooked macaroni usually cooks to about 3 cups.

Each serving equals:

HE: 2⅔ Protein, 1⅔ Vegetable, 1 Bread, ¼ Fat

273 Calories, 9 gm Fat, 22 gm Protein, 26 gm Carbohydrate, 803 mg Sodium, 2 gm Fiber

DIABETIC: 2½ Meat, 2 Vegetable, 1 Starch

Pizza Muffins

---- ❄ ----

Calling all you pizza-loving men out there! The teenage boys who taste-tested these gobbled them down with noisy enthusiasm. And Tommy asked me, "Are you sure these are healthy, Mom? Are you *sure?*" Yes, I am!

Serves 8

8 ounces ground 90% lean turkey or beef
1½ cups Bisquick Reduced Fat Baking Mix
¼ cup (¾ ounce) grated Kraft fat-free Parmesan cheese
1 teaspoon pizza or Italian seasoning
1 teaspoon dried parsley flakes
1 teaspoon dried onion flakes

¼ cup chopped green bell pepper
¾ cup chopped fresh tomato
⅓ cup (1½ ounces) shredded Kraft reduced-fat Cheddar cheese
⅓ cup skim milk
2 teaspoons vegetable oil
1 egg or equivalent in egg substitute

Preheat oven to 375 degrees. Spray 8 wells of a 12-hole muffin pan with butter-flavored cooking spray or line with paper liners. In a large skillet sprayed with olive-oil–flavored cooking spray, brown meat. Place skillet on a wire rack and allow to cool. Meanwhile, in a large bowl, combine baking mix, Parmesan cheese, pizza seasoning, parsley flakes, and onion flakes. Stir in green pepper, tomato, and Cheddar cheese. In a small bowl, combine skim milk, vegetable oil, and egg. Mix well to combine. Add milk mixture to baking mix mixture. Mix gently just to combine. Fold in cooled, browned meat. Fill 8 muffin wells full. Bake 16 to 18 minutes or until a toothpick inserted in center comes out clean. Place muffin pan on a wire rack and let set 5 minutes. Remove muffins from pan and continue cooling on wire rack. Serve at once.

Each serving equals:

HE: 1¼ Protein, 1 Bread, ¼ Vegetable, ¼ Fat, 4 Optional Calories

---

179 Calories, 7 gm Fat, 11 gm Protein, 18 gm Carbohydrate, 365 mg Sodium, 1 gm Fiber

---

DIABETIC: 1 Meat, 1 Starch, ½ Fat

Fast-Food Cheeseburger Skillet

---------------------------- ❄ ----------------------------

Now that my son Tommy lives in Arizona, he has to fix his own healthy cheeseburger meals. I keep sending him recipes for his favorite dish that are so simple to fix, it's almost like having Mom cook for you again. (Of course, now that Mom's not handy, he has to do his own dishes. . . .) *Serves 4 (1 cup)*

8 ounces ground 90% lean
 turkey or beef
½ cup (2.5-ounce jar) sliced
 mushrooms, undrained
1 (10¾-ounce) can Healthy
 Request Cream of
 Mushroom Soup
¾ cup (3 ounces) shredded
 Kraft reduced-fat Cheddar
 cheese

2 tablespoons Heinz Lite
 Ketchup
¼ cup Kraft fat-free
 mayonnaise
2 tablespoons sweet pickle
 relish
2 cups hot cooked noodles,
 rinsed and drained

In a large skillet sprayed with butter-flavored cooking spray, brown meat. Stir in undrained mushrooms and mushroom soup. Add Cheddar cheese. Mix well to combine. Stir in ketchup, mayonnaise, and pickle relish. Continue cooking, stirring often, until Cheddar cheese is melted. Add noodles. Mix well to combine. Lower heat. Continue cooking, stirring often, until mixture is heated through, about 5 minutes.

HINT: 1¾ cups uncooked noodles usually cooks to about 2 cups.

Each serving equals:

HE: 2¼ Protein, 1 Bread, ¼ Vegetable ¾ Slider, 5 Optional Calories

---

310 Calories, 10 gm Fat, 21 gm Protein, 34 gm Carbohydrate,
784 mg Sodium, 2 gm Fiber

DIABETIC: 2 Meat, 2 Starch

Tommy's Cheeseburger Turnovers

---------------------------------❄️---------------------------------

When your son asks you, as soon he's finished eating his dinner, just when you're going to make the same dish again, you know you've got a healthy-man winner! This has all his favorite flavors in it, served up quick and healthy. I bet it'll soon be a favorite around your house.   *Serves 5*

> 4 ounces 90 % lean ground
>   turkey or beef
> 1 tablespoon chopped onion
> ¼ teaspoon black pepper
> ½ teaspoon JO's Loose Meat
>   Seasoning (or any
>   preferred meat seasoning)
>
> 1 (7.5-ounce) can refrigerated
>   buttermilk biscuits
> 1½ ounces (⅓ cup) Kraft
>   shredded reduced-fat
>   Cheddar cheese

Preheat oven to 425 degrees. In a large skillet sprayed with butter-flavored cooking spray, brown meat and onion. Stir in black pepper and JO's Loose Meat Seasoning. Place 5 biscuits on a cookie sheet sprayed with butter-flavored cooking spray. Pat each biscuit with hands to form 4-inch circles. Evenly divide meat mixture over biscuits and sprinkle about 1 tablespoon shredded cheese on each. Pat remaining 5 biscuits into 4 inch circles and place on top of meat-filled biscuits. Using a fork, seal edges well. Prick top of each 3 or 4 times. Lightly spray tops with butter-flavored cooking spray. Bake 8 to 10 minutes or until golden brown.

Each serving equals:

HE: 1½ Bread, 1 Protein

---

188 Calories, 7 gm Fat, 9 gm Protein, 22 gm Carbohydrate, 617 gm Sodium, 1 gm Fiber

---

DIABETIC: 1½ Starch, 1 Meat

He-Man's Gravy and Biscuits

- ■ -

C onvinced that no one could make a satisfying and healthy version of this Midwest classic? I've always liked a challenge. You'll quickly become a believer when you devour a serving of this healthy comfort food. *Serves 5*

1 (7.5-ounce) can Pillsbury refrigerated buttermilk biscuits
8 ounces ground 90% lean turkey or beef
½ cup chopped onion
½ cup chopped green bell pepper
1¾ cups (one 15-ounce can) Hunt's Chunky Tomato

Sauce
½ cup (2.5-ounce jar) sliced mushrooms, drained
1 tablespoon Brown Sugar Twin
2 tablespoons Hormel Bacon Bits
¾ cup (3 ounces) shredded Kraft reduced-fat Cheddar cheese

Preheat oven to 450 degrees. Spray a cookie sheet with butter-flavored cooking spray. Separate biscuits and arrange on prepared cookie sheet. Lightly spray tops of biscuits with butter-flavored cooking spray. Bake 8 minutes. Place cookie sheet on a wire rack while preparing meat sauce. Meanwhile, in a large skillet sprayed with butter-flavored cooking spray, brown meat, onion, and green pepper. Stir in tomato sauce, mushrooms, Brown Sugar Twin, bacon bits, and Cheddar cheese. Continue cooking stirring often, until cheese melts and mixture is heated through. For each serving, place 2 warm biscuits on plate and spoon about ⅔ cup meat sauce over top.

Each serving equals:

HE: 2 Protein, 2 Vegetable, 1½ Bread, 10 Optional Calories

- -

264 Calories, 8 gm Fat, 19 gm Protein, 29 gm Carbohydrate, 1,020 mg Sodium, 3 gm Fiber

- -

DIABETIC: 2 Meat, 2 Vegetable, 1½ Starch

"Pot Roast" Stroganoff over Noodles

------------------------------- ∎ -------------------------------

Almost nothing is simpler in the kitchen than cooking up a rich feast in the microwave. The fat-free gravy and sour cream will fool anyone into thinking this dish is deliciously high in fat—but it's only high in flavor.   *Serves 6*

8 ounces ground 90% lean
   turkey or beef
½ cup chopped onion
1 cup frozen cut carrots
1 cup frozen cut green beans
1 (12-ounce) jar Heinz Fat
   Free Beef Gravy
½ cup (2.5-ounce jar) sliced
   mushrooms, drained

1 teaspoon dried parsley flakes
¼ teaspoon black pepper
½ cup Land O Lakes fat-free
   sour cream
3 cups hot cooked noodles,
   rinsed and drained

In a plastic colander, place meat, onion, frozen carrots, and frozen green beans. Place colander in a glass pie plate. Microwave on High (100% power) 8 minutes, stirring after 4 minutes. Pour meat mixture into an 8-cup glass measuring bowl. Add gravy, mushrooms, parsley flakes, and black pepper. Microwave on High 3 minutes. Stir in sour cream. For each serving, place ½ cup noodles on plate and spoon ¾ cup meat mixture over top.

HINT: 2½ cups uncooked noodles usually cooks to about 3 cups.

Each serving equals:

HE: 1 Protein, 1 Vegetable, 1 Bread, ¼ Slider, 15 Optional Calories

----

208 Calories, 4 gm Fat, 13 gm Protein, 30 gm Carbohydrate,
407 mg Sodium, 2 gm Fiber

DIABETIC: 1½ Starch, 1 Meat, 1 Vegetable

Easy Salisbury Steak

---◼---

For the man who enjoys real meat in his gravy, here's my Healthy Exchanges version, sauced with a true homey flavor that is every bit as tasty as the original version.

Serves 4

8 ounces ground 90% lean
    turkey or beef
1 tablespoon dried onion
    flakes
1 teaspoon dried parsley flakes
14 small fat-free soda
    crackers, made into
    crumbs
¼ cup skim milk

1 (12-ounce) jar Heinz Fat
    Free Beef Gravy
2 teaspoons Worcestershire
    sauce
2 tablespoons Heinz Light
    Harvest or Healthy Choice
    ketchup
¼ teaspoon black pepper

Preheat oven to 350 degrees. Spray an 8-by-8-inch baking dish with butter-flavored cooking spray. In a large bowl, combine meat, onion flakes, parsley flakes, cracker crumbs, and skim milk. Mix well using hands. Using a ⅓-cup measuring cup as a guide, form into 4 patties. Place patties in prepared baking dish. In a small bowl, combine gravy, Worcestershire sauce, ketchup, and black pepper. Evenly spoon gravy mixture over meat patties. Cover. Bake 1 hour. For each serving, place meat pattie on plate and evenly spoon gravy mixture over top.

Each serving equals:

HE: 2¼ Protein, ½ Bread, ¼ Vegetable, ¼ Slider

---

165 Calories, 5 gm Fat, 13 gm Protein, 17 gm Carbohydrate,
723 mg Sodium, 0 gm Fiber

DIABETIC: 2 Meat, 1 Starch

Coney Island Pasta Casserole

-------------------------- ❋ --------------------------

A s festive as a visit to the world-famous amusement park, this dish features a roller coaster of man-pleasing flavors. Enjoy!   *Serves 4*

8 ounces ground 90% lean turkey or beef
8 ounces diced Healthy Choice 97% fat free frankfurters
½ cup finely chopped onion
1¾ cups (one 15-ounce can) Hunt's Chunky Tomato Sauce

¼ cup Heinz Light Harvest or Healthy Choice ketchup
1½ teaspoons chili seasoning
2 cups hot cooked rotini pasta, rinsed and drained
⅓ cup (1½ ounces) shredded Kraft reduced-fat Cheddar cheese

Preheat oven to 350 degrees. Spray an 8-by-8-inch baking dish with butter-flavored cooking spray. In a large skillet sprayed with butter-flavored cooking spray, brown meat, frankfurters, and onion. Stir in tomato sauce, ketchup, and chili seasoning. Add rotini pasta. Mix well to combine. Spread mixture into pre-pared baking dish. Bake 20 minutes. Evenly sprinkle Cheddar cheese over top. Continue baking 10 minutes or until cheese melts. Place baking dish on a wire rack and let set 5 minutes. Cut into 4 servings.

HINT: 1½ cups uncooked rotini pasta usually cooks to about 2 cups.

Each serving equals:

HE: 2¾ Protein, 1⅓ Vegetable, 1 Bread, 7 Optional Calories

320 Calories, 8 gm Fat, 26 gm Protein, 36 gm Carbohydrate, 1,215 mg Sodium, 1 gm Fiber

DIABETIC: 3 Meat, 2 Starch, 1 Vegetable

Meatballs in Sour Cream Onion-Mushroom Sauce

I f you want a perfect party treat for a group, these saucy meatballs will keep friends and family coming back for more.

Serves 6 (4 each)

16 ounces ground 90% lean turkey or beef
6 tablespoons dried fine bread crumbs
1½ teaspoons dried parsley flakes
½ teaspoon dried minced garlic
¼ cup skim milk

1 cup coarsely chopped onion
½ cup (2.5-ounce jar) sliced mushrooms, drained
1 (12-ounce) jar Heinz Fat Free Beef Gravy
¼ cup Land O Lakes fat-free sour cream
3 cups hot cooked noodles, rinsed and drained

In a large bowl, combine meat, bread crumbs, parsley flakes, minced garlic, and skim milk. Mix well using hands. Form into 24 (¾-inch) meatballs. Place meatballs in a large skillet sprayed with butter-flavored cooking spray. Brown lightly on all sides. Remove meatballs from skillet and cover to keep warm. In the same skillet, sauté onion 5 minutes or until tender. Stir in mushrooms, beef gravy, and sour cream. Return meatballs to skillet. Lower heat. Cover and simmer 5 minutes or until mixture is heated through. For each serving, place ½ cup noodles on plate and spoon about ¾ cup meatballs in sauce over noodles.

HINT: 2½ cups uncooked noodles usually cooks to about 3 cups.

Each serving equals:

HE: 2 Protein, 1⅓ Bread, ½ Vegetable, ¼ Slider

---

280 Calories, 8 gm Fat, 20 gm Protein, 32 gm Carbohydrate, 536 mg Sodium, 2 gm Fiber

---

DIABETIC: 2 Meat, 2 Starch

Mex-Italian–Style Minute Steaks

Th**is** meat dish combines those Mexican and Italian tastes that Cliff and my sons particularly love. The Italian dressing is a secret ingredient that provides lots of taste satisfaction—and no added fat! *Serves 4*

3 tablespoons all-purpose flour
1 teaspoon chili seasoning
4 (4-ounce) lean minute
*   steaks*
3 tablespoons Kraft Fat Free
*   Italian Dressing*
1 (10¾-ounce) can Healthy

Request Tomato Soup
1 cup chunky salsa (mild,
*   medium, or hot)*
1 teaspoon Italian seasoning
¼ cup Land O Lakes fat-free
*   sour cream*

In a shallow dish, combine flour and chili seasoning. Coat both sides of minute steaks with flour mixture, reserving any leftover flour. Pour Italian dressing into a large skillet sprayed with olive oil–flavored cooking spray. Place flour-coated steaks in skillet. Cook 10 to 15 minutes or until steaks are done, turning after 6 minutes. Meanwhile, in a small saucepan, combine tomato soup, salsa, Italian seasoning, and remaining flour. Cover. Cook over medium-low heat, stirring occasionally, until meat is done. For each serving, place meat on plate and spoon about ⅓ cup soup mixture over each serving and top with 1 tablespoon sour cream.

Each serving equals:

HE: 3 Protein, ½ Vegetable, ¼ Bread, ¾ Slider, 3 Optional Calories

251 Calories, 7 gm Fat, 27 gm Protein, 20 gm Carbohydrate, 580 mg Sodium, 3 gm Fiber

DIABETIC: 3 Meat, 1 Starch, ½ Vegetable

Bar-B-Que Beef Strips

--------------------------■--------------------------

Is there a man alive who doesn't love barbecue? I've never met one, you can be sure of that! Here's a quick and easy dish that delivers all that smoky-good taste without the fat and calories of the traditional version. Can't you hear those cowboys cheer?

Serves 6

16 ounces lean round steak, cut into narrow strips

1¾ cups (one 15-ounce can) Hunt's Chunky Tomato Sauce

1 tablespoon Worcestershire sauce

2 tablespoons Brown Sugar Twin

1 tablespoon prepared mustard

⅓ cup water

⅛ teaspoon black pepper

1 cup onion slices

In a large skillet sprayed with butter-flavored cooking spray, brown meat. In a medium bowl, combine tomato sauce, Worcestershire sauce, Brown Sugar Twin, mustard, water, and black pepper. Pour sauce mixture over meat. Layer onion slices over top. Cover. Lower heat and simmer 15 minutes, stirring occasionally. Good served over rice or pasta.

Each serving equals:

HE: 2 Protein, 1½ Vegetable, 2 Optional Calories

----

127 Calories, 3 gm Fat, 19 gm Protein, 6 gm Carbohydrate, 530 mg Sodium, 2 gm Fiber

----

DIABETIC: 2 Meat, 1 Vegetable

Steak Pizzaola

------------------- ∎ -------------------

This tangy specialty is always a winner when it appears on the menu at the best Italian restaurants. That real taste and mouth feel of meat, topped by a blend of delicious flavors, make this a great dinner party dish or family night winner.

Serves 4

4 (3-ounce) lean minute
   steaks
1 cup sliced onion
½ cup (2.5-ounce jar) sliced
   mushrooms, drained
1 teaspoon Italian seasoning
2 teaspoons Sugar Twin or
   Sprinkle Sweet

½ teaspoon dried minced
   garlic
1¾ cups (one 15-ounce can)
   Hunt's Chunky Tomato
   Sauce
⅓ cup (1½ ounces) shredded
   Kraft reduced-fat
   mozzarella cheese

In a large skillet sprayed with olive oil–flavored cooking spray, brown meat on both sides. Add onion. Continue to brown meat and onion 5 minutes. Add mushrooms. In a medium bowl, combine Italian seasoning, Sugar Twin, garlic, and tomato sauce. Pour tomato sauce mixture over meat. Lower heat. Cover and simmer 20 minutes. For each serving, sprinkle mozzarella cheese over top.

Each serving equals:

HE: 2¾ Protein, 2½ Vegetable, 1 Optional Calorie

198 Calories, 6 gm Fat, 26 gm Protein, 10 gm Carbohydrate, 841 mg Sodium, 1 gm Fiber

DIABETIC: 2½ Meat, 2 Vegetable

Swiss Steak Ultra

I hope you notice that I'm including lots of recipes that call for lean beefsteaks. Why? Because men like them—and I can give you lots of ways to make them part of a healthy lifestyle. This one is truly luscious and creamy, joining hands with lots of flavors to create a true blue-ribbon meal.   *Serves 4*

1 tablespoon all-purpose flour
1 teaspoon dried parsley flakes
4 (4-ounce) lean minute or
*   cube beefsteaks*
½ cup finely chopped onion
1 cup shredded carrots
1 cup finely chopped celery
1¾ cups (one 15-ounce can)

Hunt's Chunky Tomato
*   Sauce*
1 (10¾-ounce) can Healthy
*   Request Cream of*
*   Mushroom Soup*
1 teaspoon Worcestershire
*   sauce*
¼ cup water

In a small saucer, combine flour and parsley flakes. Gently coat steaks. In a large skillet sprayed with butter-flavored cooking spray, lightly brown meat on both sides. Sprinkle onion, carrots, and celery evenly over meat. In a small bowl, combine tomato sauce, mushroom soup, Worcestershire sauce, and water. Spoon mixture evenly over vegetables and meat. Lower heat. Cover and simmer 35 to 40 minutes or until vegetables and meat are tender.

Each serving equals:

HE: 3 Protein, 3 Vegetable, ½ Slider, 9 Optional Calories

222 Calories, 6 gm Fat, 23 gm Protein, 19 gm Carbohydrate,
1,013 mg Sodium, 1 gm Fiber

DIABETIC: 3 Meat, 3 Vegetable, ½ Starch

Luau Pork

--------■--------

This is such a festive dish, you'll think you're dining in Hawaii, where sunsets and great golf courses take a back-seat to scrumptious food. Be there—Aloha! *Serves 4*

4 (4-ounce) lean pork tenderloins or cutlets
½ cup chopped onion
½ cup chopped green bell pepper
1 cup (one 8-ounce can) crushed pineapple, packed in fruit juice, undrained

⅔ cup water
½ teaspoon ground ginger
2 cups (3 ounces) Pepperidge Farm Dried Bread Cubes
2 tablespoons apricot spreadable fruit

Preheat oven to 350 degrees. Spray an 8-by-8-inch baking dish with butter-flavored cooking spray. In a large skillet sprayed with butter-flavored cooking spray, lightly brown meat on both sides. Remove meat from skillet. Add onion and green pepper to skillet. Sauté until vegetables are crisp tender, 3 to 4 minutes. Stir in undrained pineapple, water, and ginger. Add bread cubes. Mix well to combine. Spoon bread mixture into prepared baking dish. Arrange browned meat evenly over bread mixture. Spread about 1½ teaspoons spreadable fruit over each piece of meat. Cover with aluminum foil and bake 30 minutes. Uncover and continue baking 10 minutes. Place baking dish on a wire rack and let set 2 to 3 minutes. Divide into 4 servings.

Each serving equals:

HE: 3 Protein, 1 Bread, 1 Fruit, ½ Vegetable

----
306 Calories, 6 gm Fat, 28 gm Protein, 35 gm Carbohydrate, 405 mg Sodium, 1 gm Fiber

----
DIABETIC: 3 Meat, 1 Starch, 1 Fruit

Creamy "Pork and Beans"

-----------------------■-----------------------

D o the men in your house think Pork and Beans should be one of the four basic food groups and served daily? Mine do. Cliff and James can't get enough of pork and beans—and while this isn't the kind that comes out of the can, once they try it, I bet they won't be able to get enough of it!

Serves 4 (1 full cup)

1½ cups (8 ounces) diced cooked lean roast pork
1 (10¾-ounce can) Healthy Request Cream of Mushroom Soup
¼ cup skim milk
2 tablespoons Heinz Light Harvest or Healthy Choice ketchup

½ cup (2.5-ounce jar) sliced mushrooms, drained
2 cups (one 16-ounce can) cut green beans, rinsed and drained
2 cups hot cooked noodles, rinsed and drained
¼ teaspoon black pepper

In a large skillet sprayed with butter-flavored cooking spray, sauté roast pork 2 to 3 minutes. Stir in mushroom soup, skim milk, and ketchup. Add mushrooms, green beans, noodles, and black pepper. Mix well to combine. Lower heat. Simmer 5 minutes or until mixture is heated through.

HINT: 1¾ cups uncooked noodles usually cooks to about 2 cups.

Each serving equals:

HE: 2 Protein, 1¼ Vegetable, 1 Bread, ½ Slider, 14 Optional Calories

274 Calories, 6 gm Fat, 22 gm Protein, 33 gm Carbohydrate, 462 mg Sodium, 2 gm Fiber

DIABETIC: 2 Meat, 1½ Starch, 1 Vegetable

Bohemian Goulash

------------------■------------------

I created this dish in honor of my Czech grandparents, whose traditional foods always reminded us of happy childhoods and warm family feelings. It's a fast trip back to those cozy days and shared meals at Grandma Nowachek's boarding house, even if it is only through memories and taste buds.

Serves 4 (1 full cup)

¼ cup chopped onion
1½ cups (8 ounces) diced, cooked lean roast pork
1¾ cups (one 15-ounce can) Frank's Bavarian-style sauerkraut, drained
2 cups hot cooked noodles, rinsed and drained

1 (10¾-ounce) can Healthy Request Cream of Mushroom Soup
⅓ cup skim milk
¼ teaspoon black pepper

In a large skillet sprayed with butter-flavored cooking spray, sauté onion until tender. Stir in pork, sauerkraut, and noodles. Add mushroom soup, skim milk, and black pepper. Mix well to combine. Lower heat. Simmer 10 minutes, stirring occasionally.

HINTS: 1. If you can't find Bavarian sauerkraut, use regular sauerkraut, ½ teaspoon caraway seeds, and 1 teaspoon Brown Sugar Twin.
2. 1¾ cups uncooked noodles usually cooks to about 2 cups.

Each serving equals:

HE: 2 Protein, 1 Vegetable, 1 Bread, 1 Slider, 9 Optional Calories

----

298 Calories, 6 gm Fat, 23 gm Protein, 38 gm Carbohydrate, 974 mg Sodium, 3 gm Fiber

----

DIABETIC: 2 Meat, 2 Starch, 1 Vegetable

Cowpoke Pork Tenders

-------------------■-------------------

Y ou won't even need the dinner bell to "round 'em up" when
the great aroma of this dish calls from the kitchen. It's so
easy, a teenager can fix it in minutes! *Serves 4*

*4 (4-ounce) lean pork
    tenderloins
1 (10¾-ounce) can Healthy
    Request Tomato Soup*

*1 cup chunky salsa (mild,
    medium, or hot)
1 teaspoon dried parsley flakes*

In a large skillet sprayed with olive oil–flavored cooking spray,
brown meat on both sides. In a medium bowl, combine tomato
soup, salsa, and parsley flakes. Evenly spoon mixture over meat.
Lower heat. Cover and simmer 20 to 25 minutes. For each serving, place 1 piece of meat on plate and evenly spoon sauce over
top.

Each serving equals:

HE: 3 Protein, ½ Vegetable, ¾ Slider, 2 Optional Calories

219 Calories, 7 gm Fat, 26 gm Protein, 13 gm Carbohydrate,
585 mg Sodium, 3 gm Fiber

DIABETIC: 3 Meat, ½ Starch, ½ Vegetable

Ham Lasagna Toss

---- ❊ ----

Here's a great way to use up leftover ham—or just enjoy a tangy Italian treat.

Serves 4

1 full cup (6 ounces) diced Dubuque 97% fat-free ham or any extra-lean ham
½ cup chopped onion
¼ teaspoon dried minced garlic
1¾ cups (one 15-ounce can) Hunt's Chunky Tomato Sauce

1 teaspoon Italian seasoning
2 cups hot cooked rotini pasta, rinsed and drained
1 cup fat-free cottage cheese
¾ cup (3 ounces) shredded Kraft reduced-fat mozzarella cheese ☆
¼ cup (¾ ounce) grated Kraft fat-free Parmesan cheese

Preheat oven to 350 degrees. Spray an 8-by-8-inch baking dish with butter-flavored cooking spray. In a large skillet sprayed with olive oil–flavored cooking spray, sauté ham and onion. Stir in garlic, tomato sauce, and Italian seasoning. Simmer 5 minutes. Remove 1 cup meat sauce and set aside. Stir in rotini pasta. Spoon half of rotini pasta into prepared baking dish. In a small bowl, combine cottage cheese, ½ cup mozzarella cheese, and Parmesan cheese. Spread cheese mixture over top. Spoon remaining rotini mixture over cheese mixture. Top with reserved 1 cup meat sauce and remaining ¼ cup mozzarella cheese. Cover. Bake 20 minutes. Uncover. Continue baking 15 minutes. Place baking dish on a wire rack and let set 5 minutes. Cut into 4 servings.

HINT: 1½ cups uncooked rotini pasta usually cooks to 2 cups.

Each serving equals:

HE: 2¾ Protein, 2 Vegetable, 1 Bread

---

249 Calories, 5 gm Fat, 21 gm Protein, 30 gm Carbohydrate, 1,177 mg Sodium, 2 gm Fiber

---

DIABETIC: 3 Meat, 2 Vegetable, 1 Starch

Ham and Corn Scallop

---------------------■---------------------

C liff loves any kind of corn scallop, so I'm always creating new versions to please my truck-drivin' man's taste buds. The chunks of ham in this one make it even more satisfying than usual.

Serves 6

2 cups (one 16-ounce can) whole kernel corn, rinsed and drained
¼ cup finely chopped green bell pepper
½ cup finely chopped onion
Full 1½ cups (9 ounces) finely diced Dubuque 97% fat-free ham or any extra-lean ham

1 (10¾-ounce) can Healthy Request Cream of Mushroom Soup
1 teaspoon prepared mustard
1 teaspoon dried parsley flakes
1 cup (2 ounces) crushed Ritz Reduced Fat Crackers

Preheat oven to 350 degrees. Spray an 8-by-8-inch baking dish with butter-flavored cooking spray. In a large bowl, combine corn, green pepper, onion, and ham. Add mushroom soup, mustard, and parsley flakes. Mix well to combine. Stir in crushed crackers. Pour mixture into prepared baking dish. Bake 30 to 35 minutes. Place baking dish on a wire rack and allow to cool 2 to 3 minutes. Divide into 6 servings.

Each serving equals:

HE: 1 Bread, 1 Protein, ¼ Vegetable, ½ Slider, 8 Optional Calories

172 Calories, 4 gm Fat, 10 gm Protein, 24 gm Carbohydrate, 670 mg Sodium, 2 gm Fiber

DIABETIC: 1½ Starch, 1 Meat

Mexicalli Ham-Rice Dish

---------------------■---------------------

How about another quick-and-easy microwave meal that brings cries of "Viva JoAnna" when I make it? It's *that* spicy, *that* filling, and oh-so-good. It's better than *bueno,* it's *fabuloso!*

Serves 4 (1 cup)

1 full cup (6 ounces) diced
   Dubuque 97% fat-free
   ham or any extra-lean ham
½ cup chopped onion
½ cup chopped green bell
   pepper
1¾ cups (one 15-ounce can)
   Hunt's Chunky Tomato
   Sauce
1 teaspoon chili seasoning

1 tablespoon Brown Sugar
   Twin
1 cup (3 ounces) uncooked
   instant rice
6 ounces (one 8-ounce can)
   red kidney beans, rinsed
   and drained
⅓ cup (1½ ounces) shredded
   Kraft reduced-fat Cheddar
   cheese

In an 8-cup glass measuring bowl, combine ham, onion, green pepper, and tomato sauce. Cover with waxed paper and microwave on HIGH for 4 minutes. Mix well to combine. Stir in chili seasoning, Brown Sugar Twin, uncooked rice, and kidney beans. Re-cover and microwave on HIGH 4 minutes. Stir in Cheddar cheese. Continue microwaving on HIGH 1 minute or until cheese melts. Place covered bowl on a wire rack and let set 2 to 3 minutes. Divide into 4 servings.

Each serving equals:

HE: 2¼ Protein, 2¼ Vegetable, ¾ Bread, 1 Optional Calorie

203 Calories, 3 gm Fat, 15 gm Protein, 29 gm Carbohydrate, 946 mg Sodium, 4 gm Fiber

DIABETIC: 2 Meat, 2 Vegetable, 1 Starch

Creole Ham Skillet

------------■------------

C liff just can't get enough of dishes that feature ham and noodles, so I stirred up this one when we both were hungry for that great mix of spicy Southern flavors. It's kind of a Western-omelet-flavored dish, but in a healthy, tasty, skillet surprise.

Serves 4 (1 cup)

1½ full cups (9 ounces) diced Dubuque 97% fat-free ham or any extra-lean ham
½ cup chopped onion
½ cup chopped green bell pepper
1 (10¾-ounce) can Healthy Request Tomato Soup
1 teaspoon prepared mustard
1 tablespoon Brown Sugar Twin
1 teaspoon dried parsley flakes
¼ teaspoon black pepper
2 cups hot cooked noodles, rinsed and drained

In a large skillet sprayed with butter-flavored cooking spray, sauté ham, onion, and green pepper until vegetables are tender, about 5 to 10 minutes. Add tomato soup, mustard, Brown Sugar Twin, parsley flakes, and black pepper. Mix well to combine. Stir in noodles. Lower heat. Simmer 10 minutes, stirring occasionally. Divide into 4 servings.

HINT: 1¾ cups uncooked noodles usually cooks to 2 cups.

Each serving equals:

HE: 1½ Protein, 1 Bread, ½ Vegetable, ½ Slider, 6 Optional Calories

245 Calories, 5 gm Fat, 15 gm Protein, 35 gm Carbohydrate, 853 mg Sodium, 5 gm Fiber

DIABETIC: 2 Starch, 1½ Meat

Grande Macaroni and Ham Bake

I wanted this book to feature lots of recipes for that man-pleasing favorite, macaroni and cheese! Here's a tangy treat that promises spicy flavors and cozy, warm, tummy-filling goodness. ***Serves 4***

½ cup diced onion
¾ cup finely chopped celery
1 (10¾-ounce) can Healthy Request Cream of Mushroom Soup
¾ cup chunky salsa (mild, medium, or hot)
1 teaspoon dried parsley flakes
Full 1½ cups (9 ounces) diced

Dubuque 97% fat-free ham or any extra-lean ham
2 cups hot cooked elbow macaroni, rinsed and drained
4 (¾-ounce) slices Kraft reduced-fat American cheese

Preheat oven to 350 degrees. Spray an 8-by-8-inch baking dish with olive oil–flavored cooking spray. In a large skillet sprayed with olive oil–flavored cooking spray, sauté onion and celery until tender. Stir in mushroom soup, salsa, and parsley flakes. Add ham and macaroni. Mix well to combine. Spread mixture into prepared baking dish. Evenly arrange cheese slices over top. Bake 20 to 25 minutes. Place baking dish on a wire rack and let set 5 minutes. Cut into 4 servings.

HINT: 1⅓ cups uncooked elbow macaroni usually cooks to about 2 cups.

Each serving equals:

HE: 2½ Protein, 1 Vegetable, 1 Bread, ½ Slider, 1 Optional Calorie

258 Calories, 6 gm Fat, 19 gm Protein, 32 gm Carbohydrate, 1,061 mg Sodium, 1 gm Fiber

DIABETIC: 2½ Meat, 1½ Starch, 1 Vegetable

Heartland Macaroni and Cheese

--------------------------------- ❋ ---------------------------------

Men—when your wife is visiting relatives for a few days, what's to stop you from enjoying macaroni and cheese *every single night*? I'm happy to encourage you to eat the foods you love best—but in my healthy versions.   *Serves 6*

*1 (10¾-ounce) can Healthy
    Request Cream of
    Mushroom Soup
⅓ cup skim milk
1 teaspoon dried onion flakes
1 teaspoon dried parsley flakes
¼ teaspoon black pepper
1½ cups (6 ounces) shredded
    Kraft reduced-fat Cheddar
    cheese*

*2½ cups hot cooked elbow
    macaroni, rinsed and
    drained
½ cup frozen peas, thawed
Full 1½ cups (9 ounces) diced
    Dubuque 97% fat-free
    ham or any extra-lean ham*

Preheat oven to 350 degrees. Spray an 8-by-8-inch baking dish with butter-flavored cooking spray. In a large skillet, combine mushroom soup, skim milk, onion flakes, parsley flakes, and black pepper. Stir in Cheddar cheese. Cook over medium heat, stirring often, until cheese melts. Add macaroni, peas, and ham. Mix well to combine. Spread mixture into prepared baking dish. Bake 30 minutes. Place baking dish on a wire rack and let set 5 minutes. Cut into 6 servings.

HINTS: 1. 1⅔ cups uncooked macaroni usually cooks to about 2½ cups.
2. Thaw peas by placing in a colander and rinsing under hot water for one minute.

Each serving equals:

HE: 2⅓ Protein, 1 Bread, ¼ Slider, 5 Optional Calories

----

239 Calories, 7 gm Fat, 19 gm Protein, 25 gm Carbohydrate,
799 mg Sodium, 1 gm Fiber

DIABETIC: 2 Meat, 1½ Starch

Taco Chicken Bake

For all you Mexican food fans, here's a scrumptious way to savor your favorite chicken tacos in a speedy, spicy casserole. James always devours this one with a smile. ***Serves 4***

8 ounces skinned and boned
   chicken breast, cut into 12
   pieces
½ cup chopped onion
½ cup chopped green bell
   pepper
1¾ cups (one 15-ounce can)
   Hunt's Chunky Tomato
   Sauce
1½ teaspoons taco seasoning
1 teaspoon dried parsley flakes

¼ cup (1 ounce) sliced ripe
   olives
½ cup frozen whole kernel
   corn
1½ cups hot cooked noodles,
   rinsed and drained
⅓ cup (1½ ounces) shredded
   Kraft reduced-fat Cheddar
   cheese
¼ cup Land O Lakes fat-free
   sour cream

Preheat oven to 350 degrees. Spray an 8-by-8-inch baking dish with olive oil–flavored cooking spray. In a large skillet sprayed with olive oil–flavored cooking spray, brown chicken pieces, onion, and green pepper, stirring occasionally. Stir in tomato sauce, taco seasoning, parsley flakes, and olives. Add corn and noodles. Mix well to combine. Pour mixture into prepared baking dish. Evenly sprinkle Cheddar cheese over top. Bake 20 to 25 minutes. Place on a wire rack and let set 2 to 3 minutes. Cut into 4 pieces. Top each piece with 1 tablespoon sour cream.

HINT: 1¼ cups uncooked noodles usually cooks to about 1½ cups.

Each serving equals:

HE: 2¼ Vegetable, 2 Protein, 1 Bread, ¼ Fat, 15 Optional Calories

244 Calories, 4 gm Fat, 22 gm Protein, 30 gm Carbohydrate, 908 mg Sodium, 2 gm Fiber

DIABETIC: 2 Vegetable, 2 Meat, 1½ Starch

Cabbage Patch Chicken and Noodles

-----------------------------------■-----------------------------------

D oesn't this dish just bring back the cozy warmth of family
dinners in years past? You'll be pleasantly surprised at
how much tasty goodness the cabbage adds to this classic comfort meal. *Serves 4 (1 cup)*

> *3 cups coarsely chopped*
>   *cabbage*
> *½ cup chopped onion*
> *½ cup water*
> *1 (10¾-ounce) can Healthy*
>   *Request Cream of Chicken*
>   *Soup*
>
> *1½ cups (8 ounces) diced*
>   *cooked chicken breast*
> *2 cups hot cooked noodles,*
>   *rinsed and drained*
> *1 teaspoon dried parsley flakes*
> *¼ teaspoon black pepper*

In a large skillet, combine cabbage, onion, and water. Cover and
cook over medium heat for 15 to 20 minutes or until cabbage is
tender, stirring occasionally. Stir in chicken soup, chicken, and
noodles. Add parsley flakes and black pepper. Mix well to combine. Lower heat. Simmer 5 minutes, stirring occasionally.

HINT: 1¾ cups uncooked noodles usually cooks to about 2 cups.

Each serving equals:

HE: 2 Protein, 1¾ Vegetable, 1 Bread, ½ Slider, 5 Optional Calories

----

269 Calories, 5 gm Fat, 24 gm Protein, 32 gm Carbohydrate,
389 mg Sodium, 2 gm Fiber

DIABETIC: 2 Meat, 1½ Starch, 1 Vegetable

Layered Chicken Dinner

------------------------■------------------------

This dish is fun and easy to prepare—just layer each ingredient into the dish, pour on the topping, and sit down to enjoy your favorite game show while dinner bakes.

Serves 4

1 cup (3 ounces) uncooked regular white rice

2 cups (one 16-ounce can) cut green beans, rinsed and drained

16 ounces skinned and boned chicken breast, cut into 4 pieces

1 (10¾-ounce) can Healthy Request Cream of Chicken Soup

½ cup (2.5-ounce jar) sliced mushrooms, drained

2 tablespoons Hormel Bacon Bits

¾ cup water

1 teaspoon dried parsley flakes

1 teaspoon dried onion flakes

¼ teaspoon black pepper

Preheat oven to 350 degrees. Spray an 8-by-8-inch baking dish with butter-flavored cooking spray. Layer rice, green beans, and chicken in prepared baking dish. In a medium bowl, combine chicken soup, mushrooms, bacon bits, water, parsley flakes, onion flakes, and black pepper. Evenly spoon soup mixture over top. Cover and bake 90 minutes. Uncover and continue baking 15 minutes. Evenly divide into 4 servings.

Each serving equals:

HE: 3 Protein, 1¼ Vegetable, ¾ Bread, ½ Slider, 17 Optional Calories

----

284 Calories, 4 gm Fat, 32 gm Protein, 30 gm Carbohydrate, 558 mg Sodium, 2 gm Fiber

----

DIABETIC: 3 Meat, 1½ Starch, 1 Vegetable

Chicken Lovers' Pizza Casserole

T his smells so unbelievably good while it's baking, men will come peeking into the kitchen asking when it'll be ready. (Cliff did!) The mix of flavors gives the rice a real boost, and the chicken is a delightful addition.   *Serves 4*

1¾ cups (one 15-ounce can)
    Hunt's Chunky Tomato
    Sauce
1 teaspoon Italian seasoning
¼ cup (¾ ounce) grated Kraft
    fat-free Parmesan cheese
1 cup (5 ounces) diced cooked
    chicken breast

¼ cup (1 ounce) sliced ripe
    olives
2 cups hot cooked rice
⅓ cup (1½ ounces) shredded
    Kraft reduced-fat
    mozzarella cheese

Preheat oven to 375 degrees. Spray an 8-by-8-inch baking dish with olive oil–flavored cooking spray. In a large bowl, combine tomato sauce, Italian seasoning, and Parmesan cheese. Add chicken, olives, and rice. Mix well to combine. Evenly spread mixture into prepared baking dish. Bake 20 to 25 minutes. Evenly sprinkle mozzarella cheese over top. Continue baking 8 to 10 minutes or until mozzarella cheese is melted. Place baking dish on a wire rack. Let set 5 minutes. Divide into 4 servings.

HINT: 1⅓ cups uncooked rice usually cooks to about 2 cups.

Each serving equals:
HE: 2 Protein, 1¾ Vegetable, 1 Bread, ¼ Fat

241 Calories, 5 gm Fat, 21 gm Protein, 28 gm Carbohydrate, 873 mg Sodium, 2 gm Fiber

DIABETIC: 2 Meat, 2 Vegetable, 1 Starch

Italian Chicken Noodle Skillet

The sauce in this dish is so good, you'll want to lick the pan! The cheeses blend into a creamy goodness that makes all the flavors want to dance! *Serves 4*

1 cup (5 ounces) diced cooked chicken breast
1 (10¾-ounce) can Healthy Request Cream of Chicken Soup
1¾ cups (one 15-ounce can) Hunt's Chunky Tomato Sauce
½ cup (2.5-ounce jar) sliced mushrooms, drained
1 teaspoon Italian seasoning
¼ cup (¾ ounce) grated Kraft fat-free Parmesan cheese
2 cups hot cooked noodles, rinsed and drained
⅓ cup (1½ ounces) shredded Kraft reduced-fat mozzarella cheese

Preheat oven to 350 degrees. Spray an 8-by-8-inch baking dish with olive oil–flavored cooking spray. In a large skillet, combine chicken, chicken soup, and tomato sauce. Stir in mushrooms, Italian seasoning, and Parmesan cheese. Bring mixture to a boil. Add noodles. Mix well to combine. Pour mixture into prepared baking dish. Evenly sprinkle mozzarella cheese over top. Bake 20 to 25 minutes. Place baking dish on a wire rack and let set 5 minutes. Cut into 4 pieces.

HINT: 1¾ cups uncooked noodles usually cooks to about 2 cups.

Each serving equals:

HE: 2 Protein, 2 Vegetable, 1 Bread, ½ Slider, 1 Optional Calorie

277 Calories, 5 gm Fat, 23 gm Protein, 35 gm Carbohydrate, 1,125 mg Sodium, 2 gm Fiber

DIABETIC: 2 Meat, 2 Vegetable, 1½ Starch

Grande Chicken-Rice Olé!

If you're in the mood for Mexican flavors but don't want to leave home to get 'em, here's the perfect solution: an easy casserole that looks good and smells great. My son-in-law, John, cheered when I set this on the table. *Serves 6*

1½ cups (8 ounces) diced
   cooked chicken breast
1 (10¾-ounce) can Healthy
   Request Cream of Chicken
   Soup
1 cup chunky salsa (mild,
   medium, or hot) ☆

6 tablespoons Land O Lakes
   fat-free sour cream ☆
1 teaspoon dried parsley flakes
2 cups hot cooked rice
⅓ cup (1½ ounces) shredded
   Kraft reduced-fat Cheddar
   cheese

Preheat oven to 350 degrees. In a large bowl, combine chicken, chicken soup, ½ cup salsa, and 2 tablespoons sour cream. Add parsley flakes, rice, and Cheddar cheese. Mix well to combine. Pour mixture into prepared baking dish. Bake 20 minutes. In a small bowl, combine remaining ½ cup salsa and remaining 4 tablespoons sour cream. Spread mixture evenly over top of casserole. Continue baking 10 minutes. Place baking dish on a wire rack and let set 2 to 3 minutes. Cut into 6 servings.

HINT: 1⅓ cups uncooked rice usually cooks to about 2 cups.

Each serving equals:

HE: 1⅔ Protein, ⅔ Bread, ⅓ Vegetable, ½ Slider, 5 Optional Calories

179 Calories, 3 gm Fat, 17 gm Protein, 21 gm Carbohydrate,
472 mg Sodium, 1 gm Fiber

DIABETIC: 1½ Meat, 1½ Starch

"French" Chicken and Noodles

---■---

Ah, Paree—where the food is as special as the scenery! This combo of wholesome ingredients with a little extra pizazz from the creamy soup and dressing makes this *"magnifique!"*

Serves 4 (1 full cup)

1 (10¾-ounce) can Healthy Request Cream of Chicken Soup	*2 cups (one 16-ounce can) French-cut green beans, rinsed and drained*
⅓ cup Kraft Fat Free French Dressing	*1½ cups (8-ounces) diced cooked chicken breast*
1 teaspoon dried parsley flakes	*2 cups hot cooked noodles, rinsed and drained*
1 teaspoon dried onion flakes	

In a large skillet, combine chicken soup, French dressing, parsley flakes, and onion flakes. Cook over medium heat about 5 minutes, stirring often. Stir in green beans, chicken, and noodles. Continue cooking, stirring often, until mixture is heated through, about 5 minutes.

HINT: 1¾ cups uncooked noodles usually cooks to about 2 cups.

Each serving equals:

HE: 2 Protein, 1 Bread, 1 Vegetable, ¾ Slider, 12 Optional Calories

272 Calories, 4 gm Fat, 23 gm Protein, 36 gm Carbohydrate, 539 mg Sodium, 2 gm Fiber

DIABETIC: 2 Meat, 2 Starch, 2 Vegetable

Italian Grilled Chicken

-------------------◼-------------------

For those cool summer nights when the grill is fired up and you want something special to celebrate the tastes of summer, this should do the trick. ***Serves 4***

¼ cup Kraft Fat Free Italian Dressing
3 tablespoons dried fine bread crumbs
½ teaspoon Italian seasoning
16 ounces skinned and boned chicken breast, cut into 4 pieces

2 (¾-ounce) slices Kraft reduced-fat mozzarella or American cheese
½ cup shredded lettuce
½ cup thinly sliced tomatoes
4 reduced-calorie hamburger buns

Place Italian dressing in a saucer. In another saucer, combine bread crumbs and Italian seasoning. Dip chicken pieces in Italian dressing on both sides, then coat with bread crumb mixture. Place chicken on grill and brown, about 4 to 5 minutes on each side. Cut cheese slices in half. Place a piece of mozzarella cheese on top of each piece of chicken and continue grilling until cheese starts to melt. Evenly divide lettuce and tomato among 4 hamburger bun bottoms. Arrange chicken pieces over tomato slices and top with hamburger bun tops.

HINT: Can also be prepared in large skillet sprayed with olive oil–flavored cooking spray.

Each serving equals:
HE: 3½ Protein, 1¼ Bread, ½ Vegetable, 4 Optional Calories

236 Calories, 4 gm Fat, 31 gm Protein, 19 gm Carbohydrate, 562 mg Sodium, 1 gm Fiber

DIABETIC: 3½ Meat, 1 Starch, 1 Free Vegetable

Ham and Chicken Skillet

—————————————■—————————————

If you can't decide what to make for dinner—or you want to do something easy and good with leftovers—here's a man-pleasing combo that stirs up incredibly fast. No time to cook? Here's your dish! *Serves 4 (1 cup)*

1 cup (5 ounces) diced cooked chicken breast

1 full cup (6 ounces) diced Dubuque 97% fat-free ham or any extra-lean ham

2 cups hot cooked noodles, rinsed and drained

1 cup (one 8-ounce can) cut green beans, rinsed and drained

1 cup (one 8-ounce can) cut carrots, rinsed and drained

1 (10¾-ounce) can Healthy Request Cream of Chicken Soup

⅓ cup skim milk

1 teaspoon dried parsley flakes

In a large skillet sprayed with butter-flavored cooking spray, sauté chicken and ham for 2 to 3 minutes. Stir in noodles, green beans, and carrots. Add chicken soup, skim milk, and parsley flakes. Mix well to combine. Lower heat. Simmer 5 minutes, stirring often.

HINT: 1¾ cups uncooked noodles usually cooks to about 2 cups.

Each serving equals:

HE: 2¼ Protein, 1 Bread, 1 Vegetable, ¼ Slider, 12 Optional Calories

269 Calories, 5 gm Fat, 24 gm Protein, 32 gm Carbohydrate, 750 mg Sodium, 2 gm Fiber

DIABETIC: 2 Meat, 1½ Starch, 1 Vegetable

Chuck Wagon Franks and Beans

———————————————————■———————————————————

This is such an old-timey taste treat, every man who tried it starting whistling "Home on the Range," which is where it stirs up "quick and good."   *Serves 6 (scant 1 cup)*

½ cup finely chopped onion
½ cup finely chopped green bell pepper
1¾ cups (one 15-ounce can) Hunt's Chunky Tomato Sauce
2 tablespoons Brown Sugar Twin

20 ounces (two 16-ounce cans) great northern beans, rinsed and drained
8 ounces diced Healthy Choice 97% fat-free frankfurters

In a large skillet sprayed with butter-flavored cooking spray, sauté onion and green pepper until tender. Stir in tomato sauce and Brown Sugar Twin. Add great northern beans and frankfurters. Mix well to combine. Lower heat. Cover and simmer 15 minutes, stirring occasionally.

Each serving equals:

HE: 2½ Protein, 1½ Vegetable, 5 Optional Calories

181 Calories, 1 gm Fat, 14 gm Protein, 29 gm Carbohydrate, 852 mg Sodium, 5 gm Fiber

DIABETIC: 1½ Meat, 1½ Starch, 1 Vegetable

Bavarian Hash

---■---

Sauerkraut always makes a dish feel like a day out at the ball-park, which all on its own thrills men's taste buds. When you add favorites like mashed potatoes, franks, and cheese, you've got a home run every time. *Serves 4*

1⅔ cups water
1⅓ cups (3 ounces) instant potato flakes
⅓ cup Carnation Nonfat Dry Milk Powder
8 ounces diced Healthy Choice 97% fat-free frankfurters
1½ cups (one 15-ounce can)

Frank's Bavarian-style sauerkraut, well drained
1 (10¾-ounce) can Healthy Request Cream of Mushroom Soup
4 (¾-ounce) slices Kraft reduced-fat American cheese

Preheat oven to 350 degrees. Spray an 8-by-8-inch baking dish with butter-flavored cooking spray. In a large skillet, bring water to a boil. Stir in potato flakes and dry milk powder. Add frankfurters, sauerkraut, and mushroom soup. Mix well to combine. Spread mixture into prepared baking dish. Arrange cheese slices over top. Bake 20 to 25 minutes. Place baking dish on a wire rack and let set 5 minutes. Cut into 4 servings.

HINT: If you can't find Bavarian sauerkraut, use regular sauerkraut, ½ teaspoon caraway seeds, and 1 teaspoon Brown Sugar Twin.

Each serving equals:

HE: 2⅓ Protein, 1 Bread, ¾ Vegetable, ¼ Skim Milk, ½ Slider, 1 Optional Calorie

---

289 Calories, 5 gm Fat, 18 gm Protein, 43 gm Carbohydrate, 1,558 mg Sodium, 3 gm Fiber

---

DIABETIC: 2 Meat, 2 Starch, 1 Vegetable

Veggie Hot Dog Skillet

—————————————————◼—————————————————

I don't know about you, but for me combining hot dogs with a few healthy veggies is a great way to get men to gobble up the healthiest dish. This one has lots of crunch and flavor, which earned it a "yes!" from Tommy.   *Serves 4 (1 full cup)*

*8 ounces sliced Healthy
    Choice 97% fat-free
    frankfurters
1 cup shredded carrots
1 cup finely chopped celery
½ cup finely diced onion
½ cup finely diced green bell
    pepper*

*1 (10¾-ounce) can Healthy
    Request Tomato Soup
½ cup water
1 teaspoon dried parsley flakes
¼ teaspoon black pepper
1 teaspoon Worcestershire
    sauce
2 cups hot cooked rice*

In a large skillet sprayed with butter-flavored cooking spray, sauté sliced frankfurters, carrots, celery, onion, and green pepper until tender, about 6 to 8 minutes. Add tomato soup, water, parsley flakes, black pepper, and Worcestershire sauce. Mix well to combine. Stir in rice. Lower heat. Simmer 5 minutes, stirring occasionally.

HINT: 1⅓ cups uncooked rice usually cooks to about 2 cups.

Each serving equals:

HE: 1½ Vegetable, 1⅓ Protein, 1 Bread, ½ Slider, 5 Optional Calories

235 Calories, 3 gm Fat, 11 gm Protein, 41 gm Carbohydrate,
918 mg Sodium, 5 gm Fiber

DIABETIC: 2 Starch, 1½ Meat, 1 Vegetable

Corned Beef and Cabbage Quiche

◼

ere's another "meal-in-a-piecrust" that appeals to the deli lover in every man! It's a good choice for Sunday brunch or an easy supper on the weekend, and it packs lots of good nutrition into a super-tasty dish.

Serves 8

1 refrigerated unbaked 9-inch Pillsbury piecrust
½ cup chopped onion
3½ cups purchased coleslaw mix
2 (2.5-ounce) packages Carl Buddig 90% lean corned beef, finely chopped
⅓ cup (1½ ounces) shredded

Kraft reduced-fat Cheddar cheese
3 eggs or equivalent in egg substitute
1½ cups (one 12-fluid-ounce can) Carnation Evaporated Skim Milk
⅛ teaspoon black pepper

Preheat oven to 350 degrees. Place piecrust in a 9-inch pie plate. Flute edges. In a large skillet sprayed with butter-flavored cooking spray, sauté onion until tender. Add coleslaw mix and corned beef. Mix well to combine. Continue cooking until cabbage is tender, about 10 minutes. Evenly spread vegetable mixture in bottom of unbaked piecrust. Sprinkle cheese over top of mixture. In a medium bowl, beat eggs with a fork. Add evaporated skim milk and black pepper. Mix well to combine. Pour egg mixture over the cheese. Bake 35 to 40 minutes or until golden brown. Place pie plate on a wire rack and allow to set 5 minutes. Cut into 8 servings.

HINT: 3 cups shredded cabbage and ½ cup shredded carrots may be used in place of purchased coleslaw mix.

Each serving equals:

HE: 1½ Protein (⅓ limited), 1 Vegetable, ½ Bread, ⅓ Skim Milk, ½ Slider, 13 Optional Calories

222 Calories, 10 gm Fat, 12 gm Protein, 21 gm Carbohydrate, 518 mg Sodium, 1 gm Fiber

DIABETIC: 1 Meat, 1 Starch, 1 Fat, ½ Vegetable

Corned Beef Pasta Bake

-------------------------■-------------------------

This dish joins some unusual ingredients into a quick-fix casserole that the whole family will enjoy. A St. Patrick's Day buffet simply cries out for a hearty treat like this one. My Grandpa McAndrews and relatives in County Mayo would approve.   *Serves 4*

1 (2.5-ounce) package Carl Buddig 90% lean corned beef, finely chopped
½ cup finely chopped onion
2 cups (one 15-ounce can) Frank's Bavarian-style sauerkraut, well drained

1 (10¾-ounce) can Healthy Request Tomato Soup
1 teaspoon dried parsley flakes
2 cups hot cooked rotini pasta, rinsed and drained
4 (¾-ounce) slices Kraft reduced-fat Swiss cheese

Preheat oven to 350 degrees. Spray an 8-by-8-inch baking dish with butter-flavored cooking spray. In a large skillet sprayed with butter-flavored cooking spray, sauté corned beef and onion until onion is tender, about 5 to 10 minutes. Stir in drained sauerkraut, tomato soup, and parsley flakes. Add rotini pasta. Mix well to combine. Pour mixture into prepared baking dish. Arrange Swiss cheese slices evenly over top. Bake 20 to 25 minutes. Place baking dish on a wire rack and let set 5 minutes. Divide into 4 servings.

HINTS: 1. If you can't find Bavarian sauerkraut, use regular sauerkraut, ½ teaspoon caraway seeds, and 1 teaspoon Brown Sugar Twin.
2. 1½ cups uncooked rotini pasta usually cooks to about 2 cups.

Each serving equals:

HE: 1⅔ Protein, 1¼ Vegetable, 1 Bread, ½ Slider, 5 Optional Calories

276 Calories, 4 gm Fat, 15 gm Protein, 45 gm Carbohydrate, 1,092 mg Sodium, 6 gm Fiber

DIABETIC: 2½ Starch, 1 Meat, 1 Vegetable

Irresistible Endings—
Desserts Fit for
a King

───────■───────

Iread in a recent Shape *magazine article that if you want to attract a man,* bake up *some dough; don't* spend it on perfume. *Scientists studied which odors acted as aphrodisiacs to stimulate and arouse men, and they learned that home cooking worked a lot better than any floral scent. In fact, the most "stimulating" food aroma was pumpkin pie, followed by doughnuts!*

As a woman who's been serving homemade desserts to men for years now, I could have told them that. The aroma from my kitchen is better than the fanciest French perfume! Besides the Banana Split Pie stories I shared earlier, I've heard from hundreds of people that my Healthy Exchanges desserts are a real hit with the men in their lives.

Cliff's my in-home recipe tester, of course, and he's got dozens of favorite Healthy Exchanges desserts to choose from. I remember his reaction when I served him Cozumel Cloud Pudding one wintry evening. It brought back all the memories of a romantic cruise we took a few years ago, and definitely put him in a great mood!

Healthy Exchanges desserts are the crown jewels of this cookbook, as they are in every issue of my newsletter and part of every cooking demonstration I do. They include pies of every possible flavor and description, luscious cakes that make every meal a celebration, and specialty desserts like parfaits, tarts, and other special-occasion treats.

Enjoying a piece of a great dessert after a delicious, healthy meal—it just doesn't get any better than that!

(Unless the Super Bowl runs into overtime . . .)

Desserts

—————■—————

Chocolate Banana Split Parfait

Cherry Chocolate Parfait

Butterscotch Ambrosia

Rice Maple Cream

Peanut Butter Dream Pudding

Cozumel Cloud Pudding

Chunky Chocolate Pudding

Hawaiian Chocolate Banana Dessert

Pineapple Blueberry Custard Parfait

Tropical Isle Coffee Cake

Apple Dessert Pizza

Blueberry Paradise Pizza

Grasshopper Dessert Bars

Banana Split Shortcake

Georgia Peach Cobbler

Strawberry Shortcakes with Banana Cream Sauce

Lemon Cheesecake with Lemon Glaze

Raspberry-Pear Cheesecake

Orange Push-Up Cheesecake

Hawaiian Pineapple Dew
Cheesecake

Log Cabin Cheesecake

Peanut Butter and Jelly
Cheesecake

Mom's Apple Pie

Blueberry Thrill Pie

Heavenly Strawberry Pie

Hawaiian Banana Butterscotch
Pie

Chocolate Rum Pecan Pie

Better Than Candy Pie

Cherry Crumb Pie

Hawaiian Banana Split
Meringue Pie

Carrot Pineapple Cake with
Vanilla Cream Topping

Banana and Blueberry Party
Cake

Chocolate Hawaiian Dessert
Cake

Grandpa's Old-Time Spice Cake

Pineapple Graham Cracker
Scallop

Tortilla Fruit Rollups

Ambrosia Tapioca Pudding

Maple Nut Tapioca Pudding

Calypso Bread Pudding

Banana Eggnog Bread Pudding
with Rum Sauce

Peanut Butter Cup Rice
Pudding

Pineapple-Raisin Rice Pudding

■

Chocolate Banana Split Parfait

----------------------------------■----------------------------------

Did you know that "parfait" is French for "perfect"? And what could be more perfect than all these delicious flavors piled high in a tall dessert glass? How do you say "yummy" in French, I wonder? Better look it up!   *Serves 6*

2 cups sliced fresh strawberries	*1 cup (one 8-ounce can) crushed pineapple, packed in fruit juice, undrained*
1 cup (1 medium) diced bananas	
1 (4-serving) package JELL-O sugar-free chocolate cook-and-serve pudding mix	*1¼ cups water*
	1 teaspoon vanilla extract
	6 tablespoons Cool Whip Lite
⅔ cup Carnation Nonfat Dry Milk Powder	*3 maraschino cherries, halved*

In a large bowl, combine strawberries and bananas. Evenly spoon about ½ cup fruit mixture into 6 parfait dishes. In a medium saucepan, combine dry pudding mix, dry milk powder, undrained pineapple, and water. Cook over medium heat, stirring constantly, until mixture thickens and starts to boil. Remove from heat. Stir in vanilla extract. Evenly spoon a full ⅓ cup hot pudding mixture over each fruit mixture. Refrigerate at least 30 minutes. Just before serving, top each with 1 tablespoon Cool Whip Lite and garnish with cherry half.

HINT: To prevent bananas from turning brown, mix with 1 teaspoon lemon juice or sprinkle with Fruit Fresh.

Each serving equals:

HE: 1 Fruit, ⅓ Skim Milk, ¼ Slider, 12 Optional Calories

----
129 Calories, 1 gm Fat, 4 gm Protein, 26 gm Carbohydrate,
116 mg Sodium, 2 gm Fiber

DIABETIC: 1 Fruit, ½ Starch

Cherry Chocolate Parfait

-------------------------- ❄ --------------------------

This tastes just like chocolate-covered cherries. *Serves 6*

1 (4-serving) package
   JELL-O sugar-free
   chocolate cook-and-serve
   pudding mix
1 (4-serving) package
   JELL-O sugar-free cherry
   gelatin
1½ cups water ☆
2 cups (one 16-ounce can)
   tart red cherries, packed in
   water, undrained
1 teaspoon brandy extract

1 (4-serving) package JELL-O
   sugar-free instant
   chocolate pudding mix
⅔ cup Carnation Nonfat Dry
   Milk Powder
¾ cup Cool Whip Lite ☆
¼ cup + 2 tablespoons
   purchased graham cracker
   crumbs or six (2½-inch)
   squares made into crumbs
1 tablespoon (¼ ounce)
   mini–chocolate chips

In a medium saucepan, combine dry cook-and-serve pudding, dry gelatin, and ½ cup water. Stir in undrained cherries. Cook over medium heat, stirring often, until mixture thickens and starts to boil, being careful not to crush cherries. Remove from heat. Stir in brandy extract. Place pan on a wire rack and allow to cool completely, about 20 minutes. In a large bowl, combine dry instant pudding, dry milk powder, and remaining 1 cup water. Mix well using a wire whisk. Blend in full ⅓ cup Cool Whip Lite. Add cooled cherry mixture. Mix gently to combine. For each parfait, spoon about ⅓ cup pudding mixture into a parfait glass. Sprinkle 1 tablespoon graham cracker crumbs over pudding, spoon a full ¼ cup pudding mixture over crumbs, then garnish with 1 tablespoon Cool Whip Lite. Top each with ½ teaspoon chocolate chips. Refrigerate at least 15 minutes.

Each serving equals:

HE: ⅔ Fruit, ⅓ Bread, ⅓ Skim Milk, ¾ Slider, 9 Optional Calories

----

162 Calories, 2 gm Fat, 6 gm Protein, 30 gm Carbohydrate,
421 mg Sodium, 1 gm Fiber

DIABETIC: 1 Fruit, 1 Starch

Butterscotch Ambrosia

------------------------------■------------------------------

I f you remember your grandma's traditional ambrosia with its
classic flavors of pineapple, marshmallows, and nuts, I've
gone it one better with this updated version that adds the sweet
pleasure of butterscotch to all that good stuff. And since *all* the
men I know love butterscotch . . .   *Serves 6*

*1 (4-serving) package JELL-O
    sugar-free instant
    butterscotch pudding mix*
*⅓ cup Carnation Nonfat Dry
    Milk Powder*
*1 cup (one 8-ounce can)
    crushed pineapple, packed
    in fruit juice, undrained*
½ cup water

*¾ cup Yoplait plain fat-free
    yogurt*
¾ cup Cool Whip Lite
*2 cups (2 medium) sliced
    bananas*
*½ cup (1 ounce) miniature
    marshmallows*
*3 tablespoons (¾ ounce)
    chopped pecans*

In a large bowl, combine dry pudding mix, dry milk powder,
undrained pineapple, and water. Mix well using a wire whisk.
Blend in yogurt and Cool Whip Lite. Add bananas, marshmallows, and pecans. Mix gently to combine. Evenly spoon mixture
into 6 dessert dishes. Refrigerate at least 15 minutes.

HINT: To prevent bananas from turning brown, mix with 1 teaspoon lemon juice or sprinkle with Fruit Fresh.

Each serving equals:

HE: 1 Fruit, ½ Fat, ⅓ Skim Milk, ½ Slider, 5 Optional Calories

----

175 Calories, 3 gm Fat, 4 gm Protein, 33 gm Carbohydrate,
272 mg Sodium, 1 gm Fiber

DIABETIC: 1 Fruit, 1 Starch, ½ Fat

Rice Maple Cream

-----------------■-----------------

This custardy dessert blends the luscious flavors of maple and pecan with the cozy goodness of real rice pudding. You'll feel like the luckiest kid on the block when you dine on this old-fashioned classic.   *Serves 4*

1 (4-serving) package JELL-O sugar-free vanilla cook-and-serve pudding mix
⅔ cup Carnation Nonfat Dry Milk Powder
1½ cups water
½ cup Cary's Sugar Free Maple Syrup
1½ cups cold cooked rice
¼ cup Cool Whip Lite
1 tablespoon (¼ ounce) chopped pecans

In a medium saucepan, combine dry pudding mix, dry milk powder, water, and maple syrup. Cook over medium heat, stirring constantly, until mixture thickens and starts to boil. Remove from heat. Stir in rice. Evenly spoon mixture into 4 dessert dishes. Refrigerate at least 15 minutes. Just before serving, top each with 1 tablespoon Cool Whip Lite and ¾ teaspoon chopped pecans.

HINT: 1 cup uncooked rice usually cooks to about 1½ cups.

Each serving equals:
HE: ¾ Bread, ½ Skim Milk, ¼ Fat, ½ Slider, 10 Optional Calories
----
154 Calories, 2 gm Fat, 5 gm Protein, 29 gm Carbohydrate, 218 mg Sodium, 0 gm Fiber

DIABETIC: 1½ Starch, ½ Skim Milk or 2 Starch

Peanut Butter Dream Pudding

------------------------------■------------------------------

I f you're like most men, you think chocolate and peanut butter make the best team since the 1969 World Series Champion New York Mets! (My cousin, Jim McAndrews, pitched for that "dream team"!) Here's a quick treat that deserves to be called the "Dessert of Champions"! *Serves 4*

1 (4-serving) package JELL-O sugar-free instant chocolate pudding mix
⅔ cup Carnation Nonfat Dry Milk Powder
1½ cups water
2 tablespoons Peter Pan reduced-fat peanut butter

¼ cup Cool Whip Lite
1 cup (1 medium) diced bananas
6 (2½-inch) Keebler Peanut Butter Graham Crackers, made into large crumbs

In a large bowl, combine dry pudding mix, dry milk powder, and water. Mix well using a wire whisk. Blend in peanut butter and Cool Whip Lite. Stir in bananas and cracker crumbs. Evenly spoon mixture into 4 dessert dishes. Refrigerate at least 10 minutes.

Each serving equals:

HE: ½ Skim Milk, ½ Fat, ½ Protein, ½ Fruit, ½ Bread, ½ Slider

----

208 Calories, 4 gm Fat, 8 gm Protein, 35 gm Carbohydrate, 494 mg Sodium, 1 gm Fiber

----

DIABETIC: 1 Starch, ½ Skim Milk, ½ Fat, ½ Fruit

Cozumel Cloud Pudding

---- ❄ ----

Maybe you've been lucky enough to visit the sultry Mexican resort of Cozumel and taste its exotic dishes, but if, like most of us, you'll have to settle for dreaming about it, try this creamy dish that marries chocolate and cinnamon in a South-of-the-Border romance your whole family will love.

Serves 6

¾ cup purchased chocolate
    graham cracker crumbs or
    12 (2½-inch) squares
    made into crumbs ☆
1 (8-ounce) package
    Philadelphia fat-free
    cream cheese
2 (4-serving) packages
    JELL-O sugar-free instant
    chocolate pudding mix

3 cups skim milk
¾ cup Cool Whip Lite ☆
¾ cup Yoplait plain fat-free
    yogurt
¾ teaspoon ground
    cinnamon ☆
1 teaspoon vanilla extract

Evenly spoon 1½ tablespoons graham cracker crumbs into 6 dessert dishes. In a large bowl, stir cream cheese with a spoon until soft. Add dry pudding mixes and skim milk. Mix well using a wire whisk. Blend in ⅓ cup Cool Whip Lite, yogurt, ½ teaspoon cinnamon, and vanilla extract. Mix well to combine. Evenly spoon about ¾ cup pudding mixture into each dessert dish. Top each with 1 tablespoon Cool Whip Lite. In a small bowl, combine remaining 3 tablespoons chocolate crumbs and remaining ¼ teaspoon cinnamon. Evenly sprinkle mixture over top of each dessert. Refrigerate at least 15 minutes.

Each serving equals:

HE: ⅔ Bread, ⅔ Protein, ⅔ Skim Milk, ½ Slider, 13 Optional Calories

---

202 Calories, 2 gm Fat, 13 gm Protein, 33 gm Carbohydrate,
841 mg Sodium, 0 gm Fiber

DIABETIC: 1 Starch, 1 Skim Milk, ½ Meat

Chunky Chocolate Pudding

------------------------- ❈ -------------------------

R emember the thickest candy bar you ever tasted? Wouldn't you love to bite into one right now? Well, this dessert delivers those sinful taste sensations you always loved in a smooth and sweet dessert that's almost too good to be "legal."

Serves 6

1 (4-serving) package JELL-O sugar-free instant chocolate fudge pudding mix

⅔ cup Carnation Nonfat Dry Milk Powder

1½ cups water

¾ cup Yoplait plain fat-free yogurt

¾ cup Cool Whip Lite ☆

1 teaspoon vanilla extract

¼ cup (1 ounce) chopped pecans

¾ cup raisins

In a large bowl, combine dry pudding mix and dry milk powder. Add water and yogurt. Mix well using a wire whisk. Blend in ¼ cup Cool Whip Lite, vanilla extract, pecans, and raisins. Mix gently to combine. Evenly spoon mixture into 6 dessert dishes. Top each with 1 tablespoon Cool Whip Lite. Refrigerate at least 15 minutes.

HINT: To plump up raisins without "cooking," place in a glass measuring cup and microwave on HIGH for 30 seconds.

Each serving equals:

HE: 1 Fruit, ⅔ Fat, ½ Skim Milk, ½ Slider, 7 Optional Calories

176 Calories, 4 gm Fat, 6 gm Protein, 29 gm Carbohydrate, 285 mg Sodium, 1 gm Fiber

DIABETIC: 1 Fruit, 1 Fat, ½ Skim Milk, ½ Starch

Hawaiian Chocolate Banana Dessert

----------------------------- ❋ -----------------------------

This one blends the glorious flavors of the islands with rich chocolate-y goodness. You might feel moved to dance the hula after just a few bites!

Serves 8

20 (2½-inch) Nabisco Choco-
    late Graham Crackers ☆
2 (4-serving) packages
    JELL-O sugar-free instant
    chocolate pudding mix ☆
1⅓ cups Carnation Nonfat
    Dry Milk Powder ☆
2 cups (two 8-ounce cans)
    crushed pineapple, packed
    in fruit juice, undrained ☆

1 cup water ☆
2 cups (2 medium) sliced
    bananas
1 cup Cool Whip Lite
1 teaspoon coconut extract
2 tablespoons flaked coconut
2 tablespoons (½ ounce)
    chopped pecans

Evenly arrange 9 of the graham crackers in a 9-by-9-inch cake pan. In a large bowl, combine 1 package dry pudding mix, ⅔ cup dry milk powder, 1 cup undrained pineapple, and ½ cup water. Mix well using a wire whisk. Spread pudding mixture evenly over crackers. Evenly arrange banana slices over pudding mixture. Arrange 9 graham crackers over bananas. In the same bowl, combine remaining package dry pudding mix, remaining ⅔ cup dry milk powder, remaining 1 cup undrained pineapple, and remaining ½ cup water. Mix well using a wire whisk. Blend in Cool Whip Lite and coconut extract. Spread mixture evenly over crackers. Crush remaining 2 graham crackers and evenly sprinkle crumbs over pudding mix. Sprinkle coconut and pecans over top. Cover and refrigerate at least 2 hours. Cut into 8 servings.

Each serving equals:

HE: 1 Fruit, ¾ Bread, ½ Skim Milk, ¼ Fat, ¾ Slider, 1 Optional Calorie

----

228 Calories, 4 gm Fat, 6 gm Protein, 42 gm Carbohydrate,
452 mg Sodium, 2 gm Fiber

DIABETIC: 1½ Starch, 1 Fruit, ½ Skim Milk, ½ Fat

Pineapple Blueberry Custard Parfait

W hen the freshest berries are piled high at roadside stands or at your local market, why not give this colorful fruit delight a try? I bet you'll agree that this creamy-sweet dessert tastes just like a cool summer night! *Serves 4*

1½ cups fresh blueberries ☆
1 (4-serving) package JELL-O
    sugar-free vanilla cook-
    and-serve pudding mix
⅔ cup Carnation Nonfat Dry
    Milk Powder
1 cup (one 8-ounce can)
    crushed pineapple, packed
    in fruit juice, undrained

1 cup water
1 teaspoon vanilla extract
¼ teaspoon ground nutmeg
¼ cup Cool Whip Lite

Reserve ¼ cup blueberries. Evenly spoon remaining blueberries into 4 parfait glasses. In a medium saucepan, combine dry pudding mix, dry milk powder, undrained pineapple, and water. Cook over medium heat, stirring constantly, until mixture thickens and starts to boil. Remove from heat. Stir in vanilla extract and nutmeg. Evenly spoon hot mixture over blueberries. Refrigerate at least 1 hour. Just before serving, top each with 1 tablespoon Cool Whip Lite and 1 tablespoon of reserved blueberries.

Each serving equals:

HE: 1 Fruit, ½ Skim Milk, ¼ Slider, 10 Optional Calories

141 Calories, 1 gm Fat, 4 gm Protein, 29 gm Carbohydrate, 180 mg Sodium, 2 gm Fiber

DIABETIC: 1 Fruit, ½ Skim Milk, ½ Starch

Tropical Isle Coffee Cake

---- ❅ ----

Every man should have one great coffee cake he can stir up quickly and dazzle the lady of his choice. Whoever she is, she'll love this feast of sunshine and sweetness as much as you do! This was one of the top vote-getters at our Healthy Man Taste-Testing Buffet. One bite, and you'll know why.

Serves 8

1½ cups Bisquick Reduced Fat Baking Mix
1 (4-serving) package JELL-O sugar-free instant vanilla pudding mix
⅔ cup Carnation Nonfat Dry Milk Powder
2 tablespoons Sugar Twin or Sprinkle Sweet
1 cup (one 8-ounce can) crushed pineapple, packed in fruit juice, undrained

1 egg or equivalent in egg substitute, slightly beaten
½ cup Diet Mountain Dew or water
1 teaspoon coconut extract
1 cup (one 11-ounce can) mandarin oranges, rinsed and drained
¼ cup (1 ounce) chopped walnuts
2 tablespoons flaked coconut

Preheat oven to 350 degrees. Spray an 8-by-8-inch baking dish with butter-flavored cooking spray. In a large bowl, combine baking mix, dry pudding mix, dry milk powder, and Sugar Twin. Add undrained pineapple, egg, Diet Mountain Dew, and coconut extract. Mix well to combine. Fold in mandarin oranges and walnuts. Spread batter into prepared baking dish. Evenly sprinkle coconut over top. Bake 35 to 40 minutes or until a toothpick inserted in center comes out clean. Place baking dish on a wire rack to cool. Cut into 8 servings.

Each serving equals:

HE: 1 Bread, ½ Fruit, ¼ Skim Milk, ¼ Protein, 18 Optional Calories

---

185 Calories, 5 gm Fat, 5 gm Protein, 30 gm Carbohydrate, 460 mg Sodium, 1 gm Fiber

---

DIABETIC: 1½ Starch, ½ Fruit, ½ Fat

Apple Dessert Pizza

-------------------- ■ --------------------

A lmost better than (dare I say it?) Mom's apple pie, here's
an invitation to enjoy the best of the apple harvest, cou-
pled with the crunch of pecans. My son Tommy, the home-run
king, would say that this one hits the ball right out of the park!
And Cliff just loved it too! *Serves 8*

1 (4-serving) package JELL-O
sugar-free vanilla cook-
and-serve pudding mix
1 cup unsweetened apple juice
1 cup water ☆
1 teaspoon apple pie spice
3 cups (6 small) cored, peeled,
and sliced cooking apples

⅔ cup Carnation Nonfat Dry
Milk Powder
1½ cups Bisquick Reduced
Fat Baking Mix
¼ cup Sugar Twin or Sprinkle
Sweet
2 tablespoons (½ ounce)
chopped pecans

Preheat oven to 425 degrees. In a medium saucepan, combine
dry pudding mix, apple juice, ½ cup water, and apple pie spice.
Stir in apples. Cook over medium heat, stirring often, until mixture thickens and starts to boil. Place pan on a wire rack and
allow to cool. Meanwhile, in a large bowl, combine dry milk powder and remaining ½ cup water. Add baking mix, Sugar Twin, and
pecans. Mix gently to combine. Pat mixture into an ungreased
12-inch pizza pan. Evenly spoon apple mixture over top. Bake 12
to 15 minutes or until edge is golden brown. Cut into 8 wedges.

HINTS: 1. Easiest way to have dough cover pan is to slip your
hand into a plastic sandwich bag and gently pat dough
into place.
2. Good topped with 1 tablespoon Cool Whip Lite, but
don't forget to count the few additional calories.

Each serving equals:

HE: 1 Bread, 1 Fruit, ¼ Skim Milk, ¼ Fat, 13 Optional Calories

----

167 Calories, 3 gm Fat, 4 gm Protein, 31 gm Carbohydrate,
339 mg Sodium, 1 gm Fiber

DIABETIC: 1 Starch, 1 Fruit, ½ Fat

Blueberry Paradise Pizza

------------------------------■------------------------------

T he perfect day for some men I know would begin with Breakfast Pizza in the morning and end with this easy but oh-so-good dessert pizza that will convince any man he's in heaven—or at least in Iowa. Come feast in my field of sweet-tasting creamy dreams! *Serves 8*

1 refrigerated unbaked
   9-inch Pillsbury
   piecrust
1 (4-serving) package
   JELL-O sugar-free vanilla
   cook-and-serve pudding
   mix
1 (4-serving) package
   JELL-O sugar-free
   blueberry or lemon
   gelatin
1 cup water
3 cups frozen unsweetened
   blueberries

1 (8-ounce) package
   Philadelphia fat-free
   cream cheese
Sugar substitute to equal
   2 tablespoons sugar
1 cup (one 8-ounce can)
   crushed pineapple,
   packed in fruit juice,
   drained
½ cup Cool Whip Lite
1 teaspoon coconut extract
2 tablespoons flaked
   coconut

Preheat oven to 450 degrees. Place piecrust on an ungreased medium pizza pan. Prick crust freely with a fork. Bake 6 to 8 minutes or until light golden brown. Place pizza pan on a wire rack and allow to cool. Meanwhile, in a medium saucepan, combine dry pudding mix, dry gelatin, and water. Cook over medium heat, stirring constantly, until mixture thickens and starts to boil. Stir in frozen blueberries. Continue cooking, gently stirring, until blueberries start to boil. Place pan on a wire rack and allow to cool. In a medium bowl, stir cream cheese with a spoon until soft. Blend in sugar substitute and undrained pineapple. Add Cool Whip Lite and coconut extract. Mix gently to combine. Refrigerate until both crust and blueberry filling have cooled. Spread cream cheese mixture evenly over cooled crust. Evenly spoon cooled blueberry mixture over cream cheese mixture. Sprinkle coconut evenly over top. Refrigerate at least 1 hour. Cut into 8 servings.

Each serving equals:

HE: ¾ Fruit, ½ Bread, ½ Protein, ¾ Slider, 10 Optional Calories

----

216 Calories, 8 gm Fat, 6 gm Protein, 30 gm Carbohydrate,
402 mg Sodium, 2 gm Fiber

DIABETIC: 1 Fruit, 1 Starch, 1 Fat, ½ Meat

I have been a diabetic for six years and never could find any recipes I really liked or could fix so easily! Even Weight Watchers cannot even begin to compare with your recipes. I recommend them to all my friends. All are delicious and so easy to fix. My husband also likes them. He isn't a diabetic but needs to lose the weight also. He eats things now that he never would before!

—R.C., IA

Grasshopper Dessert Bars

I bet you remember, as I do, the minty marvel that is the dessert drink called a Grasshopper. I wanted to celebrate the refreshing taste of crème de menthe in a rich chocolate cookie bar, and I hope you'll agree that this does my memory justice. My son-in-law, John, thought these were great! *Serves 12*

1 (8-ounce) can Pillsbury refrigerated crescent dinner rolls

2 (8-ounce) packages Philadelphia fat-free cream cheese

¼ cup Sugar Twin or Sprinkle Sweet

1¼ teaspoons mint extract ☆

8 to 10 drops green food coloring ☆

2 (4-serving) packages JELL-O sugar-free instant chocolate pudding mix

1⅓ cups Carnation Nonfat Dry Milk Powder

2¼ cups water

1½ cups Cool Whip Lite

1 tablespoon chocolate syrup

Preheat oven to 425 degrees. Pat rolls into an ungreased 10-by-15-inch rimmed cookie sheet. Gently press dough to cover bottom of pan, being sure to seal perforations. Bake 5 to 7 minutes or until golden brown. Place cookie sheet on a wire rack and allow to cool. In a medium bowl, stir cream cheese with a spoon until soft. Stir in Sugar Twin, ¾ teaspoon mint extract, and 4 to 5 drops of green food coloring. Mix well using a wire whisk. Spread cream cheese mixture evenly over cooled crust. In a medium bowl, combine dry pudding mix and dry milk powder. Add water. Mix well using a wire whisk. Spread pudding mixture over cream cheese mixture. Refrigerate at least 30 minutes. In a medium bowl, combine Cool Whip Lite, remaining ½ teaspoon mint extract, and remaining 4 to 5 drops green food coloring. Spread evenly over chocolate layer. Drizzle chocolate syrup over top. Refrigerate at least 1 hour. Cut into 12 servings. Refrigerate leftovers.

HINT: DO NOT use inexpensive rolls. They don't cover the pan properly.

Each serving equals:

HE: ⅔ Bread, ⅔ Protein, ⅓ Skim Milk, ½ Slider, 5 Optional Calories

169 Calories, 5 gm Fat, 10 gm Protein, 21 gm Carbohydrate, 644 mg Sodium, 0 gm Fiber

DIABETIC: 1½ Starch, 1 Meat

Your cookbook sat on the shelf until last August, when my husband had a physical. His blood sugar was running too high, we were both overweight, and my cholesterol was moderately high—but it took the fear of diabetes to get us started. Since August, we have both lost 25-plus pounds, Bob's blood sugar is normal, and my cholesterol has dropped 20 points. We don't count calories, we just follow your recipes. We haven't found anything we don't like, and having delicious desserts is a bonus.

—R.C., IA

Banana Split Shortcake

You can never have enough banana split desserts, which is why I invent several new ones every year. The men who've loved Banana Split Pie (see **Man-Pleasing Classics**) always ask me for more of the same, so here's this season's sundae-in-a-shortcake! It's so full of fruit and fun, you're bound to make it a regular on your most-loved desserts list.   *Serves 8*

1½ cups Bisquick Reduced
    Fat Baking Mix
1 (4-serving) package
    JELL-O sugar-free instant
    banana cream pudding
    mix
⅔ cup Carnation Nonfat Dry
    Milk Powder
¼ cup (1 ounce) chopped
    walnuts
⅓ cup (1 medium) mashed
    ripe banana
1 egg or equivalent in egg
    substitute, slightly
    beaten

1 cup (one 8-ounce can)
    crushed pineapple,
    packed in fruit juice,
    drained and liquid
    reserved ☆
½ cup unsweetened
    applesauce
1 teaspoon vanilla extract
3 cups sliced fresh
    strawberries ☆
⅓ cup Sugar Twin or
    Sprinkle Sweet
½ cup Cool Whip Lite

Preheat oven to 350 degrees. Spray an 8-by-8-inch baking dish with butter-flavored cooking spray. In a large bowl, combine baking mix, dry pudding mix, and dry milk powder. Stir in walnuts. In a small bowl, combine banana, egg, drained pineapple, applesauce, and vanilla extract. Add enough water to reserved pineapple juice to make ½ cup liquid. Stir into banana mixture. Add banana mixture to baking mix mixture. Stir gently to combine. Pour mixture into prepared baking dish. Bake 35 minutes or until golden brown. Place baking dish on a wire rack and allow to cool. Meanwhile, in a medium bowl, mash 1 cup strawberries with a fork. Stir in Sugar Twin. Add remaining strawberries. Mix well to combine. Cover and refrigerate at least 30 minutes. Cut shortcakes into 8 pieces. For each serving, place 1 piece shortcake on dessert plate, spoon full ¼ cup strawberry mixture over shortcake, and top with 1 tablespoon Cool Whip Lite.

Each serving equals:

HE: 1 Bread, 1 Fruit, ¼ Skim Milk, ¼ Fat, ¼ Protein, ¼ Slider, 5 Optional Calories

----

213 Calories, 5 gm Fat, 6 gm Protein, 36 gm Carbohydrate, 460 mg Sodium, 1 gm Fiber

----

DIABETIC: 1½ Starch, 1 Fruit, 1 Fat

My husband has a heart condition and must really watch his cholesterol count. Ever since his bypass surgery three years ago, it has been a real chore to give him meals he enjoys. That is, until I began receiving your recipes.

—D.M., WI

Georgia Peach Cobbler

------------------- ■ -------------------

When I first visited the southern state famed for its succulent peaches, I knew I'd have to create a dessert that did justice to that sweet and beautiful fruit. Since fresh peaches have a short season out here in Iowa, I've chosen the canned variety to star in this cozy delight. Of course, if you've got 'em fresh, go for it!

Serves 6

1 (4-serving) package
  JELL-O sugar-free vanilla
  cook-and-serve pudding
  mix
1 (4-serving) package
  JELL-O sugar-free lemon
  gelatin
water
2 cups (one 16-ounce can)
  sliced peaches, packed in
  fruit juice, drained and
  liquid reserved ☆

2 tablespoons (½ ounce)
  chopped pecans
1 (7.5-ounce) can Pillsbury
  refrigerated buttermilk
  biscuits
1 tablespoon Sugar Twin or
  Sprinkle Sweet
½ teaspoon ground nutmeg

Preheat oven to 415 degrees. Spray an 8-by-8-inch baking dish with butter-flavored cooking spray. In a medium saucepan, combine dry pudding mix and dry gelatin. Add enough water to reserved fruit juice to make 1⅓ cups liquid. Add liquid to dry pudding mixture. Mix gently to combine. Stir in peaches. Cook over medium heat, stirring constantly, until mixture thickens and starts to boil. Remove from heat. Pour hot peach mixture into prepared baking dish. Sprinkle pecans evenly over hot peach mixture. Separate biscuits and cut each into 4 pieces. Evenly drop biscuit pieces over top. Lightly spray biscuit pieces with butter-flavored cooking spray. In a small bowl, combine Sugar Twin and nutmeg. Sprinkle mixture evenly over top of biscuit pieces. Bake 12 to 15 minutes or until biscuits are golden brown. Place baking dish on a wire rack and allow to cool. Divide into 6 servings. Good warm or cold.

Each serving equals:

HE: 1¼ Bread, ⅔ Fruit, ⅓ Fat, ¼ Slider, 1 Optional Calorie

167 Calories, 3 gm Fat, 4 gm Protein, 31 gm Carbohydrate, 420 mg Sodium, 3 gm Fiber

DIABETIC: 1 Starch, 1 Fruit

> *My husband is a diabetic of 40 years, and trying to get him to eat right has always been a challenge. For most of those 40 years eating low-sugar, low-fat foods was not only not very tasty, it just wasn't enjoyable. But, boy, have you made a change. My husband loves the food and it doesn't take me half a day to prepare it. You have made a wonderful change for the better in my husband's life. Keep up the marvelous work!*
>
> —B.E., IA

Strawberry Shortcakes with Banana Cream Sauce

----------------◼----------------

I used to think I loved strawberries more than anyone I ever met, but that was before I met dozens of men in towns all over the country who celebrate the ruby-colored jewel of fruits as fiercely as I do. Guys, this one's for you!

Serves 4

¾ cup Bisquick Reduced Fat Baking Mix

1 cup Carnation Nonfat Dry Milk Powder ☆

¼ cup Sugar Twin or Sprinkle Sweet

2 tablespoons Kraft reduced-fat mayonnaise

1 teaspoon vanilla extract

1⅔ cups water ☆

1 (4-serving) package JELL-O sugar-free instant banana cream pudding mix

½ cup Cool Whip Lite ☆

2 cups sliced fresh strawberries

Preheat oven to 415 degrees. Spray a cookie sheet with butter-flavored cooking spray. In a medium bowl, combine baking mix, ⅓ cup dry milk powder, and Sugar Twin. Add mayonnaise, vanilla extract, and ⅓ cup water. Mix well to combine. Drop by spoonfuls onto prepared cookie sheet to form 4 shortcakes. Bake 8 to 12 minutes. Place cookie sheet on a wire rack and allow shortcakes to cool slightly while preparing cream sauce. In a medium bowl, combine dry pudding mix, remaining ⅔ cup dry milk powder, and remaining 1⅓ cups water. Mix well using a wire whisk. Blend in ¼ cup Cool Whip Lite. For each serving, place 1 shortcake in dessert dish, arrange ½ cup strawberries over shortcake, spoon ½ cup banana cream sauce over strawberries, and top with 1 tablespoon Cool Whip Lite.

Each serving equals:

HE: 1 Bread, ½ Fruit, ¼ Skim Milk, ½ Slider, 16 Optional Calories

----

215 Calories, 3 gm Fat, 8 gm Protein, 39 gm Carbohydrate, 637 mg Sodium, 2 gm Fiber

----

DIABETIC: 2 Starch, ½ Fruit

Lemon Cheesecake
with Lemon Glaze

------------------■------------------

Would you believe I've got a Healthy Exchanges cheese-cake fan club made up entirely of men? Well, not really, but hundreds of men have volunteered to be charter members—especially if they get to enjoy a piece of healthy cheesecake *every* day!
Serves 8

2 (4-serving) packages JELL-O sugar-free instant vanilla pudding mix ☆

2 (4-serving) packages JELL-O sugar-free lemon gelatin ☆

2 (8-ounce) packages Philadelphia fat-free cream cheese

⅔ cup Carnation Nonfat Dry Milk Powder

1¾ cups Diet Mountain Dew ☆

1 cup Cool Whip Lite ☆

1 (6-ounce) Keebler shortbread or graham cracker piecrust

In a small bowl, reserve 1 tablespoon dry pudding mix and 2 teaspoons dry gelatin. In a large bowl, stir cream cheese with spoon until soft. Add dry milk powder, remaining dry pudding mix, and remaining dry gelatin to cream cheese. Stir in 1¼ cups Diet Mountain Dew. Mix well using a wire whisk. Blend in ½ cup Cool Whip Lite. Spread pudding mixture evenly into piecrust. In a small saucepan, combine reserved pudding mix and reserved gelatin with remaining ½ cup Diet Mountain Dew. Cook over medium heat, stirring constantly, until mixture starts to boil. Place saucepan on a wire rack and allow to cool 10 minutes. Drizzle mixture evenly over top of pie. Refrigerate at least 2 hours. Cut into 8 servings. Top each serving with 1 tablespoon Cool Whip Lite.

Each serving equals:

HE: 1 Protein, ½ Bread, ¼ Skim Milk, 1 Slider, 19 Optional Calories

205 Calories, 5 gm Fat, 12 gm Protein, 28 gm Carbohydrate, 830 mg Sodium, 1 gm Fiber

DIABETIC: 1½ Starch, 1 Meat, 1 Fat

Raspberry-Pear Cheesecake

———————————————————————————— ■ ————————————————————————————

This is such a colorful dish, it would easily be the centerpiece of a restaurant dessert tray.   *Serves 8*

2 cups (one 16-ounce can)   *1 (6-ounce) Keebler*
*   pears, packed in fruit*   *   shortbread piecrust*
*   juice, undrained*   *1 (4-serving) package JELL-O*
2 (8-ounce) packages   *   sugar-free vanilla cook-*
*   Philadelphia fat-free*   *   and-serve pudding mix*
*   cream cheese*   *1 (4-serving) package JELL-O*
1 (4-serving) package JELL-O   *   sugar-free raspberry*
*   sugar-free instant vanilla*   *   gelatin*
*   pudding mix*   *1 cup water*
⅔ cup Carnation Nonfat Dry   *1½ cups frozen unsweetened*
*   Milk Powder*   *   raspberries*
¼ cup Cool Whip Lite

Reserve half of pear pieces and set aside. Pour remaining pears
and juice in a blender container. Cover and process on High 10
seconds or until smooth. Set aside. In a large bowl, stir cream
cheese with a spoon until soft. Add dry instant pudding mix, dry
milk powder, and blended pear liquid. Blend in Cool Whip Lite.
Mix well using a wire whisk. Spread mixture evenly into
piecrust. Refrigerate. Meanwhile, in a medium saucepan, combine dry cook-and-serve pudding mix, dry gelatin, and water.
Cook over medium heat, stirring constantly, until mixture
thickens and starts to boil. Remove from heat. Coarsely chop remaining pear pieces. Gently stir pear pieces and frozen raspberries into hot pudding mixture. Place pan on a wire rack and let
set 5 minutes. Evenly spoon fruit mixture over filling. Refrigerate at least 1 hour. Cut into 8 servings.

Each serving equals:

HE: 1 Protein, ¾ Fruit, ½ Bread, ¼ Skim Milk, 1 Slider, 3 Optional Calories

241 Calories, 5 gm Fat, 12 gm Protein, 37 gm Carbohydrate,
718 mg Sodium, 2 gm Fiber

DIABETIC: 1½ Starch, 1 Meat, 1 Fruit, ½ Fat

Orange Push-Up Cheesecake

------------------------------ ❄ ------------------------------

T he best ice cream treat I can remember from childhood is those orange push-ups, so I just had to invent a dessert that recalled the scrumptious taste beloved by all kids—and the men they grew up to be! This tastes amazingly like the dream dessert you remember.   *Serves 8*

2 (8-ounce) packages
Philadelphia fat-free
cream cheese
1 (4-serving) package JELL-O
sugar-free instant vanilla
pudding mix
1 (4-serving) package JELL-O
sugar-free orange gelatin

⅔ cup Carnation Nonfat Dry
Milk Powder
1 cup unsweetened orange
juice
¾ cup Cool Whip Lite ☆
1 (6-ounce) Keebler
shortbread piecrust
2 tablespoons flaked coconut

In a large bowl, stir cream cheese with a spoon until soft. Add dry pudding mix, dry gelatin, dry milk powder, and orange juice. Mix well using a wire whisk. Blend in ¼ cup Cool Whip Lite. Spread mixture evenly into piecrust. Refrigerate at least 1 hour. Cut into 8 servings. Top each serving with 1 tablespoon Cool Whip Lite and 1 teaspoon coconut.

Each serving equals:

HE: ½ Bread, ½ Protein, ¼ Skim Milk, ¼ Fruit, ¾ Slider, 11 Optional Calories

205 Calories, 5 gm Fat, 12 gm Protein, 28 gm Carbohydrate, 554 mg Sodium, 1 gm Fiber

DIABETIC: 1½ Starch, 1 Fat, ½ Meat

Hawaiian Pineapple Dew Cheesecake

--------- ❋ ---------

S ometimes an ingredient inspires a wonderful new recipe, and I have to confess that when I saw the Hawaiian Pineapple JELL-O, I knew I could make a terrifically flavorful cheesecake, rich enough to make Cliff feel as though he'd had a vacation to Maui! Won't you join us at a dessert luau with this as the centerpiece?

Serves 8

2 (8-ounce) packages Philadelphia fat-free cream cheese

1 (4-serving) package JELL-O sugar-free instant vanilla pudding mix

1 (4-serving) package JELL-O sugar-free Hawaiian Pineapple Gelatin

⅔ cup Carnation Nonfat Dry Milk Powder

1 cup (one 8-ounce can) crushed pineapple, packed in fruit juice, undrained

⅔ cup Diet Mountain Dew

1 (6-ounce) Keebler graham cracker piecrust

¾ cup Cool Whip Lite

2 tablespoons (½ ounce) chopped pecans

In a large bowl, stir cream cheese with a spoon until soft. Add dry pudding mix, dry gelatin, dry milk powder, undrained pineapple, and Diet Mountain Dew. Mix well using a wire whisk. Spread mixture evenly into piecrust. Refrigerate 10 minutes. Spread Cool Whip Lite evenly over set filling. Sprinkle pecans evenly over the top. Refrigerate at least 1 hour. Cut into 8 servings.

Each serving equals:

HE: ½ Bread, ½ Protein, ¼ Skim Milk, ¼ Fruit, ¼ Fat, 1 Slider, 3 Optional Calories

227 Calories, 7 gm Fat, 12 gm Protein, 29 gm Carbohydrate, 701 mg Sodium, 1 gm Fiber

DIABETIC: 2 Starch, 1 Fat, ½ Meat

Log Cabin Cheesecake

----------------- ❄ -----------------

D o the men you know like a little pancake with their maple syrup? My son James is a big fan of the sweet goodness of syrup, so this cheesecake pleased him no end. It may remind you of winter in New England, snow, and roaring fires—or you just may think of nothing else but how luscious it is.

Serves 8

2 (8-ounce) packages
    Philadelphia fat-free
    cream cheese
1 (4-serving) package JELL-O
    sugar-free instant vanilla
    pudding mix
⅔ cup Carnation Nonfat Dry
    Milk Powder
1 cup Cary's Sugar Free Maple
    Syrup

1 cup Cool Whip Lite ☆
1 (6-ounce) Keebler graham
    cracker piecrust
1 teaspoon coconut extract
2 tablespoons flaked coconut
2 tablespoons (½ ounce)
    chopped pecans

In a large bowl, stir cream cheese with a spoon until soft. Add dry pudding mix, dry milk powder, and maple syrup. Mix well using a wire whisk. Blend in ¼ cup Cool Whip Lite. Spread mixture evenly into piecrust. Refrigerate while preparing topping. In a small bowl, combine remaining ¾ cup Cool Whip Lite and coconut extract. Spread mixture evenly over filling. Evenly sprinkle coconut and pecans over top. Refrigerate at least 1 hour. Cut into 8 servings.

Each serving equals:

HE: 1 Protein, ½ Bread, ¼ Skim Milk, ¼ Fat, 1 Slider, 14 Optional Calories

223 Calories, 7 gm Fat, 11 gm Protein, 29 gm Carbohydrate, 714 mg Sodium, 1 gm Fiber

DIABETIC: 2 Starch, 1 Meat, ½ Fat

Peanut Butter and Jelly Cheesecake

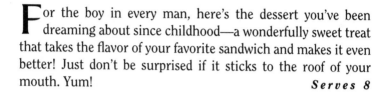

For the boy in every man, here's the dessert you've been dreaming about since childhood—a wonderfully sweet treat that takes the flavor of your favorite sandwich and makes it even better! Just don't be surprised if it sticks to the roof of your mouth. Yum!

Serves 8

2 (8-ounce) packages
    Philadelphia fat-free
    cream cheese
¼ cup Peter Pan reduced-fat
    peanut butter
1 (4-serving) package JELL-O
    sugar-free instant vanilla
    pudding mix
⅔ cup Carnation Nonfat Dry
    Milk Powder

1 cup water
¾ cup Cool Whip Lite ☆
1 (6-ounce) Keebler graham
    cracker piecrust
½ cup grape spreadable fruit
    spread
2 tablespoons (½ ounce) dry-
    roasted peanuts

In a large bowl, stir cream cheese and peanut butter with a spoon until blended and soft. Add dry pudding mix, dry milk powder, and water. Mix well using a wire whisk. Blend in ¼ cup Cool Whip Lite. Spread mixture evenly into piecrust. Refrigerate while preparing topping. In a small bowl, stir fruit spread with a spoon until soft. Add remaining ½ cup Cool Whip Lite. Mix gently to combine. Evenly spread topping mixture over filling mixture. Sprinkle peanuts evenly over top. Refrigerate at least 30 minutes. Cut into 8 servings.

Each serving equals:

HE: 1½ Protein, 1 Fruit, ½ Fat, ½ Bread, ¼ Skim Milk, 1 Slider,
6 Optional Calories

289 Calories, 9 gm Fat, 13 gm Protein, 39 gm Carbohydrate,
721 mg Sodium, 1 gm Fiber

DIABETIC: 1½ Meat, 1½ Starch, 1 Fruit, 1 Fat

Mom's Apple Pie

------------- ❋ -------------

She used to make it for you just to see you smile, but now you can make it for yourself! This healthy version still looks, tastes, and smells like the one that brought you racing to the kitchen for a taste hot from the oven. *Mmmmm . . . it's good.*   *Serves 8*

1 (4-serving) package JELL-O
    sugar-free vanilla cook-
    and-serve pudding mix
1 cup unsweetened apple juice
1½ teaspoons apple pie
    spice ☆

3 cups (6 small) cored,
    unpeeled, chopped cooking
    apples
1 (6-ounce) Keebler graham
    cracker piecrust
¾ cup Cool Whip Lite

Preheat oven to 375 degrees. In a medium saucepan, combine dry pudding mix, apple juice, and 1 teaspoon apple pie spice. Add apples. Mix well to combine. Cook over medium heat, stirring often, until mixture thickens and starts to boil. Pour hot mixture into piecrust. Bake 20 minutes. Place pie on a wire rack and allow to cool completely. When cooled, spread Cool Whip Lite evenly over apple mixture. Evenly sprinkle remaining ½ teaspoon apple pie spice over top. Refrigerate until ready to serve. Cut into 8 servings.

Each serving equals:

HE: 1 Fruit, ½ Bread, ¾ Slider, 12 Optional Calories

170 Calories, 6 gm Fat, 1 gm Protein, 28 gm Carbohydrate, 193 mg Sodium, 1 gm Fiber

DIABETIC: 1 Fruit, 1 Starch, 1 Fat

Blueberry Thrill Pie

------------ ❄ ------------

R emember how Richie Cunningham on *Happy Days* used to sing Fats Domino's hit "Blueberry Hill" (where he found his "thrill") when he was really excited? Well, here's the cheesecake that just may drive you to burst uncontrollably into song!

Serves 8

3 cups fresh blueberries ☆
1 (6-ounce) Keebler
  shortbread piecrust
1 (4-serving) package JELL-O
  sugar-free vanilla cook-
  and-serve pudding mix

1 (4-serving) package JELL-O
  sugar-free lemon gelatin
1¼ cups water
1 teaspoon coconut extract ☆
¾ cup Cool Whip Lite
2 tablespoons flaked coconut

Layer 2½ cups blueberries in bottom of piecrust. In a medium saucepan, combine dry pudding mix, dry gelatin, water, and remaining ½ cup blueberries. Cook over medium heat, stirring constantly, until mixture starts to boil and blueberries soften. Remove from heat. Stir in ½ teaspoon coconut extract. Pour hot mixture over blueberries. Refrigerate at least 2 hours. In a small bowl, combine Cool Whip Lite and remaining ½ teaspoon coconut extract. Spread mixture evenly over top of pie. Evenly sprinkle coconut over top. Refrigerate at least 1 hour. Cut into 8 servings.

Each serving equals:

HE: ½ Bread, ½ Fruit, 1 Slider

178 Calories, 6 gm Fat, 2 gm Protein, 29 gm Carbohydrate, 228 mg Sodium, 2 gm Fiber

DIABETIC: 1½ Starch, 1 Fat, ½ Fruit

Heavenly Strawberry Pie

---------------------❋---------------------

he sky's no limit when it comes to the out-of-this-world flavor of that gem of all fruits, the strawberry. This one looks as good as it tastes—and it tastes *soooo* good.   *Serves 8*

2 cups sliced fresh
strawberries
1 (6-ounce) Keebler
shortbread piecrust
1 (4-serving) package JELL-O
sugar-free strawberry
gelatin
1 (4-serving) package JELL-O
sugar-free vanilla cook-
and-serve pudding mix

1½ cups + ½ teaspoon
water ☆
1 cup Cool Whip Lite
1 teaspoon coconut extract
5 to 6 drops red food
coloring ☆
2 tablespoons flaked coconut

Place sliced strawberries in piecrust. In a medium saucepan, combine dry gelatin, dry pudding mix, and 1½ cups water. Cook over medium heat, stirring constantly, until mixture thickens and starts to boil. Remove from heat. Spoon hot mixture evenly over strawberries. Refrigerate at least 2 hours. In a small bowl, combine Cool Whip Lite, coconut extract, and 2 to 3 drops red food coloring. Spread mixture evenly over set filling. In a plastic sandwich bag, combine remaining ½ teaspoon water and remaining 2 to 3 drops red food coloring. Add flaked coconut. Close bag and shake until coconut is evenly tinted pink. Place coconut in a small dish for 1 to 2 minutes to dry. Evenly sprinkle dried coconut over top of pie. Refrigerate at least 15 minutes or until ready to serve. Cut into 8 servings.

Each serving equals:

HE: ½ Bread, ¼ Fruit, 1 Slider, 9 Optional Calories

---

154 Calories, 6 gm Fat, 2 gm Protein, 23 gm Carbohydrate,
183 mg Sodium, 1 gm Fiber

DIABETIC: 1½ Starch, 1 Fat

Hawaiian Banana Butterscotch Pie

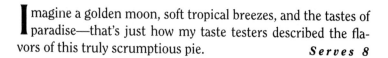

Imagine a golden moon, soft tropical breezes, and the tastes of paradise—that's just how my taste testers described the flavors of this truly scrumptious pie.

Serves 8

2 cups (2 medium) sliced
   bananas
1 (6-ounce) Keebler graham
   cracker piecrust
2 (4-serving) packages JELL-
   O sugar-free instant
   butterscotch pudding
   mix ☆
1⅓ cups Carnation Nonfat
   Dry Milk Powder ☆

2⅓ cups water ☆
½ cup Cool Whip Lite
1 teaspoon coconut extract
1 tablespoon purchased
   graham cracker crumbs or
   one (2½-inch) square
   made into crumbs
2 tablespoons (½ ounce)
   chopped pecans
1 tablespoon flaked coconut

Layer bananas in bottom of piecrust. In a medium bowl, combine 1 package dry pudding mix, ⅔ cup dry milk powder, and 1⅓ cups water. Mix well using a wire whisk. Pour pudding mixture evenly over bananas. Refrigerate while preparing topping. In same bowl, combine remaining dry pudding mix, remaining ⅔ cup dry milk powder and remaining 1 cup water. Mix well using a wire whisk. Blend in Cool Whip Lite and coconut extract. Spread topping mixture evenly over set layer. In a small bowl, combine graham cracker crumbs, pecans, and coconut. Evenly sprinkle crumb mixture over top. Refrigerate at least 1 hour. Cut into 8 servings

HINT: To prevent bananas from turning brown, mix with 1 teaspoon lemon juice or sprinkle with Fruit Fresh.

Each serving equals:

HE: ½ Bread, ½ Fruit, ½ Skim Milk, ¼ Fat, 1 Slider, 10 Optional Calories

231 Calories, 7 gm Fat, 5 gm Protein, 37 gm Carbohydrate,
545 mg Sodium, 1 gm Fiber

DIABETIC: 1½ Starch, 1 Fat, ½ Fruit, ½ Skim Milk

Chocolate Rum Pecan Pie

This is my version of chocolate rum balls, but in pie form. It couldn't be simpler to stir up, and it couldn't be a better dessert to win the heart of every man who loves the blend of chocolate, rum, and pecans. *Serves 8*

1 (4-serving) package JELL-O
   sugar-free chocolate cook-
   and-serve pudding mix
⅔ cup Carnation Nonfat Dry
   Milk Powder
1½ cups water

1 teaspoon rum extract
½ cup (2 ounces) chopped
   pecans
1 (6-ounce) Keebler chocolate
   piecrust

In a medium saucepan, combine dry pudding mix, dry milk powder, and water. Cook over medium heat, stirring constantly, until mixture thickens and starts to boil. Remove from heat. Stir in rum extract and pecans. Pour hot mixture into piecrust. Refrigerate at least 2 hours. Cut into 8 servings.

Each serving equals:

HE: 1 Fat, ½ Bread, ¼ Skim Milk, ¾ Slider

194 Calories, 10 gm Fat, 4 gm Protein, 22 gm Carbohydrate,
296 mg Sodium, 1 gm Fiber

DIABETIC: 1½ Starch, 1 Fat

Better Than Candy Pie

--------------------■--------------------

The name for this outrageous dessert came right from the men who tried it. Each one took a big bite, then smiled and said, "This is better than candy." That's saying a lot.

Serves 8

1 cup (1 medium) diced
  banana
1 (6-ounce) Keebler chocolate-
  flavored piecrust
¼ cup (1 ounce) chopped dry-
  roasted peanuts ☆
1 (4-serving) package JELL-O
  sugar-free instant
  butterscotch pudding mix
⅔ cup Carnation Nonfat Dry
  Milk Powder

1¼ cups water
2 tablespoons Peter Pan
  reduced-fat peanut butter
¾ cup Cool Whip Lite
2 (2½-inch) Nabisco
  Chocolate Graham
  Crackers, made into fine
  crumbs

Layer bananas in bottom of piecrust. Sprinkle 2 tablespoons peanuts over bananas. In a large bowl, combine dry pudding mix, dry milk powder, and water. Mix well using a wire whisk. Blend in peanut butter until mixture is smooth. Pour pudding mixture evenly over bananas and peanuts. Refrigerate 5 minutes. Spread Cool Whip Lite evenly over set filling. In a small bowl, combine remaining 2 tablespoons peanuts and cracker crumbs. Evenly sprinkle mixture over top. Refrigerate at least 1 hour. Cut into 8 servings.

HINT: To prevent bananas from turning brown, mix with 1 teaspoon lemon juice or sprinkle with Fruit Fresh.

Each serving equals:

HE: ½ Bread, ½ Fat, ⅓ Protein, ¼ Fruit, ¼ Skim Milk

----

217 Calories, 9 gm Fat, 5 gm Protein, 29 gm Carbohydrate,
324 mg Sodium, 1 gm Fiber

DIABETIC: 2 Starch, 1 Fat

Cherry Crumb Pie

------------------ ❄ ------------------

Here's an old-fashioned, wholesome, and oh-so-sweet version of cherry pie, made even better by the addition of crumb topping just like the kind Grandma used to make. I bet George Washington isn't the only man who'd chop down a cherry tree in order to enjoy this dessert. Cliff raved about this pie for two months to anyone who came within earshot.

Serves 8

1 (4-serving) package JELL-O
    sugar-free vanilla cook-
    and-serve pudding mix
1 (4-serving) package JELL-O
    sugar-free cherry gelatin
½ cup water
2 cups (one 16-ounce can)
    tart red cherries, packed in
    water, undrained
1 (6-ounce) Keebler graham
    cracker piecrust

6 tablespoons purchased
    graham-cracker crumbs or
    6 (2½-inch) squares made
    into crumbs
2 tablespoons Sugar Twin or
    Sprinkle Sweet
2 tablespoons (½ ounce)
    chopped pecans

Preheat oven to 375 degrees. In a medium saucepan, combine dry pudding mix, dry gelatin, and water. Stir in undrained cherries. Cook over medium heat, stirring often, until mixture thickens and starts to boil, being careful not to crush cherries. Place pan on a wire rack and let set 5 minutes. Spoon cherry mixture into piecrust. In a medium bowl, combine graham cracker crumbs, Sugar Twin, and pecans. Evenly sprinkle crumb mixture over top. Bake 12 to 15 minutes. Place pie plate on a wire rack and allow to cool completely. Cut into 8 servings.

Each serving equals:

HE: ¾ Bread, ½ Fruit, ¼ Fat, ¾ Slider, 17 Optional Calories

183 Calories, 7 gm Fat, 3 gm Protein, 27 gm Carbohydrate, 259 mg Sodium, 2 gm Fiber

DIABETIC: 1½ Starch, 1 Fat, ½ Fruit

Hawaiian Banana Split Meringue Pie

-----------------------------------■-----------------------------------

I created this pie on Christmas Day 1995. It was the first
Christmas since I became a mom that I didn't have my kids
here, so it was just Cliff and me. I decided to invent something
really special because of the holiday. Cliff thought it was the best
Christmas present I'd ever given him! With the meringue
mounded high, it looks out of this world, smells gorgeous, and
tastes great! *Serves 8*

1 refrigerated unbaked 9-inch
   Pillsbury piecrust
1 (4-serving) package JELL-O
   sugar-free vanilla cook-
   and-serve pudding mix
1 (4-serving) package JELL-O
   sugar-free strawberry
   gelatin
1 cup (one 8-ounce can)
   crushed pineapple, packed
   in fruit juice, undrained

½ cup water
2 cups frozen unsweetened
   strawberries
1 cup (1 medium) diced
   banana
6 egg whites
½ cup Sugar Twin or Sprinkle
   Sweet
1 teaspoon coconut extract
2 tablespoons flaked coconut

Preheat oven to 415 degrees. Place piecrust in a 9-inch pie plate.
Flute edges and prick bottom and sides with a fork. Bake 9 to 11
minutes or until lightly browned. Place pie plate on a wire rack
and allow to cool completely. Meanwhile, lower oven temperature to 350 degrees. In a large saucepan, combine dry pudding
mix, dry gelatin, undrained pineapple, and water. Stir in frozen
strawberries. Cook over medium heat, stirring often, until mixture thickens and begins to boil, and strawberries start to thaw.
Remove from heat. Stir in bananas. Place on a wire rack and
allow to cool 5 minutes. Meanwhile, in a medium bowl, whip egg
whites with an electric mixer, whipping until soft peaks form.
Add Sugar Twin and coconut extract. Continue beating until stiff
peaks form. Spoon partially cooled fruit mixture into piecrust.
Spread meringue mixture evenly over filling, being sure to seal
completely to edges of piecrust. Evenly sprinkle coconut over

top. Bake 15 minutes or until meringue starts to turn golden brown. Place pie plate on a wire rack and allow to cool 15 minutes. Refrigerate for at least 1 hour. Cut into 8 servings.

HINTS: 1. Egg whites beat best at room temperature.
2. Meringue pie cuts easily if you dip a sharp knife in warm water before slicing.

Each serving equals:

HE: ¾ Fruit, ½ Bread, ¼ Protein, ¾ Slider, 15 Optional Calories

---

195 Calories, 7 gm Fat, 4 gm Protein, 29 gm Carbohydrate, 273 mg Sodium, 1 gm Fiber

---

DIABETIC: 1 Fruit, 1 Starch, 1 Fat

> *My husband is not only diabetic, he had a bypass surgery last December, so you can see that we have to change a lot of old habits to improve our health and keep it that way. I really like the recipes using foods that we used to use before we started falling apart as we reached our sixties. Thanks for the help I've been wanting and not finding in other cookbooks!*
>
> —M.R., IA

Carrot Pineapple Cake with Vanilla Cream Topping

------------------------------ ❄ ------------------------------

Cliff loves carrot cake, and this one got his attention so fast, even I was surprised. He praised the blend of spice cake and creamy topping, then showed he meant what he said by asking to have it again the next day. *Serves 8*

1½ cups all-purpose flour
1 teaspoon baking powder
1 teaspoon baking soda
1 teaspoon apple pie spice
½ cup Sugar Twin or Sprinkle Sweet ☆
2 tablespoons vegetable oil
2 eggs or equivalent in egg substitute
1½ teaspoons vanilla extract ☆
1 cup (one 8-ounce can)

crushed pineapple, packed in fruit juice, drained and liquid reserved ☆
¼ cup Yoplait plain fat-free yogurt
1 cup finely shredded carrots
¼ cup raisins
1 (8-ounce) package Philadelphia fat-free cream cheese
¼ cup Cool Whip Lite

Preheat oven to 350 degrees. Spray an 8-by-8-inch baking dish with butter-flavored cooking spray. In a large bowl, combine flour, baking powder, baking soda, apple pie spice, and 6 tablespoons Sugar Twin. In a small bowl, combine oil, eggs, 1 teaspoon vanilla extract, ¼ cup reserved pineapple juice, pineapple, and yogurt. Mix well using a wire whisk. Add to flour mixture. Stir just to combine. Add carrots and raisins. Mix gently to combine. Pour into prepared baking dish. Bake 20 to 25 minutes. Place baking dish on a wire rack and allow to cool. In a medium bowl, stir cream cheese with a spoon until soft. Add 2 tablespoons reserved pineapple juice, remaining ½ teaspoon vanilla extract, remaining 2 tablespoons Sugar Twin, and Cool Whip Lite. Mix well to combine. Spread cream cheese mixture evenly over cooled cake. Cut into 8 servings.

Each serving equals:

HE: 1 Bread, ¾ Fat, ¾ Protein (¼ limited), ½ Fruit, ¼ Vegetable, ¼ Slider

----

205 Calories, 5 gm Fat, 9 gm Protein, 31 gm Carbohydrate,
418 mg Sodium, 2 gm Fiber

DIABETIC: 1½ Starch, 1 Meat, ½ Fat, ½ Fruit

*Your recipes are great, really wonderful. My husband is such a big
eater, but using your recipes, I don't need to feel like I have to stop
from enjoying his food, because they are so good for him. I can't
begin to count how many times I've fixed your Healthy JO's—they are
the greatest thing next to making love, my husband says. Isn't he
the cute one?*

—S.F., IA

Banana and Blueberry Party Cake

----------------------------■----------------------------

I named this cake a "party" because of how all these flavors make merry in your mouth. It's a perfect blend of sweet and creamy, fruity and nutty—and anyone who tries it will probably want to give you a thank-you party!   *Serves 12*

> *1½ cups all-purpose flour*
> *½ cup Sugar Twin or Sprinkle Sweet*
> *½ teaspoon baking powder*
> *1 teaspoon baking soda*
> *1 teaspoon apple pie spice*
> *¼ cup (1 ounce) chopped pecans ☆*
> *⅔ cup (2 ripe medium) mashed bananas*
> *¾ cup Kraft fat-free mayonnaise*
> *2 teaspoons vanilla extract ☆*
>
> *3 cups water ☆*
> *1 (4-serving) package JELL-O sugar-free vanilla cook-and-serve pudding mix*
> *1 (4-serving) package JELL-O sugar-free lemon gelatin*
> *1½ cups fresh blueberries*
> *1 (4-serving) package JELL-O sugar-free instant banana cream pudding mix*
> *1 cup Carnation Nonfat Dry Milk Powder*
> *1 cup Cool Whip Lite*

Preheat oven to 350 degrees. Spray a 9-by-9-inch cake pan with butter-flavored cooking spray. In a large bowl, combine flour, Sugar Twin, baking powder, baking soda, apple pie spice, and 2 tablespoons pecans. Mix well to combine. In a small bowl, combine mashed bananas, mayonnaise, 1 teaspoon vanilla extract, and ½ cup water. Add banana mixture to flour mixture. Mix gently just to combine. Spread mixture into prepared cake pan. Bake 20 to 24 minutes or until a toothpick inserted in center comes out clean. Meanwhile, in a medium saucepan, combine dry cook-and-serve pudding mix, dry gelatin, and 1¼ cups water. Cook over medium heat, stirring constantly, until mixture thickens and starts to boil. Stir in blueberries. Remove from heat. Place cake pan on a wire rack and allow to cool 30 minutes. Spread cooled blueberry mixture over cooled cake. In a medium bowl, combine dry instant pudding mix, dry milk powder, and remaining 1¼ cups water. Mix well using a wire whisk. Blend in Cool Whip Lite and remaining 1 teaspoon vanilla extract. Spread pudding mixture evenly over cooled cake. Sprinkle remaining 2 tablespoons pecans evenly over top. Refrigerate at least 30 minutes. Cut into 12 servings. Refrigerate leftovers.

HINT: Frozen, unsweetened blueberries, thawed and drained, may be used instead of fresh.

Each serving equals:

HE: ⅔ Bread, ½ Fruit, ⅓ Fat, ¼ Skim Milk, ½ Slider, 6 Optional Calories

150 Calories, 2 gm Fat, 4 gm Protein, 29 gm Carbohydrate,
455 mg Sodium, 1 gm Fiber

DIABETIC: 1½ Starch, ½ Fruit

My hubby, "Sonnie," and I started cooking healthy six weeks ago. I got your cookbook sometime ago but couldn't get started. Well, now we have—and Sonnie has lost 24 pounds and 17 for me.

Chocolate Hawaiian Dessert Cake

------------------------------■------------------------------

I t's no surprise that the favored honeymoon destination of
men everywhere is those romantic islands where soft breezes
blow and you can enjoy so much good food. This dessert is easy
to fix but tastes as though hours of hard labor were required. My
grandbabies gobbled it down as fast as they could!

Serves 12

1½ cups all-purpose flour	*sugar-free instant*
¼ cup unsweetened cocoa	*chocolate pudding mix*
1¼ teaspoons baking soda	*1 cup (one 8-ounce can)*
½ cup Sugar Twin or Sprinkle	*crushed pineapple, packed*
Sweet	*in fruit juice, undrained*
1 cup Carnation Nonfat Dry	*1 cup (1 medium) finely diced*
Milk Powder ☆	*banana*
¾ cup Kraft fat-free	*1 teaspoon coconut extract*
mayonnaise	*½ cup Cool Whip Lite*
1¾ cups water ☆	*3 tablespoons (¾ ounce)*
1½ teaspoons vanilla extract	*chopped pecans*
1 (4-serving) package JELL-O	*2 tablespoons flaked coconut*

Preheat oven to 350 degrees. Spray a 9-by-9-inch cake pan with
butter-flavored cooking spray. In a large bowl, combine flour,
cocoa, baking soda, Sugar Twin, and ⅓ cup dry milk powder. Add
mayonnaise, 1 cup water, and vanilla extract. Mix well to combine. Spread mixture into prepared cake pan. Bake 20 to 24 minutes or until a toothpick inserted in center comes out clean. Do
not overbake. Place cake pan on a wire rack and allow to cool 30
minutes. In a medium bowl, combine dry pudding mix, remaining ⅔ cup dry milk powder, remaining ¾ cup water, and
undrained pineapple. Mix well, using a wire whisk. Stir in bananas. Add coconut extract and Cool Whip Lite. Mix gently to
combine. Spread pudding mixture evenly over cooled cake.
Sprinkle pecans and coconut evenly over top. Refrigerate at least
30 minutes. Cut into 12 servings. Refrigerate leftovers.

HINT: To prevent bananas from turning brown, mix with 1 teaspoon lemon juice or sprinkle with Fruit Fresh.

Each serving equals:

HE: ⅔ Bread, ⅓ Fruit, ¼ Skim Milk, ¼ Fat, ½ Slider, 6 Optional Calories

150 Calories, 2 gm Fat, 4 gm Protein, 29 gm Carbohydrate,
356 mg Sodium, 2 gm Fiber

DIABETIC: 1½ Starch, ½ Fruit

> *My husband and I are really enjoying your recipes. My husband says*
> *they taste "like real food"!*
>
> —M.H., IL

Grandpa's Old-Time Spice Cake

This one's for Cliff, the youngest grandpa I know. He'd be glad to have me serve spice cake three times a day—especially one that tastes this old-fashioned and this good. When I want to convince Cliff to do it "my way," this cake can be *very* persuasive!

Serves 8

1½ cups all-purpose flour
¾ cup Sugar Twin or Sprinkle
   Sweet
1½ teaspoons baking soda
1 teaspoon apple pie spice
¾ cup raisins

½ cup Kraft fat-free
   mayonnaise
¼ cup Yoplait plain fat-free
   yogurt
1 cup unsweetened apple juice
1 teaspoon vanilla extract

Preheat oven to 350 degrees. Spray an 8-by-8-inch baking dish with butter-flavored cooking spray. In a large bowl, combine flour, Sugar Twin, baking soda, and apple pie spice. Stir in raisins. Add mayonnaise, yogurt, apple juice, and vanilla extract. Mix well to combine. Spread mixture into prepared baking dish. Bake 30 to 35 minutes or until a toothpick inserted in center comes out clean. Place baking dish on a wire rack and allow to cool. Cut into 8 servings.

HINT: Also good with ¼ cup chopped walnuts stirred in with raisins.

Each serving equals:

HE: 1 Fruit, 1 Bread, ¼ Slider, 4 Optional Calories

164 Calories, 0 gm Fat, 3 gm Protein, 38 gm Carbohydrate,
354 mg Sodium, 1 gm Fiber

DIABETIC: 1 Fruit, 1 Starch

Pineapple Graham Cracker Scallop

------------------------------ ❄ ------------------------------

Warm, cozy fruit desserts bring back such delicious family memories, don't they? Here's a fragrant treat that combines lush pineapple with the crunch of nuts and graham crackers. It's downright mouthwatering, according to my male taste testers, even little Josh with his two-year-old taste buds.

Serves 8

1 cup + 2 tablespoons purchased graham cracker crumbs or 18 (2½-inch) squares made into crumbs
1 (4-serving) package JELL-O sugar-free instant butterscotch pudding mix
1 teaspoon baking powder
1 teaspoon ground cinnamon
¼ cup (1 ounce) chopped walnuts
2 cups (two 8-ounce cans) crushed pineapple, packed in fruit juice, drained and liquid reserved
water
1 egg, beaten, or equivalent in egg substitute
1 teaspoon vanilla extract
2 tablespoons skim milk

Preheat oven to 350 degrees. Spray an 8-by-8-inch baking dish with butter-flavored cooking spray. In a large bowl, combine cracker crumbs, dry pudding mix, baking powder, and cinnamon. Blend in walnuts. Add enough water to reserved pineapple juice to make ½ cup liquid. In a small bowl, combine egg, vanilla extract, and skim milk. Add liquid mixture to cracker mixture. Mix gently to combine. Fold in pineapple. Pour into prepared baking dish. Bake 35 to 40 minutes. Place baking dish on a wire rack and allow to cool. Cut into 8 servings. Good served warm or cold.

HINT: Good served with Cool Whip Lite, but don't forget to count the few additional calories.

Each serving equals:

HE: ¾ Bread, ½ Fruit, ¼ Fat, ¼ Protein, 14 Optional Calories

156 Calories, 4 gm Fat, 3 gm Protein, 27 gm Carbohydrate, 344 mg Sodium, 1 gm Fiber

DIABETIC: 1 Starch, ½ Fruit, ½ Fat

Tortilla Fruit Rollups

---■---

These were even better than I imagined when we tested them one afternoon in JO's Kitchen Cafe. I think they're a fun end to a spicy Mexican meal and a sweet way to enjoy ripe, fresh fruit and custard. These are easy to make for a party or a crowd, so go for it. Olé!   *Serves 8*

> 2 (4-serving) packages JELL-O sugar-free vanilla cook-and-serve pudding mix
> 2 (4-serving) packages JELL-O sugar-free strawberry gelatin
> 2¾ cups water
> 2 cups sliced fresh strawberries
> 8 (6-inch) flour tortillas
> 1 teaspoon vanilla extract
> ½ teaspoon ground cinnamon
> 2 tablespoons (½ ounce) chopped pecans

Preheat oven to 400 degrees. Spray a 9-by-13-inch cake pan with butter-flavored cooking spray. In a large saucepan, combine dry pudding mixes, dry gelatin, and water. Cook over medium heat, stirring constantly, until mixture thickens and starts to boil. Remove from heat. Place strawberries in a large bowl. Pour 1½ cups hot mixture over strawberries. Mix well to combine. Spoon about ¼ cup warm strawberry mixture into center of each tortilla. Roll each and place seam side down in prepared cake pan. Stir vanilla extract, cinnamon, and pecans into remaining warm pudding mixture. Evenly spoon mixture over top of tortillas. Bake 10 minutes. For each serving, place 1 tortilla in dessert dish and evenly spoon any remaining sauce in pan over top.

HINT: Also good topped with 1 teaspoon fat-free sour cream. If using, don't forget to count the few additional calories.

Each serving equals:

HE: 1 Bread, ¼ Fruit, ¼ Fat, ¼ Slider, 10 Optional Calories

---

135 Calories, 3 gm Fat, 4 gm Protein, 23 gm Carbohydrate, 296 mg Sodium, 1 gm Fiber

---

DIABETIC: 1½ Starch

Ambrosia Tapioca Pudding

----------------------------------■----------------------------------

Cliff is a real fan of tapioca, so I'm always looking for ways to give him the tastes he loves. When I combined these scrumptious ingredients that Grandma put in her ambrosia salad, he stood up and cheered the result. *Serves 4*

1 (4-serving) package JELL-O sugar-free vanilla cook-and-serve pudding mix	crushed pineapple, packed in fruit juice, undrained
⅔ cup Carnation Nonfat Dry Milk Powder	1 teaspoon coconut extract
3 tablespoons Quick Cooking Minute Tapioca	1 cup (one 11-ounce can) mandarin oranges, rinsed and drained
1¼ cups water	¼ cup Cool Whip Lite
1 cup (one 8-ounce can)	1 tablespoon + 1 teaspoon flaked coconut

In a medium saucepan, combine dry pudding mix, dry milk powder, tapioca, and water. Mix well using a wire whisk. Let set 5 minutes. Stir in undrained pineapple. Cook over medium heat, stirring constantly, until mixture thickens and comes to a full boil. Remove from heat. Stir in coconut extract and mandarin oranges. Place pan on a wire rack and allow to cool 20 minutes. Evenly spoon mixture into 4 dessert dishes. Top each with 1 tablespoon Cool Whip Lite and 1 teaspoon coconut. Refrigerate at least 30 minutes.

Each serving equals:

HE: 1 Fruit, ½ Skim Milk, ½ Slider

----
165 Calories, 1 gm Fat, 4 gm Protein, 35 gm Carbohydrate, 184 mg Sodium, 1 gm Fiber
----

DIABETIC: 1 Fruit, ½ Skim Milk, ½ Starch

Maple Nut Tapioca Pudding

T his is such a great way to offer the men in the family a cozy treat full of maple-nutty goodness. For the tapioca lover in your house, here's a dish to savor again and again. *Serves 4*

1 (4-serving) package JELL-O sugar-free vanilla cook-and-serve pudding mix
⅔ cup Carnation Nonfat Dry Milk Powder
3 tablespoons Quick Cooking Minute Tapioca

1¼ cups water
½ cup Cary's Sugar Free Maple Syrup
¼ cup (1 ounce) chopped walnuts

In a medium saucepan, combine dry pudding mix, dry milk powder, tapioca, water, and syrup. Let set 5 minutes. Cook over medium heat, stirring constantly, until mixture thickens and starts to boil. Remove from heat. Stir in walnuts. Evenly spoon mixture into 4 dessert dishes. Refrigerate at least 30 minutes.

Each serving equals:

HE: ½ Fat, ½ Skim Milk, ¼ Protein, ¾ Slider, 7 Optional Calories

144 Calories, 4 gm Fat, 5 gm Protein, 22 gm Carbohydrate, 217 mg Sodium, 0 gm Fiber

DIABETIC: 1 Starch, ½ Fat, ½ Skim Milk

Calypso Bread Pudding

----------------------■----------------------

Bread pudding is my absolute favorite dessert, and Cliff agrees it's surely one of his. The rum flavor and plump raisins in this version will make every man's heart beat fast, his hips sway, and his feet want to tap tap tap! *Serves 6*

1 (4-serving) package JELL-O sugar-free vanilla cook-and-serve pudding mix
⅔ cup Carnation Nonfat Dry Milk Powder
1 cup (one 8-ounce can) crushed pineapple, packed in fruit juice, undrained

1½ cups water
1 teaspoon coconut extract
½ cup raisins
8 slices reduced-calorie white bread, torn into pieces
2 tablespoons flaked coconut

Preheat oven to 350 degrees. Spray an 8-by-8-inch baking dish with butter-flavored cooking spray. In a large saucepan, combine dry pudding mix, dry milk powder, undrained pineapple, and water. Cook over medium heat, stirring often, until mixture thickens and starts to boil. Remove from heat. Stir in coconut extract and raisins. Add bread pieces. Mix gently to combine. Spoon mixture into prepared baking dish. Evenly sprinkle coconut over top. Bake 30 to 35 minutes. Divide into 6 servings.

Each serving equals:
HE: 1 Fruit, ⅔ Bread, ⅓ Skim Milk, 13 Optional Calories

164 Calories, 0 gm Fat, 7 gm Protein, 34 gm Carbohydrate, 240 mg Sodium, 1 gm Fiber

DIABETIC: 1 Fruit, 1 Starch

Pineapple-Raisin Rice Pudding

— — — — — — — — — — ■ — — — — — — — — — — — —

Oh, won't this bring back sweet and cozy memories of eating Grandma's rice pudding when you tuck into this wonderfully old-time dessert! Isn't it a comfort that you can still eat what you thought was only a sweet memory? My grandbabies like to eat this when they visit Grandma and "Papa Cliff."

Serves 4

1 (4-serving) package JELL-O
    sugar-free vanilla cook-
    and-serve pudding mix
⅔ cup Carnation Nonfat Dry
    Milk Powder
1 cup (one 8-ounce can)
    crushed pineapple, packed
    in fruit juice, undrained

1 cup water
¼ cup raisins
1 teaspoon vanilla extract
½ teaspoon apple pie spice
2 cups cold cooked rice

In a medium saucepan, combine dry pudding mix, dry milk powder, undrained pineapple, water, and raisins. Mix well using a wire whisk. Cook over medium heat, stirring constantly, until mixture thickens and starts to boil. Remove from heat. Stir in vanilla extract and apple pie spice. Add rice. Mix well to combine. Spoon into 4 dessert dishes. Good warm or cold.

HINT: 1⅓ cups uncooked rice usually cooks to about 2 cups.

Each serving equals:

HE: 1 Bread, 1 Fruit, ½ Skim Milk, ¼ Slider

204 Calories, 0 gm Fat, 6 gm Protein, 45 gm Carbohydrate, 181 mg Sodium, 1 gm Fiber

DIABETIC: 1½ Starch, 1 Fruit, ½ Skim Milk

Peanut Butter Cup Rice Pudding

― ■ ―

" **D** ownright decadent" is the only way to describe a rice pudding dessert flavored with chocolate and peanut butter. What could be better than this "cup" of good cheer in a bowl? *Serves 6*

1 (4-serving) package JELL-O	*1⅔ cups water*
sugar-free chocolate cook-	*1 teaspoon vanilla extract*
and-serve pudding mix	*6 tablespoon Peter Pan*
⅔ cup Carnation Nonfat Dry	*reduced-fat peanut butter*
Milk Powder	*2 cups cold cooked rice*

In a medium saucepan, combine dry pudding mix, dry milk powder, and water. Cook over medium heat, stirring constantly, until mixture thickens and starts to boil. Remove from heat. Stir in vanilla extract and peanut butter. Mix well until smooth. Add rice. Mix gently to combine. Spoon mixture evenly into 6 dessert dishes. Refrigerate at least 30 minutes.

HINT: 1⅓ cups uncooked rice usually cooks to about 2 cups.

Each serving equals:

HE: 1 Fat, 1 Protein, ⅔ Bread, ⅓ Skim Milk, 17 Optional Calories

198 Calories, 6 gm Fat, 8 gm Protein, 28 gm Carbohydrate, 186 mg Sodium, 1 gm Fiber

DIABETIC: 1½ Starch, 1 Fat, 1 Meat

Banana Eggnog Bread Pudding with Rum Sauce

I never saw a dessert disappear so fast as when I was testing this one! It could have been the nutmeg wafting from the oven, or maybe the lush sauce that topped the warm pudding. All I know is, one moment it was in the pan, and the next it was GONE! Then I saw the men standing around with smiles on their faces. . . .

Serves 6

2 (4-serving) packages JELL-O sugar-free vanilla cook-and-serve pudding mix ☆
4 cups skim milk ☆
½ cup raisins
1½ teaspoons rum extract ☆
¼ teaspoon ground nutmeg
12 slices reduced-calorie white bread, cubed
1 cup (1 medium) sliced banana
1 tablespoon Brown Sugar Twin
1 tablespoon reduced-calorie margarine

Preheat oven to 350 degrees. Spray an 8-by-8-inch baking dish with butter-flavored cooking spray. In a large saucepan sprayed with butter-flavored cooking spray, combine 1 package dry pudding mix and 2½ cups skim milk. Add raisins. Mix well to combine. Cook over medium heat, stirring constantly, until mixture starts to boil. Remove saucepan from heat. Stir in ½ teaspoon rum extract and nutmeg. Add bread cubes and banana. Mix gently to combine, Spoon bread mixture into prepared baking dish. Bake 35 to 45 minutes or until knife inserted in center comes out clean. In a medium saucepan, combine remaining package dry pudding mix, remaining 1½ cups skim milk, and Brown Sugar Twin. Mix well to combine. Let set until five minutes before bread pudding has completed baking. Then, cook over medium heat, stirring constantly, until mixture thickens and starts to boil. Lower heat. Add margarine and remaining 1 teaspoon rum extract. Mix well to combine. Continue cooking on low until bread pudding has completed baking, stirring occasionally. Remove baking dish from oven and cut warm bread pudding into 6 servings. For each serving, place piece of bread pudding on serving dish and spoon about ¼ cup warm rum sauce over top.

Each serving equals:

HE: 1 Bread, 1 Fruit, ⅔ Skim Milk, ¼ Fat, 15 Optional Calories

-----

233 Calories, 1 gm Fat, 12 gm Protein, 44 gm Carbohydrate, 427 gm Sodium, 1 gm Fiber

-----

DIABETIC: 1 Starch, 1 Fruit, 1 Skim Milk

This and That

------■------

Real Breakfasts for Real Men (Plus a Few Guy "Gulps" and Superbowl Snacks)

I like to say that my recipes appeal to men from 4 to 94, and I'm blessed by having two very young taste testers close to home!

My grandbabies love my food, especially Zachary James Dierickx, whom we call "the pancake kid." He likes to get up early with "Granny Wanny" (his name for me) and help me make breakfast, especially when I'm mixing up Blueberry Dew Pancakes or Zach's Tropical Isle Pancakes, which I created especially for his third birthday. They're full of fruit, crunchy with pecans, garnished with coconut—and so easy to make, you don't have to save them for special occasions. His younger brother, Joshua Michael, will get up extra early for a taste of my Pineapple Raisin Muffins. I've always said, start feeding men delicious healthy food when they're young—and they'll be yours for life!

From scrumptious pancakes and French toast to warm-from-the-oven breads and biscuits, this section provides great ideas for filling breakfasts every man will love. I've also included some tasty party beverages perfect for tailgate parties and picnics, and some crunchy snacks that go perfectly with Monday-night football and NBA playoffs.

This and That

Pineapple Raisin Muffins

Blueberry Dew Pancakes

Zach's Tropical Isle Pancakes

Apple-Walnut Pancakes

Stuffed French Toast

Banana Buster Bread

Mexican Cornbread

Italian Biscuit Ring

Breakfast Pleasure Pita

Deviled Ham Muffins

Breakfast Biscuit Bake

Breakfast Ham and Eggs Pizza

Bacon Crunch Deviled Eggs

Creamy Taco Dip

French Pickle Relish Dressing

Spiced Apple Cooler

Mocha-Cream Shake

JO's Trail Mix

Reuben Roll-Ups

Pineapple Raisin Muffins

------------------------------ ❄ ------------------------------

There's nothing better than enjoying warm muffins on a weekend morning, and these smell delicious enough to get any man out of bed! In fact, you might even get him to do a few "honey-do" jobs after serving these.

Serves 8

1½ cups all-purpose flour
2 teaspoons baking powder
½ teaspoon apple pie spice
2 tablespoons Sugar Twin or
    Sprinkle Sweet
½ cup raisins
½ cup skim milk
2 eggs beaten or equivalent in
    egg substitute

1 tablespoon + 1 teaspoon
    vegetable oil
1 cup (one 8-ounce can)
    crushed pineapple, packed
    in fruit juice, drained and
    liquid reserved

Preheat oven to 400 degrees. Spray 8 wells of a 12-hole muffin pan with butter-flavored cooking spray or line with paper liners. In a medium bowl, combine flour, baking powder, apple pie spice, Sugar Twin, and raisins. In a small bowl, combine skim milk, eggs, oil, and pineapple. Add enough water to reserved pineapple juice to make ¼ cup liquid. Add liquid to milk mixture. Mix well to combine. Add milk mixture to flour mixture. Mix just until combined. Fill prepared muffin wells with batter. Bake 25 to 30 minutes or until a toothpick inserted in center comes out clean. Place muffin pan on a wire rack and let set 5 minutes. Remove muffins from pan and continue cooling on wire rack.

HINT: Fill unused muffin wells with water. It protects the muffin tin and ensures even baking.

Each serving equals:

HE: 1 Bread, ¼ Protein (limited), ¾ Fruit, ½ Fat, 7 Optional Calories

----

180 Calories, 4 gm Fat, 5 gm Protein, 31 gm Carbohydrate, 148 mg Sodium, 1 gm Fiber

----

DIABETIC: 1 Starch, 1 Fruit

Blueberry Dew Pancakes

------------------------ ❋ ------------------------

The secret ingredient in these irresistible treats is the fizz of the Diet Dew, which makes them lemony and light. You'll devour a stack in no time at all—just the way Cliff did!

Serves 6 (2 each)

1 cup Diet Mountain Dew
¼ cup Yoplait plain fat-free yogurt
1 cup + 2 tablespoons fresh or frozen blueberries, thawed and well drained

1½ cups Bisquick Reduced Fat Baking Mix

In a medium bowl, combine Diet Mountain Dew and yogurt. Stir in blueberries. Add baking mix. Mix gently to combine. Using a ¼ cup measure as a guide, pour batter on large hot skillet or griddle sprayed with butter-flavored cooking spray. Brown pancakes on both sides.

Each serving equals:

HE: 1⅓ Bread, ¼ Fruit

135 Calories, 3 gm Fat, 3 gm Protein, 24 gm Carbohydrate, 339 mg Sodium, 1 gm Fiber

DIABETIC: 1 Starch, ½ Fruit

Apple-Walnut Pancakes

------------------------- ❋ -------------------------

The best kitchen aroma there is, according to most men, is the homey scent of brown sugar, apples, and Mom's apple pie. Now you can savor that wonderful taste in these quick and easy pancakes that serve up in seconds! *Serves 6*

1½ cups all-purpose flour
1½ teaspoons baking powder
1 tablespoon Brown Sugar
Twin
1½ cups (one 12-fluid-ounce
can) Carnation Evaporated
Skim Milk
1 egg or equivalent in egg
substitute

2 tablespoons Land O Lakes
fat-free sour cream
1 cup (2 small) cored,
unpeeled, finely chopped
cooking apples
¼ cup (1 ounce) chopped
walnuts

In a large bowl, combine flour, baking powder, and Brown Sugar Twin. Add evaporated skim milk, egg, and sour cream. Mix well to combine. Stir in apples and walnuts. Using a ½ cup measure as a guide, pour batter on griddle or in a skillet sprayed with butter-flavored cooking spray to form 6 pancakes. Brown lightly on both sides. Good as is or topped with either reduced-calorie maple syrup or apple butter. If using either, count optional calories accordingly.

Each serving equals:

HE: 1⅓ Bread, ¼ Skim Milk, ⅓ Protein, ⅓ Fat, ⅓ Fruit, 6 Optional Calories

220 Calories, 4 gm Fat, 10 gm Protein, 36 gm Carbohydrate,
214 mg Sodium, 1 gm Fiber

DIABETIC: 1½ Starch, ½ Skim Milk, ½ Fat, ½ Fruit

Zach's Tropical Isle Pancakes
------------------------- ❋ -------------------------

My grandson Zach thinks every meal is better with dessert, so for his third birthday I stirred up these special treats.

Serves 4

*1 cup (one 8-ounce can)
crushed pineapple, packed
in fruit juice, drained and
liquid reserved
1 teaspoon cornstarch
1 tablespoon Brown Sugar
Twin
1 cup (one 11-ounce can)
mandarin oranges, rinsed
and drained*

*1 teaspoon coconut extract
¾ cup Hungry Jack Extra
Light & Fluffy pancake
and waffle mix
½ cup unsweetened orange
juice
1 tablespoon (¼ ounce)
chopped pecans
1 tablespoon plus 1 teaspoon
flaked coconut*

In a medium saucepan, combine reserved pineapple juice and cornstarch. Cook over medium heat, stirring constantly, until mixture thickens. Stir in Brown Sugar Twin and drained pineapple. Add mandarin oranges and coconut extract. Mix gently to combine. Lower heat. Simmer while preparing pancakes. In a medium bowl, combine pancake mix and orange juice. Mix well. Stir in pecans. Using a ¼ cup as measure, pour batter onto hot griddle or skillet sprayed with butter-flavored cooking spray to form 4 pancakes. Cook 1 to 1½ minutes, or until the edges look cooked and bubbles begin to break on top. Turn and continue to cook 1 to 1½ minutes or until pancakes are lightly browned. For each serving, place 1 pancake on a plate, spoon about ⅓ cup pineapple mixture over pancake, and sprinkle 1 teaspoon flaked coconut over top.

Each serving equals:

HE: 1¼ Fruit, 1 Bread, ¼ Fat, 9 Optional Calories

----
191 Calories, 3 gm Fat, 3 gm Protein, 38 gm Carbohydrate,
344 mg Sodium, 1 gm Fiber

DIABETIC: 1 Fruit, 1 Starch, ½ Fat

Stuffed French Toast

If you always enjoyed this breakfast classic, prepare to be amazed at the impossibly delicious surprise this version delivers! The oohs and aahs shouldn't surprise the cook, because this dish is a winner every time.

Serves 4

8 slices reduced-calorie white
    bread
¼ cup (2 ounces) Philadelphia
    fat-free cream cheese
¼ cup strawberry spreadable
    fruit spread

2 eggs or equivalent in egg
    substitute
2 tablespoons skim milk
½ teaspoon vanilla extract

Spread 1 teaspoon cream cheese onto each slice of bread. Spread 1 teaspoon fruit spread over top of each. Put bread together to form 4 sandwiches. In a medium bowl, combine eggs, skim milk, and vanilla extract. Beat well, using a fork. Spray a griddle or large skillet with butter-flavored cooking spray. Dip each sandwich into egg mixture, coating both sides evenly. Place on griddle and cook 2 to 3 minutes on each side or until golden brown. Serve at once.

Each serving equals:

HE: 1 Bread, ¾ Protein (½ limited), 1 Fruit, 3 Optional Calories

182 Calories, 2 gm Fat, 13 gm Protein, 28 gm Carbohydrate,
400 mg Sodium, 1 gm Fiber

DIABETIC: 1 Starch, 1 Meat, 1 Fruit

Banana Buster Bread

Ask any man about his favorite tea bread, dense and fruity and oh-so-good, and he's more than likely to say "banana bread." But when he tastes this decadent creation, he'll surely have a new "best-loved"—it's so full of goodies it ought to be illegal, but it's not. Enjoy!

Serves 8 (1 thick or 2 thin slices)

1½ cups all-purpose flour
1 (4-serving) package JELL-O instant sugar-free banana cream pudding mix
1 teaspoon baking soda
1 teaspoon baking powder
¼ cup (1 ounce) chopped dry-roasted peanuts
¼ cup (1 ounce) mini–chocolate chips

⅔ cup (2 medium) mashed ripe bananas
1 egg or equivalent in egg substitute
½ cup unsweetened applesauce
½ cup unsweetened apple juice
1 teaspoon vanilla extract

Preheat oven to 350 degrees. Spray a 9-by-5-inch loaf pan with butter-flavored cooking spray. In a large bowl, combine flour, dry pudding mix, baking soda, and baking powder. Stir in peanuts and chocolate chips. In a medium bowl, combine mashed bananas, egg, applesauce, apple juice, and vanilla extract. Add banana mixture to flour mixture. Mix just until combined. Pour mixture into prepared loaf pan. Bake 55 to 60 minutes or until top tests done. Set pan on a wire rack to cool. Remove from pan and continue cooling on rack. Cut into 8 thick or 16 thin slices.

Each serving equals:

HE: 1 Bread, ⅔ Fruit, ¼ Protein, ¼ Fat, 13 Optional Calories

150 Calories, 2 gm Fat, 3 gm Protein, 30 gm Carbohydrate, 398 mg Sodium, 1 gm Fiber

DIABETIC: 1 Starch, 1 Fruit

Mexican Cornbread

------------------- ❋ -------------------

I've always found the hearty, tangy goodness of cornbread to be the perfect accompaniment to a Mexican meal, but this one is special enough to be savored all by itself. The cheese and mayo give it a smooth, silky texture, and the corn, onion, and pepper spice it up just perfectly. At the tasting buffet, a man tried to bribe me to give him the recipe!

Serves 8

⅔ cup Carnation Nonfat Dry Milk Powder

1 cup water

1 teaspoon white vinegar

1 cup yellow cornmeal

6 tablespoons all-purpose flour

1 teaspoon baking powder

½ teaspoon baking soda

½ teaspoon dried minced garlic

1 teaspoon dried parsley flakes

1 cup frozen whole kernel corn

¾ cup (3 ounces) shredded Kraft reduced-fat Cheddar cheese

½ cup chopped onion

½ cup chopped green bell pepper

2 tablespoons canned diced pimiento

⅓ cup Kraft fat-free mayonnaise

Preheat oven to 350 degrees. Spray an 8-by-8-inch baking dish with olive-oil–flavored cooking spray. In a small bowl, combine dry milk powder, water, and vinegar. Set aside. In a large bowl, combine cornmeal, flour, baking powder, baking soda, garlic, and parsley flakes. Add corn, Cheddar cheese, onion, green pepper, and pimiento. Mix well to combine. Stir in milk mixture and mayonnaise. Mix just to combine. Pour mixture into prepared baking dish. Bake 45 to 50 minutes or until golden brown. Place pan on a wire rack and allow to cool. Cut into 8 servings.

Each serving equals:

HE: 1½ Bread, ½ Protein, ¼ Skim Milk, ¼ Vegetable, 7 Optional Calories

162 Calories, 2 gm Fat, 8 gm Protein, 28 gm Carbohydrate, 373 gm Sodium, 2 gm Fiber

DIABETIC: 2 Starch

Italian Biscuit Ring

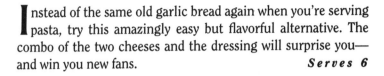

Instead of the same old garlic bread again when you're serving pasta, try this amazingly easy but flavorful alternative. The combo of the two cheeses and the dressing will surprise you—and win you new fans.   *Serves 6*

1 (7.5-ounce) can Pillsbury
refrigerated buttermilk
biscuits
¼ cup Kraft Fat Free Italian
Dressing
¼ cup (¾ ounce) grated Kraft
fat-free Parmesan cheese

⅓ cup (1½ ounces) shredded
Kraft reduced-fat
mozzarella cheese
1 teaspoon dried parsley flakes

Preheat oven to 425 degrees. Spray a 9-inch pie plate with olive-oil–flavored cooking spray. Separate biscuits. Cut each into 2 pieces. Dip pieces in Italian dressing, then into Parmesan cheese. Place pieces in prepared pie plate. Sprinkle any remaining Parmesan cheese and Italian dressing evenly over biscuits. Evenly sprinkle mozzarella cheese and parsley flakes over top. Bake 15 to 20 minutes. Cool slightly on a wire rack. Cut into 6 wedges.

Each serving equals:

HE: 1¼ Bread, ½ Protein, 2 Optional Calories

118 Calories, 2 gm Fat, 6 gm Protein, 19 gm Carbohydrate,
517 mg Sodium, 2 gm Fiber

DIABETIC: 1 Starch, ½ Meat

Breakfast Pleasure Pita

--------------------❄--------------------

Here's a simply scrumptious fast food–style pocket sandwich that you can enjoy at home. Every bite offers a medley of flavors guaranteed to put a smile on the sleepiest face.

Serves 4

1 cup (5 ounces) frozen hash brown potatoes
¼ cup chopped onion
¼ cup chopped green bell pepper
4 ounces ground 90% lean turkey or beef
4 eggs or equivalent in egg substitute

¼ cup skim milk
½ teaspoon poultry seasoning
¼ teaspoon ground sage
¼ teaspoon garlic powder
⅓ cup (1½ ounces) shredded Kraft reduced-fat Cheddar cheese
2 pita rounds

In a large skillet sprayed with butter-flavored cooking spray, brown hash browns, onion, green pepper, and meat, stirring occasionally. In a medium bowl, combine eggs, skim milk, poultry seasoning, ground sage, and garlic powder using a wire whisk. Pour egg mixture into potato mixture. Cook, stirring occasionally, until eggs are set. Add Cheddar cheese and mix lightly to combine. Cut pita rounds in half and evenly spoon about 1 cup potato mixture into each half. Serve at once.

HINTS: 1. Mr. Dell's frozen shredded potatoes arc a good choice for this recipe or raw shredded potatoes may be used in place of frozen potatoes.
2. To make opening pita rounds easier, place pita halves on a paper towel and microwave on HIGH 10 seconds. Remove and gently press open.

Each serving equals:

HE: 2½ Protein (1 limited), 1¼ Bread, ¼ Vegetable, 6 Optional Calories

257 Calories, 9 gm Fat, 18 gm Protein, 26 gm Carbohydrate, 349 mg Sodium, 1 gm Fiber

DIABETIC: 2 Meat, 2 Starch

Deviled Ham Muffins

-------------------- ❋ --------------------

This is just like those wonderful dishes Mom used to make when the children came home from school for lunch. You'll feel like a contented lad when you gobble it down and say "Um-um-good." *Serves 4*

1 (10¾-ounce) can Healthy Request Tomato Soup
1 teaspoon prepared mustard
½ teaspoon prepared horseradish
1 teaspoon dried parsley flakes
1 full cup (6 ounces) finely diced Dubuque 97% fat-free ham or any extra-lean ham
¾ cup (3 ounces) shredded Kraft reduced-fat Cheddar cheese
2 English Muffins, split and toasted

In a medium saucepan, combine tomato soup, mustard, horseradish, and parsley flakes. Stir in ham and Cheddar cheese. Cook over medium heat, stirring often until mixture is heated through and cheese is melted. For each serving, place English Muffin half on a plate and spoon about ⅔ cup ham sauce over top.

Each serving equals:

HE: 2 Protein, 1 Bread, ½ Slider, 5 Optional Calories

222 Calories, 6 gm Fat, 16 gm Protein, 26 gm Carbohydrate, 964 mg Sodium, 4 gm Fiber

DIABETIC: 2 Meat, 1½ Starch

Breakfast Biscuit Bake

---------------- ❋ ----------------

There's no more romantic gesture than when a man makes breakfast for the woman he loves. Here's a dish you can both enjoy, without the man worrying about ease of preparation or the woman worrying about her waistline! Leave the dishes for later. . . .

Serves 6

1 (7.5-ounce) can Pillsbury refrigerated buttermilk biscuits
6 eggs or equivalent in egg substitute
¼ cup skim milk

1 teaspoon parsley flakes
1 teaspoon dried onion flakes
½ teaspoon lemon pepper
¾ cup (3 ounces) shredded Kraft reduced-fat Cheddar cheese ☆

Preheat oven to 450 degrees. Spray both a cookie sheet and an 8-by-8-inch baking dish with butter-flavored cooking spray. Separate biscuits and arrange on prepared cookie sheet. Lightly spray tops of biscuits with butter-flavored cooking spray. Bake 8 minutes. Place cookie sheet on a wire rack and allow to cool. Reduce oven temperature to 375 degrees. Break each biscuit into 3 pieces and set aside. In a large bowl, combine eggs, skim milk, parsley flakes, onion flakes, and lemon pepper. Mix well using a wire whisk. Stir in the biscuit pieces and ½ cup Cheddar cheese. Pour mixture into prepared baking dish. Bake 15 to 20 minutes or until the center is set. Sprinkle remaining ¼ cup Cheddar cheese evenly over top. Continue baking 5 minutes or until cheese starts to melt. Place baking dish on a wire rack and let set 5 minutes. Cut into 6 servings.

Each serving equals:

HE: 1⅔ Protein (1 limited), 1¼ Bread, 4 Optional Calories

----

200 Calories, 8 gm Fat, 13 gm Protein, 19 gm Carbohydrate, 482 mg Sodium, 2 gm Fiber

----

DIABETIC: 1½ Meat, 1½ Starch

Breakfast Ham and Eggs Pizza

I suggested this to one lady who needed a post-sleepover breakfast for her sons and their friends. She reported that the kids woke up instantly when the scent of this lively dish reached their attic playroom. It's a great choice for kids and Dad alike.

Serves 8

1 (11-ounce) can Pillsbury refrigerated French loaf
8 eggs or equivalent in egg substitute
¼ cup skim milk
½ teaspoon lemon pepper
½ teaspoon pizza or Italian seasoning
1 cup (one 8-ounce can)
Hunt's Tomato Sauce
1 full cup (6 ounces) diced Dubuque 97% fat-free ham or any extra-lean ham
¾ cup (3 ounces) shredded Kraft reduced-fat Cheddar cheese
2 teaspoons dried parsley flakes

Preheat oven to 425 degrees. Unroll French loaf. Pat into jelly roll pan and up sides of pan to form a rim. Bake 5 minutes. Meanwhile in a large bowl, combine eggs, skim milk, and lemon pepper. Mix well using a wire whisk. Pour into a large skillet sprayed with butter-flavored cooking spray. Scramble eggs, until firm but not browned. Remove from heat. Stir pizza seasoning into tomato sauce. Spread sauce mixture evenly over partially baked French loaf. Spoon the scrambled eggs and ham evenly over tomato sauce. Sprinkle Cheddar cheese evenly over eggs and ham. Evenly sprinkle parsley flakes over top. Continue to bake 8 to 12 minutes or until cheese is melted and crust is golden brown. Cut into 8 servings.

Each serving equals:

HE: 2 Protein (1 limited), ⅔ Bread, ½ Vegetable, 3 Optional Calories

207 Calories, 7 gm Fat, 18 gm Protein, 18 gm Carbohydrate, 735 mg Sodium, 1 gm Fiber

DIABETIC: 2 Meat, 1 Starch, ½ Vegetable

Bacon Crunch Deviled Eggs

— ■ —

When I featured these at my Healthy Man Taste-Testing Buffet, there was a stampede to grab for seconds! All the men I spoke to mentioned how much they liked these special eggs—and told me they might have to learn to cook just to make them!

Serves 4 (2 halves each)

4 hard-boiled eggs
3 tablespoons Kraft fat-free
  mayonnaise
1 teaspoon Worcestershire
  sauce
¼ teaspoon celery seed

1 teaspoon dried onion flakes
1 teaspoon dried parsley flakes
1 tablespoon Hormel Bacon
  Bits

Cut eggs in half lengthwise and remove yolks. Place yolks in a medium bowl and mash well using a fork. Add mayonnaise, Worcestershire sauce, celery seed, onion flakes, parsley flakes, and bacon bits. Mix well to combine. Refill egg white halves by spooning a full 1 tablespoon yolk mixture into each. Cover and refrigerate at least 30 minutes.

Each serving equals:

HE: 1 Protein (limited), 14 Optional Calories

81 Calories, 5 gm Fat, 7 gm Protein, 2 gm Carbohydrate, 162 mg Sodium, 0 gm Fiber

DIABETIC: 1 Meat

Creamy Taco Dip

--------------■--------------

Try this spicy, cheesy concoction at your next tailgate party, offering it with baked tortilla chips or cut-up veggies. You'll hear cheers, even if your team isn't winning.

Serves 8 (⅓ cup)

*2 (8-ounce) packages
  Philadelphia fat-free
  cream cheese
1 teaspoon taco seasoning
1 teaspoon dried parsley flakes
1 cup chunky salsa (mild,*

*medium, or hot)
⅓ cup (1½ ounces) shredded
  Kraft reduced-fat Cheddar
  cheese
⅓ cup (2 ounces) finely
  chopped ripe olives*

In a medium bowl, stir cream cheese with a spoon until soft. Stir in taco seasoning, parsley flakes, and salsa. Add Cheddar cheese and olives. Mix well to combine. Cover and refrigerate at least 1 hour.

Each serving equals:

HE: 1¼ Protein, ¼ Fat, ¼ Vegetable

----

65 Calories, 1 gm Fat, 9 gm Protein, 5 gm Carbohydrate, 673 mg Sodium, 0 gm Fiber

----

DIABETIC: 1 Meat, ½ Starch

French Pickle Relish Dressing

This is great as a dip or a salad dressing, prepared for a party or just an evening at home. It's simple to make double or triple the recipe if you're expecting a crowd.

Serves 8 (3 tablespoons)

1 cup Kraft Fat Free French Dressing
¾ cup Kraft fat-free mayonnaise

⅓ cup sweet pickle relish

In a medium bowl, combine French dressing and mayonnaise. Add sweet pickle relish. Mix well to combine. Cover and refrigerate at least 1 hour.

Each serving equals:

HE: ½ Slider, 18 Optional Calories

56 Calories, 0 gm Fat, 0 gm Protein, 14 gm Carbohydrate, 451 mg Sodium, 0 gm Fiber

DIABETIC: 1 Starch

Spiced Apple Cooler

-------------------◆-------------------

Fan for fans of apple cider who can't wait until cider season, here's a tasty alternative that's sure to succeed with thirsty men everywhere.   *Serves 6 (1 cup)*

3 cups unsweetened apple juice	*½ teaspoon apple pie spice*
1 tablespoon lemon juice	*1 cup chopped ice*
	3 cups Diet Mountain Dew

In a blender container, combine apple juice, lemon juice, and apple pie spice. Cover and blend on HIGH, 15 seconds. Add chopped ice. Cover and process on HIGH 30 seconds. Pour mixture into a large pitcher. Add Diet Mountain Dew. Mix well to combine. Serve over ice.

Each serving equals:

HE: 1 Fruit

----

60 Calories, 0 gm Fat, 0 gm Protein, 15 gm Carbohydrate, 22 mg Sodium, 0 gm Fiber

----

DIABETIC: 1 Fruit

Mocha-Cream Shake

Most men can't resist a milk shake, and this one is especially good. Isn't it great to be able to drink this thick and creamy treat without fear of flab?   *Serves 4*

3 cups skim milk
1 (4-serving) package JELL-O
   sugar-free instant
   chocolate pudding mix
2 teaspoons instant coffee
   crystals

2 cups Wells' Blue Bunny
   Sugar Free and Fat Free
   Vanilla Ice Cream or any
   sugar- and fat-free ice
   cream
¼ cup Cool Whip Lite

In a blender container, combine skim milk, dry pudding mix, and coffee crystals. Cover and process on BLEND 15 seconds. Add ice cream. Cover and process on BLEND until smooth, about 20 seconds. Evenly pour into 4 glasses and top each with 1 tablespoon Cool Whip Lite.

Each serving equals:

HE: ¾ Skim Milk, 1 Slider, 8 Optional Calories

161 Calories, 1 gm Fat, 10 gm Protein, 28 gm Carbohydrate,
475 mg Sodium, 0 gm Fiber

DIABETIC: 1 Skim Milk, 1 Starch

JO's Trail Mix

--------- ❊ ---------

W hat would a cookbook created for men's appetites be without a super snack or two? This healthy version of trail mix is popular with men of all ages (and women, too!). It's crunchy, nutty, sweet, and tangy—and it's a treat to enjoy without guilt. *Serves 8 (¾ cup)*

1 cup (¾ ounce) Cheerios
½ cup (¾ ounce) Wheat Chex
2⅔ cups (2¼ ounces) Rice Chex
1 cup (¾ ounce) Corn Chex
6 (2½-inch) graham crackers, very coarsely broken
½ cup raisins

½ cup (3 ounces) chopped dried apricots
¼ cup (1 ounce) chopped pecans
½ teaspoon apple pie spice
2 tablespoons Sugar Twin or Sprinkle Sweet

In a large bowl, combine Cheerios, Wheat Chex, Rice Chex, Corn Chex, and graham crackers. Stir in raisins, apricots, and pecans. In a small bowl, combine apple pie spice and Sugar Twin. Add mixture to cereal mixture. Mix gently to combine. Place in an airtight container to store. Shake well before serving.

HINT: To plump up raisins without "cooking," place in a glass measuring cup and microwave on High for 20 seconds.

Each serving equals:
HE: 1 Bread, 1 Fruit, ½ Fat, 2 Optional Calories

171 Calories, 3 gm Fat, 3 gm Protein, 33 gm Carbohydrate, 183 mg Sodium, 2 gm Fiber

DIABETIC: 1 Starch, 1 Fruit, ½ Fat

Reuben Roll-Ups

— ■ —

If you've got a hankering for a delicatessen sandwich, here's a hot treat you can serve during halftime any night you choose. You'll cheer right along with the cheerleaders at the kind of teamwork the ingredients in this recipe deliver!

Serves 8 (1 piece)

1 (8-ounce) can Pillsbury refrigerated crescent dinner rolls

1 cup (one 8-ounce can) regular sauerkraut, drained

¼ cup Kraft Fat Free Thousand Island Dressing

1 (2.5-ounce) package Carl Buddig 90% lean corned beef, finely chopped

2 (¾-ounce) slices Kraft reduced-fat Swiss cheese

Preheat oven to 375 degrees. Unroll and separate crescent rolls. In a small bowl, combine sauerkraut, Thousand Island dressing, and chopped corned beef. Spoon a full 2 tablespoons of mixture on large end of each roll. Cut Swiss cheese slices into 4 pieces. Place quarter slice of cheese on top of each. Roll up as for jelly rolls. Place on ungreased cookie sheet. Bake 12 to 14 minutes or until rolls are golden brown. Serve hot.

Each serving equals:

HE: 1 Bread, ¼ Protein, ¼ Vegetable, 16 Optional Calories

134 Calories, 6 gm Fat, 5 gm Protein, 15 gm Carbohydrate, 628 mg Sodium, 1 gm Fiber

DIABETIC: 1 Starch, ½ Meat, ½ Fat

---■---

Healthy Exchanges has made some terrific changes in my life. I had lost 23 pounds and had just about given up getting the other 27 off. I was frustrated and could not stay on a diet and could simply not face up to trying to prepare two meals anymore. And what I would try to eat and lose weight, my husband did not want to eat. But now I have done a complete turnaround. I am having a ball making all your wonderful recipes. . . . As my husband and I sat last evening eating a piece of Hawaiian Strawberry Pie, I said when food tastes this good and I can look forward to eating like this the rest of my life, I can finish getting the weight off and keep it off.

—J.Z., NE

---■---

Man-Pleasing Classics

---◾---

H ere's my little gift to you, a "lucky seven" of Healthy Exchanges recipes that men have loved best over the years. Because they have appeared in other books and in my newsletter, I'm calling this a "bonus" section; you're still getting more than two hundred new recipes in this book. I make it a point of pride not to repeat recipes, but these just seem to belong in my *Cooking Healthy with a Man in Mind* book! Once you taste them, I'm sure you'll agree.

Mustard Coleslaw	"Grandma's" Lemonade
Healthy JOs	Banana Split Pie
Mexicalli Pie	Triple Layer Party Pie
Party Turkey Tetrazzini	

Mustard Coleslaw

----------------■----------------

After tasting this winning combination of Dijon mustard and cabbage, you will never be satisfied with "plain" coleslaw again.   *S e r v e s   6   (¾   c u p)*

4 cups purchased coleslaw
    mix
1 cup finely chopped celery
1 tablespoon dried parsley
    flakes
½ cup Kraft fat–free
    mayonnaise

1 tablespoon white vinegar
Sugar substitute to equal 2
    tablespoons sugar
1 tablespoon Dijon mustard
⅛ teaspoon black pepper

In a large bowl, combine coleslaw mix and celery. In a small bowl, combine parsley flakes, mayonnaise, vinegar, sugar substitute, Dijon mustard, and black pepper. Add to vegetables. Mix gently to combine. Cover and refrigerate until ready to serve.

HINT: 3½ cups shredded cabbage and ½ cup shredded carrots can be used in place of purchased coleslaw mix.

Each serving equals:

HE: 1⅔ Vegetable, 13 Optional Calories

----

36 calories, less than 1 gm Fat, 1 gm Protein, 8 gm Carbohydrate, 243 mg Sodium, 1 gm Fiber

----

DIABETIC: 1 Vegetable, 1 Free Vegetable

Healthy JO'S

-------- ❄ --------

Here's my version of the old standby. It's an easy meal to make for a crowd, or perfect for those weekend suppers in front of the TV when a favorite movie is on. Cliff says he could eat this every week and never get tired of it. One of my newsletter subscribers' husbands says it's the *next*-best thing to making love! *Serves 6 (⅓ cup filling)*

*16 ounces ground 90% lean
 turkey or beef*
½ cup chopped onions
1 cup Hunt's tomato sauce
½ cup chunky salsa

*1 tablespoon Brown Sugar
 Twin*
*6 reduced-calorie hamburger
 buns (80 calories each)*

In a large skillet sprayed with olive-oil–flavored cooking spray, brown meat and onion. Add tomato sauce, salsa, and Brown Sugar Twin. Lower heat and simmer 15 to 20 minutes. Serve on hamburger buns.

Each serving equals:

HE: 2 Protein, 1 Bread, 1 Vegetable, 1 Optional Calorie
----
209 calories, 7 gm Fat, 17 gm Protein, 19 gm Carbohydrate,
567 mg Sodium, 2 gm Fiber

DIABETIC: 2 Meat, 1 Starch, 1 Vegetable

Mexicalli Pie

----------■----------

This is the recipe that started the whole thing, that launched Healthy Exchanges. It's the first one I ever created—and when I served it to Cliff, he told me he would eat anything else I prepared, no matter how healthy, as long as it tasted this good! That's about as high a compliment a "truck-drivin' man" can give.

Serves 8

16 ounces ground 90% lean
   turkey or beef
½ cup chopped onion
½ cup chopped green and/or
   red bell peppers
1½ cups frozen whole kernel
   corn

1 cup chunky salsa
¾ cup (3 ounces) Kraft
   shredded reduced-fat
   Cheddar cheese
⅛ teaspoon black pepper
1 cup (3 ounces) crushed corn
   chips

Preheat oven to 350 degrees. In a large skillet sprayed with olive-oil–flavored cooking spray, brown meat, onions, and green pepper. Add corn, salsa, Cheddar cheese, and black pepper. Spray a 10-inch pie plate with olive-oil–flavored cooking spray. Place meat mixture in pie plate. Top with crushed corn chips. Bake 30 minutes. Cool 10 minutes before serving.

Each serving equals:

HE: 2 Protein, ¾ Bread, ½ Vegetable, ¼ Slider, 10 Optional Calories

204 Calories, 10 gm Fat, 15 gm Protein, 14 gm Carbohydrate, 324 mg Sodium, 2 gm Fiber

DIABETIC: 2 Meat, 1 Starch

Party Turkey Tetrazzini

----------------------■----------------------

I fell in love with this dish the first time I prepared it—and five years later, it's still one of my favorites. I hope it makes your list of best-loved recipes, too!   *Serves 4*

½ cup chopped onion
8 ounces (1½ cups) diced cooked turkey breast
1 (10¾-ounce) can Campbell's Healthy Request Cream of Mushroom Soup
¾ cup (3 ounces) Kraft shredded reduced-fat
Cheddar cheese
2 cups cooked spaghetti
2 tablespoons chopped pimiento
2 tablespoons chopped fresh parsley or 1 teaspoon dried parsley flakes
⅛ teaspoon black pepper

In a large skillet sprayed with butter-flavored cooking spray, sauté onion and turkey until onion is tender. Blend in mushroom soup and Cheddar cheese. Cook over low heat until cheese is melted, stirring often. Add spaghetti, pimiento, parsley, and black pepper. Continue cooking until heated through.

HINTS: 1. Chicken or ham may be substituted for turkey.
2. 1½ cups uncooked spaghetti usually cooks to about 2 cups.
3. Break the spaghetti into about four-inch pieces before cooking.
4. Purchase a chunk of turkey breast from your local deli and dice it when you get home.

Each serving equals:

HE: 3 Protein, 1 Bread, ¼ Vegetable, ½ Slider, 1 Optional Calorie

----

271 Calories, 5 gm Fat, 27 gm Protein, 29 gm Carbohydrate, 516 mg Sodium, 1 gm Fiber

----

DIABETIC: 2½ Meat, 2 Starch

"Grandma's" Lemonade

----------------------■----------------------

R emember when you used to go to Grandma's house and enjoy her homemade lemonade in the middle of summer? If you were lucky, you got to help her squeeze the lemons on her old-fashioned glass lemon juicer. Invariably some of the seeds and some of the pulp got into the lemonade, and that's what made it taste so good. Well, we're just doing that on purpose with today's modern conveniences. *Serves 8 (1 cup)*

1 tub Crystal Light sugar-free   *¼ lemon, unpeeled and*
  lemonade mix   *unseeded*
8 cups water

Prepare sugar-free lemonade according to package directions. Slice ¼ to ⅓ of a lemon, *including skin and seeds,* into chunks. Pour 2 cups of prepared lemonade into a blender; add lemon chunks and blend on HIGH for 30 to 45 seconds. Pour into the pitcher of lemonade mixture and mix well.
Serve over ice and enjoy!

HINT: You can also use ¼ to ⅓ of an orange for Lemon-Orange Ade, or ⅛ to ¼ of a lime for Lemon-Lime Ade.

Each serving equals:

HE: 1 optional calorie

----

1 Calorie, 0 gm Fat, 0 gm Protein, 0 gm Carbohydrate,
less than 1 mg Sodium, 0 Fiber

DIABETIC: free food

Banana Split Pie

C liff likes to call this his "heaven on earth" pie because this is what he imagines the best taste there is might be like! That's quite a compliment from my "truck-drivin' man," who honed his taste buds in truck stops and restaurants coast-to-coast during his years as a long-distance trucker. Now he's traded his eighteen-wheeler for computers and printing presses, but he's never lost his taste for my banana split recipes.

Serves 8

1 (6-ounce) Keebler chocolate piecrust
1 cup sliced banana (1 medium)
1 cup (one 8-ounce can) canned crushed pineapple, packed in fruit juice, drained

1 (4-serving) package JELL-O sugar-free instant vanilla pudding mix
2 cups skim milk
1 cup sliced strawberries
¾ cup Cool Whip Lite
2 teaspoons chocolate syrup
4 maraschino cherries, halved

Place sliced bananas in piecrust. Sprinkle drained crushed pineapple over sliced bananas. In a medium bowl, combine dry pudding mix and skim milk. Mix well using a wire whisk. Pour pudding mixture over fruit. Refrigerate 1 hour. Sprinkle sliced strawberries over set pudding. Spread Cool Whip Lite evenly over strawberries. Drizzle chocolate syrup over Cool Whip Lite. Garnish top evenly with maraschino cherry halves. Refrigerate at least 1 hour. Cut into 8 pieces.

HINT: For a firmer pie, substitute ⅔ cup nonfat dry milk powder and 1⅓ cups water for 2 cups skim milk.

Each serving equals:

HE: ⅔ Fruit, ½ Bread, ¼ Skim Milk, 1 Slider, 5 Optional Calories

198 Calories, 6 gm Fat, 3 gm Protein, 33 gm Carbohydrate, 203 mg Sodium, 2 gm Fiber

DIABETIC: 1 Starch, 1 Fruit, 1 Fat

Triple Layer Party Pie

-------------------- ❈ --------------------

The more layers in a dessert, the more possibilities—don't you agree? You can have a party in your mouth with the flavors of this pie. I think of this one as the "Pie That Wowed New York" because back in 1994, when I served it to all the publishers, they literally fought one another off with their forks to see who was going to work with "that lady from Iowa."

Serves 8

1 (4-serving) package JELL-O
   sugar-free instant
   butterscotch pudding mix
1⅓ cups Carnation Nonfat
   Dry Milk Powder ☆
2½ cups water ☆
1 6-ounce Keebler chocolate
   piecrust

1 (4-serving) package JELL-O
   sugar-free instant
   chocolate pudding mix
½ cup Cool Whip Lite
2 tablespoons (½ ounce)
   chopped pecans
1 tablespoon (¼ ounce)
   mini–chocolate chips

In a medium bowl, combine dry butterscotch pudding mix, ⅔ cup dry milk powder, and 1¼ cups water. Mix well using a wire whisk. Pour mixture into piecrust. In a medium bowl, combine dry chocolate pudding mix, remaining ⅔ cup dry milk powder, and remaining 1¼ cups water. Mix well using a wire whisk. Pour mixture over butterscotch layer. Refrigerate about 15 minutes. Before serving, spread ½ cup Cool Whip Lite evenly over chocolate layer. Sprinkle pecans and mini–chocolate chips evenly over top. Refrigerate until ready to serve.

Each serving equals:

HE: ½ Bread, ½ Skim Milk, ¼ Fat, 1 Slider, 8 Optional Calories

----

217 calories, 7 gm Fat, 6 gm Protein, 32 gm Carbohydrate, 487 mg Sodium, 1 gm Fiber

----

DIABETIC: 2 Starch, 1 Fat, ½ Skim Milk

Menus Men Will Love for All Occasions

-------------------■-------------------

New Year's Eve Party
Dilled Salmon Pasta Salad
Reuben Roll-Ups
Meatballs in Sour Cream Onion-Mushroom Sauce
Orange Push-Up Cheesecake
Chocolate Hawaiian Dessert Cake

-------■-------

Valentine's Day à Deux
Heavenly Cherry Salad
Ruby Rio Stroganoff
Carrot French Pennies
Cherry Chocolate Parfaits

-------■-------

St. Paddy's Day Dinner
Pistachio Creme Fruit Salad
Corned Beef and Cabbage Quiche
Corn and Onion au Gratin
Grasshopper Dessert Bars

-------■-------

"I Survived Tax Day" Poker Night
Blazing Glory Chili
Ham Pasta Salad with Maize Dressing
Swiss Steak Ultra

Butterscotch Ambrosia
JO's Trail Mix

------■-------

NBA Playoffs Potluck
Creamy Taco Dip
Macho Burritos
Spanish Green Beans
Mexican Cornbread
Tortilla Fruit Roll-Ups

------■-------

Father's Day Brunch
Blueberry Dew Pancakes
He-Man's Gravy and Biscuits
Banana Buster Bread
Mocha-Cream Shake

------■-------

Fourth of July Cookout
Bacon Crunch Deviled Eggs
Grande Potato Salad
Bar-B-Que Beef Strips
Banana Split Shortcake

------■-------

Labor Day Weekend Family Reunion
Western Macaroni Salad
Celery Seed Cole Slaw
Ham and Corn Scallop
Bavarian Meat Loaf
Banana Blueberry Party Cake
Cherry Crumb Pie

------■------

Back to School Blast
Decadent "Candy Bar" Salad
Green Bean Mushroom Casserole
Pizza Skillet
Peanut Butter and Jelly Cheesecake

------■------

Oktoberfest Beer Tasting
German Potato Soup
Heartland Macaroni and Cheese
Mom's Apple Pie

------■------

Tailgate Thanksgiving
Grandma's "Homemade" Harvest Time Soup
Cabbage Patch Meat Loaf
Turkey Club Casserole
Carrot Pineapple Cake with Vanilla Cream Topping

------■------

Santa's Late Supper
Buffalo Chicken Macaroni Salad
Hamburger-Potato Casserole
Banana Eggnog Bread Pudding with Rum Sauce
Grandpa's Old Time Spice Cake

------■------

Making Healthy Exchanges Work for You

------------■------------

Y ou're ready now to begin a wonderful journey to better health. In the preceding pages, you've discovered the remarkable variety of good food available to you when you begin eating the Healthy Exchanges way. You've stocked your pantry and learned many of my food preparation "secrets" that will point you on the way to delicious success.

But before I let you go, I'd like to share a few tips that I've learned while traveling toward healthier eating habits. It took me a long time to learn how to eat *smarter*. In fact, I'm still working on it. But I am getting better. For years, I could *inhale* a five-course meal in five minutes flat—and still make room for a second helping of dessert!

Now I follow certain signposts on the road that help me stay on the right path. I hope these ideas will help point you in the right direction as well.

1. **Eat slowly** so your brain has time to catch up with your tummy. Cut and chew each bite slowly. Try putting your fork down between bites. Stop eating as soon as you feel full. Crumple your napkin and throw it on top of your plate so you don't continue to eat when you are no longer hungry.

2. **Smaller plates** may help you feel more satisfied by your food portions *and* limit the amount you can put on the plate.

3. **Watch portion size.** If you are *truly* hungry, you can always add more food to your plate once you've finished your initial

serving. But remember to count the additional food accordingly.

4. **Always eat at your dining-room or kitchen table.** You deserve better than nibbling from an open refrigerator or over the sink. Make an attractive place setting, even if you're eating alone. Feed your eyes as well as your stomach. By always eating at a table, you will become much more aware of your true food intake. For some reason, many of us conveniently "forget" the food we swallow while standing over the stove, munching in the car, or on the run.

5. **Avoid doing anything else while you are eating.** If you read the paper or watch television while you eat, it's easy to consume too much food without realizing it, because you are concentrating on something else besides what you're eating. Then, when you look down at your plate and see that it's empty, you wonder where all the food went and why you still feel hungry.

Day by day, as you travel the path to good health, it will become easier to make the right choices, to eat *smarter.* But don't ever fool yourself into thinking that you'll be able to put your eating habits on cruise control and forget about them. Making a commitment to eat good healthy food and sticking to it takes some effort. But with all the good-tasting recipes in this Healthy Exchanges cookbook, just think how well you're going to eat—and enjoy it—from now on!

Healthy Lean Bon Appétit!

Index

------■------

Flour, as gravy base, 41
Food exchanges, 15–23
Frankfurters:
Bavarian Hash, 224
and beans, 223
Coney Island Pasta Casserole, 198
and corn soup 88
and potato salad, 114
and vegetable soup, 87
Veggie Hot Dog Skillet, 225
Free foods, 20
Freezing leftovers, 33–34
French toast, stuffed, 288
Frozen dinners, 54
Fruits, 18–19, 39–41. *See also individual fruits*

Gelatins, 43
German Potato Soup, 73
Graham crackers:
chocolate:
and banana dessert, Hawaiian, 238
Better Than Candy Pie, 262
and cherry cloud salad, 140
Cozumel Cloud Pudding, 236
Decadent "Candy Bar" Salad, 139
Citrus Cinnamon Salad, 138
and pineapple scallop, 273
Grasshopper Dessert Bars, 244–45
Gravy, 40–41
Ground meat, browning, 36. *See also* Beef, ground

Ham, 54
and bean soup, Cliff's, 91
and bean soup, garden, 90
and chicken skillet, 222
and corn chowder, 89
and corn scallop, 209
deviled, muffins, 293
Dixieland Green Beans, 149
and eggs pizza, breakfast, 295
and lasagna toss, 208

macaroni and cheese with, 213
and macaroni bake, 212
and macaroni salad, Mexican, 97
and pasta salad with maize dressing, 96
and rice dish, Mexicalli, 210
skillet, Creole, 211
Hash, Bavarian, 224
Healthy Exchanges, 21–23, 317–18
recipes, 2–3, 8–9, 17
favorites, 304–11
ingredients, 24–28
reading, 61–62
Healthy Exchanges Food Newsletter, 321–22
Healthy JO's, 306
Homemade foods, 44–45
Hot dogs, 53–54. *See also* Frankfurters

Instant pudding mixes, 41–42
Italian Biscuit Ring, 291
Italian Chicken Noodle Skillet, 218
Italian Chicken Spaghetti Soup, 79
Italian Green Bean Salad, 103
Italian Grilled Chicken, 221
Italian Pea Salad, 105

Jewel Box Salad, 125
JO's Kitchen Cafe, 1
JO's Spices, 320
JO's Trail Mix, 301

Key West Raspberry Salad, 132
Kiwi fruit: Jewel Box Salad, 125

Labels, food, 25, 52, 56
Layered BLT Salad, 115
Layered Chicken Dinner, 216
Leftovers, freezing, 33–34
Lemonade, "Grandma's," 309
Lemon Cheesecake with Lemon Glaze, 251
Lemon juice, fruits and vegetables sprayed with, 39–40
Lemon yogurt, 43

Salads, 94–95

savory:

buffalo chicken macaroni, 98

Cabbage and Apple Slaw with Walnuts, 112

Carrot French Pennies, 106

carrot-raisin, 108

Celery Seed Coleslaw, 111

corn, quick, 109

corn and kidney bean, 110

cucumber harvest, 100

dilled cucumber, 101

dilled salmon-pasta, 99

English pea, 104

frankfurter potato, 114

ham pasta, with maize dressing, 96

Italian green bean, 103

Italian pea, 105

layered BLT, 115

maple nut carrot, 107

Mexican ham macaroni, 97

pizza bacon-lettuce-and-tomato, 121

potato, Father's classic, 113

potato, grande, 120

potluck sauerkraut, 102

ranch pasta-carrot, 118

shrimp cocktail, 119

tomato rigatoni pasta, 116

western macaroni, 117

sweet, 122–23

apple sunshine, 128

banana rice, 131

carrot marshmallow, 142

cherry-chocolate cloud, 140

citrus cinnamon, 138

creamy strawberry fruit, 135

decadent "candy bar," 139

fruit cloud, 126

heavenly cherry, 124

jewel box, 125

Key West raspberry, 132

New England apple, 129

orange-pecan tapioca, 136

pear-mint, 133

pistachio apple cream, 130

pistachio creme fruit, 134

southern blueberry fruit, 137

strawberry-pineapple fluff, 141

Waldorf, basic, 127

Salisbury Noodle Skillet, 188

Salmon:

cheese loaf, 176

dilled, and pasta salad, 199

Salsa, 35

baked fish topped with, 171

Creamy Taco Dip, 297

Healthy JO's, 306

Macho Burritos, 181

Mexicalli Pie, 307

Mexican Cheese Soup, 72

Mexican Chicken Soup, 77

Mexican Ham Macaroni Salad, 97

Texas Jo Casserole, 185

with vegetables, 40

Saturated fat, 26–27

Sauerkraut:

Bavarian Hash, 224

Bavarian Meat Loaf, 189

Bohemian Goulash, 206

Corned Beef Pasta Bake, 227

Reuben Roll-Ups, 302

salad, potluck, 102

Seasoning extracts, 42

Shopping, 51–57

Shrimp:

cocktail salad, 119

and rice, Cajun country, 175

Skim milk, food exchanges, 19

Sliders, 20–21, 22

Snack foods, 54

JO's Trail Mix, 301

Sodium, 24–25

Solids, measuring, 65

Soups, 68–69

Blazing Glory Chili, 84

cabbage noodle, 74

cabbage patch, 82

canned, fat-free, 25

cheese, Mexican, 72

ground, 32, 54. *See also* Beef,
   ground
peppers stuffed with, 177
skillet, creamy, 180
tetrazzini, 308
Turkey ham, 54

Vegetables, 19, 39–41, 144–45
   and beef soup, creamy, 80
   California Beef Bake, 186
   Carrot-Cabbage Casserole, 152
   Carrots with Mushrooms, 150
   Cheesy Broccoli and Corn Casse-
      role, 156
   Corn and Onion au Gratin, 155
   Country Scalloped Tomatoes,
      160
   Dixieland Green Beans, 149
   Easy Marinated Mushrooms, 154
   French Squaw Corn, 157
   German Green Beans, 146
   Green Bean Mushroom Casse-
      role, 147
   and hot dog skillet, 225

Mustard Cauliflower and
   Broccoli, 153
Mustard Coleslaw, 305
Polynesian Carrots, 151
Potato Corn Bake, 159
Potluck Corn, 158
Spanish Green Beans, 148
See also Salads; *individual
   vegetables*
Vitamins, 22

Walnuts. *See* Nuts
Water, 22
Weight Loss Choices / Exchanges,
   15–17, 21–23
Western Macaroni Salad, 117
Whipped topping, thawing, 41
White sauce for vegetables, 40
Women, diet for, 21

Yogurt, 37–38, 41
   fruit-flavored, 43

Zach's Tropical Isle Pancakes, 287

I want to hear from you . . .

---■---

Besides my family, the love of my life is creating "common folk" healthy recipes and solving everyday cooking questions in *The Healthy Exchanges Way*. Everyone who uses my recipes is considered part of the Healthy Exchanges Family, so please write to me if you have any questions, comments, or suggestions. I will do my best to answer. With your support, I'll continue to stir up even more recipes and cooking tips for the Family in the years to come.

Write to: JoAnna M. Lund
          c/o Healthy Exchanges, Inc.
          P.O. Box 124
          DeWitt, IA 52742

If you prefer, you can fax me at 1-319-659-2126 or contact me via E-mail by writing to HealthyJo @ aol.com.

If you're ever in the DeWitt, Iowa, area, stop in and visit me at "The House That Recipes Built" and dine at JO's Kitchen Cafe, "Grandma's Comfort Food Made Healthy!"

JO's Kitchen™ Cafe
Grandma's Comfort Food Made Healthy!™

110 Industrial Street • DeWitt, Iowa 52742 • (319) 659-8234

--------■--------

Ever since I began stirring up Healthy Exchanges recipes, I've wanted every dish to be rich in flavor and lively in taste. As part of my pursuit of satisfying eating and healthy living for a lifetime, I decided to create my own line of spices.

JO's Spices are salt-, sugar-, wheat-, and MSG-free, and you can substitute them in any of the recipes calling for traditional spice mixes. If you're interested in hearing more about my special blends, please call Healthy Exchanges at 1-319-659-8234 for more information or to order. If you prefer, write to JO's Spices, c/o Healthy Exchanges, P.O. Box 124, DeWitt, IA 52742.

JO'S SPICES . . . A Healthy Way to Spice Up Your Life!™

Now That You've Read *Cooking Healthy with a Man in Mind,* Why Not Order *The Healthy Exchanges Food Newsletter?*

If you enjoyed the recipes in this cookbook and would like to cook up even more of these "common folk" healthy dishes, you may want to subscribe to *The Healthy Exchanges Food Newsletter.*

This monthly twelve-page newsletter contains thirty-plus new recipes *every month* in such columns as:

■ Reader Exchange ■ Reader Requests

■ Recipe Makeover ■ Micro Corner ■ Dinner for Two

■ Crock Pot Luck ■ Meatless Main Dishes

■ Rise & Shine ■ Our Small World ■ Brown Bagging It

■ Snack Attack ■ Side Dishes ■ Main Dishes ■ Desserts

In addition to all the recipes, other regular features include:

- The Editor's Motivational Corner
- Dining Out Question & Answer
- Cooking Question & Answer
- New Product Alert
- Success Profiles of Winners in the Losing Game
- Exercise Advice from a Cardiac Rehab Specialist
- Nutrition Advice from a Registered Dietitian
- Positive Thought for the Month

Just as in this cookbook, all *Healthy Exchanges Food Newsletter* recipes are calculated in three distinct ways: (1) Weight Loss Choices, (2) Calories with Fat and Fiber Grams, and (3) Diabetic Exchanges.

The cost for a one-year (12-issue) subscription with a special Healthy Exchanges three-ring binder to store the newsletters in is $28.50, or $22.50 without the binder. To order, simply complete the form and mail to us *or* call our toll-free number and pay with your VISA or MasterCard.

_____ Yes, I want to subscribe to *The Healthy Exchanges Food Newsletter* $28.50 Yearly Subscription Cost with Storage Binder $_____; $22.50 Yearly Subscription Cost without binder $_____

_____ Foreign orders please add $6.00 for money exchange and extra postage $_____

_____ I'm not sure, so please send me a sample copy at $2.50 $_____

Please make check payable to HEALTHY EXCHANGES or pay by VISA/MasterCard

Card Number: _____ Expiration Date: _____

Signature: _____

Signature required for all credit card orders.

Or Order Toll-Free, using your credit card, at 1-800-766-8961

NAME: _____

ADDRESS: _____

CITY _____ STATE _____ ZIP _____

TELEPHONE: (   ) _____

If additional orders for the newsletter are to be sent to an address other than the one listed above, please use a separate sheet and attach to this form.

MAIL TO: **HEALTHY EXCHANGES**
P.O. BOX 124
DeWitt, IA 52742-0124

1-800-766-8961 For Customer Orders
1-319-659-8234 For Customer Service

Thank you for your order, and for choosing to become a part of the Healthy Exchanges Family!